Revolt in Louisiana

REVOLT in LOUISIANA

The Spanish Occupation, 1766–1770

JOHN PRESTON MOORE

LOUISIANA STATE UNIVERSITY PRESS

Baton Rouge

LIBRARY OF CONGRESS CATALOGING IN PUBLICATION DATA

Moore, John Preston.
  Revolt in Louisiana.

  Bibliography: p.
  Includes index.
  1. Louisiana—History—To 1803. 2. Spain—
Colonies—North America. 3. France—Colonies—
North America. 4. Ulloa, Antonio de, 1716–1795.
I. Title.
F373.M75   976.3'03   75–5349
ISBN 0–8071–0180–X

Contents

Illustrations

Tables

Preface

The futile uprising of the French colonists in 1768 against the imposition of Spanish authority was a signal event in the history of colonial Louisiana in the eighteenth century. It marked the termination of French rule and the beginning of thirty-odd years under the Spanish crown. Changes in administrative procedure, in the legal system, and in the economy accompanied the transfer of sovereignty. The occurrence .of the revolt less than ten years before the American Revolution had overtones of anticolonialism that resounded, bold and unmuffled, elsewhere in North America in 1776.

With the hope of answering the all-important historical questions of how and why, I have undertaken to investigate, or (to use the term of one of my professors at Harvard, the late Crane Brinton) to observe the "anatomy" of, the revolution that was centered in New Orleans and encompassed a four-year period. There is perhaps no apter metaphor for a revolution than the physiological one of a "fever," which develops and runs its course before the patient returns to normality. What were the causes, phases, and outcome of the rebellion? Who were the principal conspirators? Why did their plans fail of realization? These are points that must be adequately treated. That the revolution was limited in scope and incomplete when compared with the American Revolution is evident. Its objectives were never attained. Yet there were immediate and long-term results, and one must conclude that Louisiana profited from Spanish rule.

The timing of the revolt in the fall of 1768 raises the pertinent query of its influence. Did the insurrection of the French settlers constitute a prelude to the American Revolution? Clearly, the two events had something in common. Both were protests against a restriction of economic liberties that had been enjoyed for a long time. The insurrectionists voiced also a feeling of separatism between the European and the colonial. And, like the American Revolution, the uprising produced a remarkable document that defended the acts of the rebels by appealing to political theory. To the Spanish ambassador at the Court of St. James's there was a distinct connection between the disaffection in the English colonies and the discontent in Louisiana. His prophetic words concerning the future of Louisiana, uttered in response to an inquiry from a British statesman in February, 1769, after the occurrence of the revolt, are to be found in a dispatch to the Spanish secretary of state: "I told him that the citizens of New Orleans had anticipated what the English colonies were ready to undertake, from whom they [the French colonists] had pursued a bad example." Yet, despite these similarities and the views of a Spanish diplomat, divergences of ultimate objectives, of popular participation, and of economic and social attitudes are numerous. The connection between the two movements is too tenuous to form a link in a chain of events leading to the independence of the English colonies.

In the history of Louisiana the means of crushing the uprising gave rise to a *cause célèbre*. The trial and execution of five prominent citizens of New Orleans by General Alexander O'Reilly prejudiced many early Louisiana historians against Spain. The change of sovereignty, with the adoption of different laws and customs and a new official language, created apprehensiveness and antipathy among the Louisianians, the recollection of which perpetuated the bias. In this atmosphere of resentment, the myths, legends, and misconceptions have flourished. The historian's task is to set the record straight.

I hope also that this study will place Louisiana in the proper context of the Spanish colonial system. To a greater extent than in past treatments the effort is made to view the colony, the people and its problems, from the Spanish standpoint. An understanding of the crown's objectives and the methods adopted to realize them should illumine not only the history of Louisiana but also the functioning of the Spanish Empire in the eighteenth century. At the same time there is no intention of discounting the continuity of Gallic customs and institutions and the basic contributions of the creoles in the future.

To enhance perspective, conditions in British West Florida are referred to from time to time. The turmoil in government in Louisiana was not unique in frontier North America, as the rivalry between civilian and military components of the British regime obstructed the conduct of policy.

In order to make this monograph as thorough as possible, I have sought to consult all important sources. A special effort has been made to utilize the material in the Spanish archives and libraries, including the Archivo General de Indias in Seville, the Archivo General in Simancas, and the Archivo Histórico Nacional, the Biblioteca Nacional, and the Biblioteca de Palacio of Madrid. Other foreign archives from which information has been secured are the Archives Nationales and the Archives de Ministère des Affaires Etrangères of Paris and the Public Record Office and the British Museum in London. In addition, the documents, transcriptions, and microfilm in the Library of Congress, the Louisiana State University Library in Baton Rouge, and the many repositories in New Orleans at Tulane University, Loyola University, the Cabildo, and the public library have all been of inestimable value.

Any author aspiring to scholarship must recognize his indebtedness to researchers in the field and others who have assisted in the preparation of the manuscript. Above all, I should like to acknowledge the wise counsel and cooperation of Admiral Julio F. Guillén Tato, director of the Museo Naval of Madrid; Señorita Rosario Parra, director of the Archivo General de Indias in Seville; Señorita Matilde López, director of the Biblioteca de Palacio of Madrid; and Professor Marcel Giraud of the Collège de France, Paris. I am indebted also to Professor Edwin Davis, former chairman, and Professors James D. Hardy, Jr., and Jane L. DeGrummond, of the history department at Louisiana State University; Miss Evangeline Lynch, custodian of the Louisiana Room of the LSU Library; Dr. Connie Griffith, head of the archives department at Tulane University; and the personnel of the libraries at Washington and Lee University and the Virginia Military Institute. Professor Charles O'Neill of Loyola University, New Orleans, deserves special thanks for permitting me to see a valuable manuscript that he recently found in the Spanish archives. In these acknowledgments should be two former students: Dr. David K. Texada, Saint Mary's Dominican College, and Dr. Donald J. Lemieux, director of the Louisiana Archives and Records Service, whose investigations have illuminated this era of colonial history. The style of the manuscript has been improved by the suggestions of Marie Carmichael of the LSU Press. Without the sympathetic understanding and encouragement of my wife this work could not have been accomplished.

Revolt in Louisiana

I

The Coming of the Spaniards

The rain beat down in a steady torrent on the flagstones of the Place d'Armes of the city of Nouvelle Orléans on this momentous day of March 5, 1766. It was a *gran borrasca,* a storm, combining a downpour and wind customary at this time of the year. At noon a single vessel, of eighteen cannons, displaying the red and yellow banner of Charles III of Spain, moved slowly upstream toward the landing place. The anchor of the *Volante* was dropped, and a small boat conveyed a group of thoroughly drenched Spanish officials to shore. The ship that symbolized Spanish might was technically a packet, but was commonly referred to as a frigate owing to its armaments. The storm was not a good omen for the successful completion of the mission to occupy the province of Louisiana, which now belonged to the cadet branch of the Bourbon family. Only a small crowd of French officials and colonists gathered to witness the arrival by ship of the Spanish governor, Antonio de Ulloa. Accounts differ on the details of the reception, but all agree that there was little cordiality or enthusiasm.[1] It was bad judgment to come in foul weather,

1. An official accompanying Ulloa on the *Volante* described the reception as "respectful but cold and somber, which announced only too clearly the dissatisfaction of the citizenry," and Jean Bochart, the chevalier de Champigny, a French nobleman in the colony, expressed the strong attachment of the populace to France: "I was an eyewitness of the consternation which the overwhelming news [the cession of Louisiana] produced at New Orleans. A general despair would have followed, had they not fondly hoped that the cession would never actually take place." Decrees and memorials of the rebels during the uprising suggest that formal gestures of welcome were extended to the new governor. See the statement of Esteban Gayarré, given at the trial of the conspirators, October, 1769, quoted in Vicente Rodríguez Casado, *Primeros años de dominación española en la*

1

as the turnout was bound to be small. The need to finally make a public appearance was, however, overriding.

Upon disembarking at the levee Governor Ulloa formally greeted the French officials and the inhabitants of New Orleans. To the astonishment of the assembled colonists he refrained from proclaiming the formal possession of the province for the Spanish crown. Nor did he order the French flag to be lowered and the Spanish colors hoisted in its place. This omission he may well have regretted subsequently, for the pretext for a conspiracy was provided on the grounds that Spanish authority in the province had no legal basis. But the governor felt there were good reasons for this inaction, principally that his force consisted of only ninety men. With this tiny contingent, much of the success or failure of the mission would obviously depend on the character and personality of the governor.

The man appointed to the responsible position of governor was an experienced official in the colonial bureaucracy. He had been administrator of an important province in the viceroyalty of Peru. In addition, he was a naval officer by profession, an author, and a scientist. In this latter capacity he was well known to European intellectuals, enjoying a reputation equal to that of any other Spaniard of his day in the special field of natural science.

Like many officials in the colonial service, Don Antonio de Ulloa y de la Torre Guiral hailed from the lesser nobility. He was born on January 12, 1716, in a mansion on Clavel Calle (in present-day Triana), Seville.[2] This metropolis, in effect the capital of the colonial empire, was the birthplace of many celebrated

---

Luisiana (Madrid, 1942), 100, 101; Jean Bochart Champigny, "Memoir of the Present State of Louisiana" in B. F. French (ed.), *Historical Collections of Louisiana Embracing Transactions of Many Rare and Valuable Documents Relating to the Natural, Civil, and Political History of That State, Compiled with Historical and Biographical Notes* (5 vols.; New York, 1846–53); Decreto del consejo superior de la provincia de Luisiana expulsando a Don Antonio de Ulloa, in Leg. 20,854, Consejo de Indias, Archivo Histórico Nacional, Madrid, hereinafter cited as AHN.

2. I was unable to identify the actual place of birth because the section has changed greatly since the eighteenth century.

explorers, navigators, administrators, and churchmen. Although the name Ulloa is a common one in Spain, this particular family derived from the town of Toro in Old Castile. His father Don Bernardo de Ulloa y Sousa had considerable renown as an economist.[3] On his mother's side he was descended from an old Andalusian family. From the union there were ten children, among whom was Martín de Ulloa who obtained prominence as a judge in the *audiencia,* or administrative court, of Havana.

Although a naval officer by training, Antonio de Ulloa did not possess the robust constitution usually associated with those combating the rigors of the sea and warfare. Hoping to strengthen his son's physique, his father sent Ulloa at the age of thirteen to a friend, an admiral, who commanded a vessel bound for America. For three years the lad was a cabin boy aboard the ship in its cruise to Cartagena and other ports in the Caribbean. Upon his return to Cádiz in 1733 he was admitted to the naval academy there, established in 1717 by Cardinal Giulio Alberoni, chief minister for Philip V. Here, as a member of the select Compañía de Caballeros Guardias Marinas, he obtained most of his formal education. Like a modern military academy, it stressed a lofty code of honor, with inculcation of loyalty to the ruler, respect for authority, integrity, and personal courage. The founding of the academy contributed to the renaissance of the Spanish navy in the late 1740s, the specter of which caused serious apprehension in the British admiralty.[4] In addition to a thorough grounding in mathematics, in which he received the grade of *sobresaliente,* or excellent, the youthful cadet imbibed a love of the natural sciences that led him in later life to explore many areas of knowledge and to make significant contributions in a number of them.

In 1734 an unusual opportunity presented itself to two Spaniards with scientific predilections. The prestigious Royal

3. He was the author of *Restablecimiento de las fábricas, y comercio español: Errores que se padecen en las causales de su cadencia* (Madrid, 1740).
4. Rodríguez, *Primeros años,* 55. Peter the Great of Russia paid the school a compliment by sending several young nobles to be enrolled in its classes.

Academy of Science of Paris proposed to solve the Newtonian debate then raging in learned circles in Europe over the shape of the earth by dispatching expeditions to measure an arc of the meridian, one to the North Pole and a second to the equator. The region selected for the latter measurement was Ecuador, a province of the Spanish Empire in South America. In response to a petition from the academy, Philip V granted permission for the use of his territory, with the stipulation, however, that two Spanish officials be allowed to accompany the distinguished French delegation. Instead of appointing mature mathematicians to work with such eminent scientists as Louis Godin and Charles de La Condamine, the king unexpectedly nominated two young, unknown cadets from the Guardias Marinas, Jorge Juan y Santacilia and Antonio de Ulloa.[5] Although considerably younger than their French counterparts, being twenty-one and nineteen respectively, they nevertheless proved to be exceedingly able.[6]

The expedition was an unqualified success. In 1736 the two cadets, promoted to the rank of lieutenant, joined in Quito the French scientists who had proceeded by a different route. Despite the hazards and handicaps of working in the rarefied atmosphere of the Andes, the delegation might have completed its labors in a short time had it not been for the outbreak of war in Europe.[7] The danger for this part of the empire came from a foray by the English admiral George Anson around Cape Horn and into the Pacific. From 1740 to 1744 the viceroy of Peru

5. *Ibid.*, 56, 57, 58; Leg. 590, Audiencia de Lima, Archivo General de Indias, Seville, hereinafter cited as AGI. Fortune played into Ulloa's hands, for he was not the first choice for one of the two positions. The original appointee, whom he replaced, happened to be away from Cádiz at the time. A royal order of June 4, 1735, officially confirmed the appointments.

6. As was natural, the differences in age and experience were a source of irritation to the French associates. See Charles de La Condamine, *Histoire des pyramides de Quito* (Paris, 1751).

7. The citizens of Quito humorously referred to the group as the *caballeros del punto fijo*, or "knights of the fixed point," since the intense preoccupation of the young Spanish scientists with their astronomical labors was a matter of common knowledge. See Julio F. Guillén, *Los tenientes de navío Jorge Juan y Santacilia y Antonio de Ulloa y de la Torre-Guiral y la medición del meridiano* (Madrid, 1936), 67. Guillén has the fullest and most accurate

employed Juan and Ulloa in putting the limited naval contingent in these waters in fighting condition and in constructing adequate fortifications for the ports. With the reduced threat in the Pacific and the completion of their scientific work, the two friends sailed for Europe on separate vessels to ensure the safety of their records and reports. Ulloa was not as lucky as Juan in reaching his destination, as his ship had the misfortune to be captured by the British and he himself was taken as a prisoner of war to London. Owing to the intercession of Lord Charles Stanhope, an influential member of the Royal Society of London, Ulloa was released and permitted to join his companion in Madrid.[8] At the instigation of the king's minister, Zenón de Somodevilla, the marqués de la Ensenada, Juan and Ulloa collaborated in the publication in 1748 of the results of their labors under the title *Relación histórica del viaje a la América meridional*. To Ulloa's pen we owe the first four sections containing significant expositions of geography, ethnology, Indian and creole customs, flora and fauna, and other aspects of the fascinating regions that they had visited; to Juan, the fifth section, with the mathematical and astronomical calculations for the confirmation of Newton's conception of the earth.[9] Numerous translations in the next two decades attested to its widespread appeal to the scientific world.[10]

account of their scientific work. One should note that Ulloa and Juan were engaged in a quarrel with the president of the *audiencia,* the highest royal official of the district. The origin of the dispute was of a trivial nature, the condescending salutation employed by the official in a letter to the two naval officers. Ulloa's insistence on full observance of protocol invoked the incident. Only the intervention of the viceroy in Lima, a friend of Juan's, saved the two young men from imprisonment. This was the first of a series of controversies that plagued Ulloa's career in the colonial service and the navy. See Leg. 133, Audiencia de Quito, AGI.

8. For an account of his experience as a prisoner in England and his relations with British scientists, see Arthur P. Whitaker, "Antonio de Ulloa, the *Deliverance,* and the Royal Society," *Hispanic American Historical Review,* XLVI (November, 1966), 357–70.

9. The full title was *Relación histórica del viaje a la América meridional, hecho de orden de S. M. para medir algunos grados de meridiano terrestre, y venir por ellos en conocimiento de la verdadera figura de la tierra, con otras varias observaciones astronómicas y físicas* (4 vols.; Madrid, 1748). Its appearance so soon after the expedition aroused the envy of their French colleagues, who brought out their versions later on.

10. See Guillén, *Los tenientes de navío,* 177, 178. In the following year, 1749, Juan and Ulloa proposed to terminate the long controversy between Spain and Portugal over the

Historians of the Spanish Empire of the eighteenth century are almost unanimous in their praise of Ulloa and Juan's second collaborative production, an investigative work commonly known as the *Noticias secretas de América*. Prepared secretly at the request of Ensenada, it is an extraordinarily accurate report of political, social, and religious conditions existing in the viceroyalty of Peru in the middle of the century. Penetrating, candid, and objective, it not only brings out in clear perspective the corruption and oppression of the natives that existed in Peru and Ecuador, but it offers meaningful suggestions for correcting the ills.[11]

In the seven or eight years following the completion of his studies and reports on America, Ulloa carried out specific missions for the crown in Spain and in other parts of Europe. He inspected shipyards and fortifications throughout the kingdom. His engineering skill was put to use in constructing a canal for Castile to improve transportation in the central part of the country. At the orders of his patron Ensenada, he undertook a journey to France, Holland, the Scandinavian countries, and the Germanies to observe the nature and extent of naval facilities and to note the progress of the scientific Enlightenment.[12] Of

exact location of the boundary of Brazil and the Spanish Empire by publishing a study on this subject. Although it established a fairly accurate geographical line, it did not lead to a rectification of frontiers that were being determined by this time on the basis of exploration and actual occupation of territory. See Rodríguez, *Primeros años*, 64, 65.

11. The full title of the manuscript is "Discourso y Reflexiones sobre el estado presente de la marina de los reynos del Perú, su gobierno, arsenales, maestranzas, viajes, armamentos, plana mayor de sus oficiales, sus sueldos, de los navios, marchantes, govierno, resumen particular de aquellos avitadores y abusos que se han introducido en uno y otro" (Ms. 1468 in América del Sur, Manuscritos de América, Biblioteca de Palacio, Madrid, hereinafter cited as BP). The first publication occurred abroad in 1826 when Spanish policies and institutions in Europe and America were under attack by liberals. Hence, this edition is far from satisfactory, and a definitive version awaits future scholarship. There is evidence that the manuscript was written by 1749 and used thereafter as a guide by administrators assigned to posts in South America. See Arthur P. Whitaker, "Antonio de Ulloa," *Hispanic American Historical Review*, XV (May, 1935), 155–94; Guillén, *Los tenientes de navío*, 163–67; and Rodríguez, *Primeros años*, 65–73.

12. On his return trip he stopped in Berlin, where he was for a short time the guest of Frederick the Great. Ulloa's correspondence with Ensenada is extensive. See, in particular, Leg. 377 and 712, Marina, Archivo General de Simancas, Simancas, hereinafter cited as AGS.

special interest in this latter category were the innovations in mining technology.[13]

Ulloa's next important assignment enabled him to revisit Peru. The steady decline at the Huancavelica mine in the production of mercury—essential in the amalgamation process for the extraction of silver—had been a serious preoccupation of the crown for many years.[14] It was necessary to introduce new techniques and above all to check the graft and inefficiency characterizing the system of mine operation. The choice of Ulloa as governor of Huancavelica was logical in view of his knowledge of mining and his unassailable probity. After some hesitation, due in part to the contrary advice of his old friend Jorge Juan, who was then prominent in governmental circles in Madrid and who sensed the deep opposition to reform by local administrators within the viceroyalty, Ulloa accepted and sailed from Cádiz in January, 1758, by way of Cape Horn to the Pacific.

Was it possible for Ulloa to succeed where others had given up and resigned? The downward trend in the output of quicksilver was partly due to the exhaustion of the veins. Other factors reduced production: graft and venality of governmental officials, including the powerful viceroy and members of the *audiencia,* the greed and irresponsibility of the guild of miners who conducted operations under the supervision of the governor of Huancavelica, the wasteful and archaic methods used in the extraction of the ore, and finally the scarcity of Indian labor.[15] Ulloa's recommendations for improving conditions were sound. If they had been followed, the production of ore would have materially increased, at least for a short time.

As Jorge Juan had predicted, the resistance of local interests to

---

13. Guillén, *Los tenientes de navío,* 236, 237.

14. So significant was the maintenance of the output regarded by the crown that a phrase expressing this concern was coined: "Without Huancavelica, good-bye to America."

15. There is an excellent study of the problems involved and the fruitless efforts by various reformers to solve them. See Arthur P. Whitaker, *The Huancavelica Mercury Mine: A Contribution to the History of the Bourbon Renaissance in the Spanish Empire* (Cambridge, 1941).

any modification of the system at Huancavelica was well intrenched. Ulloa's efforts to expose the extortion and wastefulness strengthened the opposition. In Professor Arthur P. Whitaker's words, "ties of friendship, family, and interests united miners, clergy and his own subordinate officials at Huancavelica with the highest officials at Lima in a solid phalanx dedicated to the defense of a system which was thoroughly corrupt." By 1763 Ulloa was deeply discouraged at his inability to bring about reforms. Complaining bitterly "of the heavy weight of anxieties that are dragging me down to complete dejection," he petitioned the crown to be relieved of his post.[16] A royal order of January 4, 1764, confirmed his resignation as "superintendant of Huancavelica and governor of the province of Angares." There was no mention of the *residencia,* or judicial enquiry, customarily held at the end of the term of office.[17]

Thus relieved of his position in Peru, Ulloa anticipated a speedy return to Spain. The crown had, however, other plans for his future. In obedience to royal command he sailed from Callao on November 19 on the frigate *Soledad* and by February 3, 1765, he had arrived in Havana. His orders required him to remain indefinitely in the Cuban capital.[18] There is no indication that he knew what was in store for him as administrator until receiving an April 24 dispatch from the minister of the Indies.[19]

In the light of his subsequent inability to deal satisfactorily

16. *Ibid.,* 43, 44. He undoubtedly added to his unpopularity by issuing regulations restricting gambling and dancing. A straitlaced, puritanical governor was sure to be disliked in a mining community where prostitution, debauchery, and games of chance were the normal way of life. See "Relación del gobierno del capitán del navío Don Antonio de Ulloa en la villa de Huancavelica" (Ms. 2453 in América del Sur, Manuscritos de América, BP).

17. The enquiry was postponed because of the feeling in Madrid that the governor could not obtain a fair, unprejudiced hearing as long as Manuel de Amat was viceroy of Peru. The *residencia* probably never took place, since Amat remained in office until 1776.

18. He would have preferred a billet in Spain. "Although I have an aversion to serving here [in America]," he wrote Minister of the Indies Julián de Arriaga, "owing to the reproofs I have endured at so much cost to my honor and career, you may rest assured that I have no other wish than to fulfill the royal command." See Ulloa to Arriaga, February 3, 1765, in Leg. 775, Audiencia de Lima, AGI.

19. Ulloa to Arriaga, June 21, 1765, *ibid.*

with the people of the former French province, why was Ulloa tendered the appointment of governor of Louisiana by Marqués Jerónimo Grimaldi? This question has puzzled historians of colonial Louisiana. He had failed as administrator of the Huancavelica mine if he is judged by the attainment of the twin objectives of the crown, the increase in the output of quicksilver and the elimination of corruption. Yet this was an assignment that had baffled many before him. His conduct in Peru had shown nothing dishonorable in his character. On the other hand there are many reasons to explain the crown's decision. He had numerous qualifications as a capable public servant: intelligence, initiative, industry, integrity, and loyalty. Moreover, he possessed a knowledge of the French language and culture, gained through his sojourn in France and his association with the French scientists in Ecuador and Peru.[20] This would be of the utmost importance in establishing a rapport with the settlers of the newly acquired province.

At the same time it is hardly likely that the minister of the Indies, Julián de Arriaga, was blind to certain unfavorable traits of personality. Ulloa was overly painstaking, unduly assiduous in issuing and enforcing regulations, sometimes brusque in manner with a habit of discounting the opinions of others—in short, a person with many of the features of a martinet.[21] Of less than ordinary height and hence physically unimpressive, he could not

20. La Condamine, the foremost figure in the French group, mentions Ulloa's ability to speak French. See Jerónimo Rubio, *Un amigo español de La Condamine: Armona* (Madrid, 1952), 17.

21. The observations of Ulloa's contemporaries confirmed a certain pettiness or excessive attention to minutiae. The French governor Charles Aubry had this to say about him: "It appears to me that M. de Ulloa is sometimes too punctilious and often makes problems out of things that are scarcely worth the trouble to bother with. It is necessary for us sometimes to argue over the plainest matters about which there would have been no debate were it not for insignificant particulars." In an earlier communication Aubry pointed out another defect: "The governor that His Catholic Majesty has sent is a man of ability, knowledge, and talent, but contrary to the custom of his nation he is extremely quick and it seems to me that he does not listen sufficiently to the remonstrances that are made to him. This angers those who have business with him." Quoted in Charles Gayarré, *Histoire de la Louisiane* (2 vols.; New Orleans, 1846–47), II, 163, 157, 158. This work, which is largely documentary, lacks the interpretation and depth of Gayarré's later study, but is useful for accurate records.

Antonio de Ulloa. Courtesy Museo Naval, Madrid

effectively symbolize the might and grandeur of Spain. Nor was he inclined to curry favor with the populace by gala receptions and sumptuous dinners. Obviously, it was not easy to find a person possessing all the qualifications for this difficult position. Ulloa was, furthermore, at hand and available.[22] He was also personally acquainted with the minister of state Grimaldi, whom he had met many years before in Stockholm when the Italian was the Spanish ambassador at the Swedish court. And, in his compadre Jorge Juan, Ulloa had an intimate friend enjoying prestige and influence in high governmental circles.[23]

To complete the portrait of the first governor of Louisiana, one must remember that Ulloa was a child of the eighteenth-century Enlightenment, a complex, many-sided person. Highly intelligent, he was a man of culture and of encyclopedic interests—surely not the type to be appreciated in a French colony where learning was not the mark of distinction. His fondness for letter writing made him one of the most prolific Spanish correspondents of his age. Although more introverted than extroverted, he had one conspicuously commendable characteristic as an administrator, an unusual drive and energy. Despite an ordinary physical makeup, he carried out many tasks requiring exceptional physical and mental exertion.[24] This then was the image of Antonio de Ulloa. Myths and legends arising in a hostile creole climate have obscured some good traits and unduly magnified undesirable ones. His personality was not that of the ideal administrator. Yet it is doubtful that this fact is the key element in the ultimate failure of his administration.

22. Whitaker attaches importance to this. See Whitaker, "Antonio de Ulloa," 183.

23. To render an opinion on the conflicting reports from Peru concerning the operation of the Huancavelica mine, Arriaga turned to Jorge Juan, who drew up an *informe,* citing Ulloa "as one of the most intelligent men to be found in Spain." In a dictamen of February 12, 1765, Juan continued his exoneration of Ulloa, which apparently convinced Arriaga, because a marginal comment in the minister's handwriting refers to the former governor as "persecuted" by the viceroy. See Juan's report, July 18, 1763, and Juan to Arriaga, February 12, 1765, both in Leg. 1631, Indiferente, AGI.

24. José de Loyola, the Spanish commissary, alluded to Ulloa's wish to make an unobtrusive entry into New Orleans after his marriage at Balize: "I understand the aversion with which Your Excellency looks upon public demonstrations." Loyola to Ulloa, July 2, 1767, in Leg. 109, Papeles de Cuba, AGI.

Although probably aware that the long delay in the receipt of orders spelled another assignment in America, Ulloa did not learn of his new destination until June, 1765,[25] when Arriaga's note of April 24 arrived announcing his appointment as governor of Louisiana: "By letter of February last the king was informed of Your Excellency's arrival at that port [Havana] and having designated you to proceed to Louisiana and take possession of those territories at the recommendation of the marqués de Grimaldi, secretary of state, in whose charge are all regulations relative to its development, I instruct you by royal command to be at the disposition of this minister and wait in this place for the orders to be passed to you, for which purpose a frigate is being outfitted to sail from El Ferrol to transport you to your destination." A week later, on May 1, 1765, the king signed the formal commission. Ulloa acknowledged receipt of his appointment by Arriaga the last of June, expressing his gratitude and pleasure at the honor bestowed upon him by his sovereign.[26]

Eager to establish contact with his new subjects, Ulloa dispatched three weeks later a message to the Superior Council of Louisiana in New Orleans to inform this body of his appointment as governor: "Having received recently orders from His Catholic Majesty to go to your city and take possession of it in his name and in fulfillment of orders of His Most Christian Majesty, I take this occasion to inform you and to notify you that I shall soon have the honor to be among you to carry out this commission. I flatter myself beforehand that it will give me many opportunities of rendering to you all the services that you and the inhabitants of the city can wish for; and in which function I beg to assure you sincerely that I shall be only carrying out my duties and gratifying my own inclination."[27]

25. The French ambassador at Madrid informed Choiseul in December, 1763, that Grimaldi had already selected a governor "who is at this time in the Indies but has not yet received orders to go to his destination." If this is true, then Ulloa had been under consideration for some time. See Marc de Villiers du Terrage, *Les dernières années de la Louisiane française* (Paris, 1903), 224.

26. Arriaga to Ulloa, April 24, 1765, and Ulloa to Arriaga, June 21, 1765, both in Leg. 775, Audiencia de Lima, AGI. See Chapter III, herein, for the instructions contained in the commission of office.

27. Quoted in Gayarré, *Histoire de la Louisiane*, II, 136, 137.

It is clear that Ulloa devoted much time and thought during the summer and fall of 1765 to the problems of Louisiana.[28] With his accustomed zeal he must have gleaned from records in Havana, from reports from Spain, and from interviews with captains of merchant ships trading in the Gulf of Mexico considerable information about the land and customs of the people of the province. During the interim, officials of the colony opened correspondence with the governor-designate. In August the Superior Council replied politely to his letter of July 10. Early in October the French commissary Nicolas Foucault in a friendly note urged the Spanish governor to assume authority in the colony as soon as possible because of dire economic conditions. Ulloa replied that he awaited the arrival of the frigate that was to convey him to New Orleans. "I do not know," he continued, "the cause of its delay. I am extremely appreciative of your attentiveness and ardently wish that there will be many opportunities in which I will be able to convince you of the desire that I have to render to you any services that are in my power."[29]

In a lengthy letter of October 19 to Ulloa the French governor Charles Aubry painted a gloomy picture of deteriorating relations with the Indians:

> I find myself in a very difficult position. It is very hard to be able to satisfy at the same time the demands and customs of the various nations that present themselves. The arrival of the English has upset everything and occasions much disorder. . . . It has been two years since we have received any supplies, our magazines are empty. I cannot give any more to the savages who come from everywhere to New Orleans to find out when you will be here. I try to make them happy by soothing words; but that does not suffice; munitions are the most essential thing and I have at present no more than fifty pounds of powder. . . . I await this moment [your arrival] with the greatest impatience.

28. But he was not unmindful of the morass from which he had narrowly escaped, for his letters to Madrid testify that he was also engaged in preparing reports for the judgment to be made by the Council of the Indies in his controversy with the viceroy of Peru. See Ulloa to Arriaga, with enclosures, July 12, October 28, and November 5, 1765, all in Leg. 775, Audiencia de Lima, AGI.

29. Foucault to Ulloa, October 8, 1765, and Ulloa to Foucault, November 10, 1765, both in Leg. 187, Papeles de Cuba, AGI.

Ulloa's reply to this appeal for assistance was sympathetic but noncommittal. Without orders from his superiors he could not officially dispatch gunpowder to Louisiana. He promised, however, to petition the intendant in Havana to purchase thirty to forty quintals (three thousand to four thousand pounds) against the appropriation for the colony and arrange for its safe transportation to New Orleans.[30] Whether this request was ever approved by the authorities in Havana is uncertain.

The "soon," inserted by Ulloa in his letter of July 10 to the Superior Council, was translated into six months. It was not until January of the following year that he left Havana for New Orleans. The delay arose primarily from the somewhat puzzling policy adopted by the court in Madrid toward the assumption of authority in the province.[31] The frigate bearing men and supplies for the expedition did not reach the Cuban capital until late in November or early December, 1765.

Initial preparations for the expedition to occupy the province had begun in January, 1764. The prime mover in developing the plans was Grimaldi, architect with Duc Etienne François de Choiseul of the Treaty of Fontainebleau, which contained the terms of the transfer.[32] The apparent uniqueness of Louisiana in the Spanish colonial empire, namely its French-speaking inhabitants, its climate, and the seminomadic aborigines, pointed to the advisability of limited cooperation with the French crown in establishing a viable government. To Grimaldi the essentials in the organization of the expedition were the procurement of supplies for the settlers and the Indians and the recruitment of soldiers to maintain Spanish authority. In the realization of these objectives there were offers of assistance from the French government.

30. Aubry to Ulloa, October 19, 1765, and Ulloa to Aubry, November 10, 1765, both *ibid*.

31. An explanation of this strange but obviously extremely cautious policy is offered in Chapter II, herein.

32. The Spanish records on the question of Louisiana are silent for over a year after the signing of the act of cession. See Grimaldi to Arriaga, January 29, 1764, in Leg. 2542, Audiencia de Sto. Domingo, AGI.

Among the supplies to be shipped to the colony, the major item constituted presents for the natives. Realizing the importance of placating the savages but ignorant of their demands in this part of North America, the Spanish ambassador at Versailles, Joaquín Atanasio Pignatelli de Aragón, the conde de Fuentes, solicited from Choiseul a list of the gifts bestowed annually by the French government on the chiefs and braves of the various tribes in the region. On March 9, 1764, Fuentes forwarded to Grimaldi this information. Knowing that these items might be difficult to find readily in Spain, the secretary of state ordered the ambassador to purchase in France a large supply of blankets, knives, and other articles, so that there would be no shortage for several years. It was hoped that in the future Spanish sources would furnish the requisite items. Every effort was to be made to expedite the delivery of the goods. For the procurement of the various items the French agent was Monsieur Le Moyne, a merchant of Rouen and relative of Pierre Le Moyne, Sieur d'Iberville, a founder of the French colony of Louisiana. As his firm had acted as commissary for the court since 1732, he was thoroughly familiar with the diversity of gifts to be obtained. On May 22, 1764, he signed with Fuentes a contract for the goods to be secured and delivered to La Rochelle, having previously assured the ambassador that it would take at least three or four weeks to assemble the goods in the correct sizes, colors, and designs "in order not to offend the savages."[33]

Somewhat later Grimaldi authorized the purchase in France of flour and other general supplies for the colony to be shipped from Bayonne to La Coruña. Unfortunately, delays occurred in the purchase and assembly of the cargo at the French port. Inexplicably, Choiseul bore a measure of the blame, having withheld for a short time the issuance of a license for the exportation of guns and powder. The lack of shipping between Bayonne and the Galician port resulted in an additional delay. It

33. Fuentes to Grimaldi, March 9, 1764, Grimaldi to Fuentes, March 29, 1764, and Fuentes to Grimaldi, May 18, 1764, Expediente, Louisiana, Nos. 2 and 3, all *ibid.*

Jerónimo Grimaldi. Courtesy Biblioteca Nacional, Madrid

was not until February, 1765, that the conde de Fuentes informed Grimaldi that he had learned of the imminent departure of the goods for Spain. Contrary circumstances prevented the ship from dropping anchor in the harbor of El Ferrol, near La Coruña, before the middle of June. The barrels of flour, which were to form an integral part of the general supplies for the colony, did not reach Spain until July 27.[34]

It was somewhat easier to recruit and train soldiers to occupy the colony. Only a small force was deemed necessary, as Choiseul had generously agreed to the enlistment in the Spanish army of 250 men of the French guard for patrolling New Orleans and for manning the posts.[35] Perhaps because of this offer the crown made no move in this direction until the spring of 1765. At the king's command, Secretary of War Leopoldo de Gregorio, the marqués de Esquilache, directed Marqués Carlos Francisco de Croix, captain general of Galicia, with headquarters in La Coruña, to form a company consisting of 4 officers and 100 men to be drawn from the 4 regiments stationed in this province. "The king wishes that they be volunteers, of Spanish nationality, unmarried, robust, seasoned, and reliable," he wrote. "They should be assembled in the castle of Felipe in El Ferrol, clothed, equipped, trained, and ready to depart in a frigate for America."[36] Haste was essential.

Croix took immediate steps to carry out the order. Having arranged the cadre, he recommended the appointment of Captain Francisco Riu y Morales, a veteran of over thirty years' service with combat experience in Savoy and Piedmont, as com-

34. Fernando Magallón to Grimaldi, October 1, 1764, Magallón to Grimaldi, December 21, 1764, Fuentes to Grimaldi, February 4, 1765, the marqués de Monteverde, the navy intendant, to Grimaldi, June 12, 1765, and Croix to Grimaldi, August 3, 1765, all *ibid.*

35. The French minister pointed out the advantages of incorporating this force, many of the men "being in a position to furnish useful information to the Spanish governor and officers who will command concerning the relations of the settlers and the savages, both friendly and hostile." See Choiseul to d'Ossun, April 25, 1764, in Leg. 174A, Papeles de Cuba, AGI.

36. Esquilache to Croix, May 2, 1765, in Leg. 2088, Audiencia de Sto. Domingo, AGI.

mander of the troop. Lieutenant Pedro Joseph Piernas, of the regiment of León, would be promoted to the rank of captain. In view of Croix's reputation as a soldier, the king approved all his recommendations except the elevation of Piernas to a higher status.[37] Croix expressed pride in the recruitment of a company worthy of dispatch to the former French colony: "The greater number of the men comprising the company are of more than average height and have volunteered for service in America." To maintain morale he had, however, considered ordering the company to be isolated in the castle of Felipe. Grimaldi and Arriaga were both informed of the readiness of the troops. Expecting momentarily the arrival of three treasury officials, two French officers, and three Capuchins, Croix on July 7 ordered the company to the fortress to forestall desertions. (Some of the "volunteers" had already had a change of heart about service in Louisiana.) The frigate *Liebre* (the hare), a vessel of thirty cannons, which was to transport men and supplies to America, had for some weeks been at anchor at El Ferrol. However, the departure of the expedition for Louisiana again was postponed. Owing to the rumor of hostile warships along the coast, Croix held up the sailing of the frigate until a man-of-war, the *Guerrero,* arrived from Cartagena, to provide a convoy for one hundred leagues from the coast. With the warship at hand and weather favorable, the frigate finally raised anchor and sailed for Havana on September 5.[38]

The delays in the organization and departure of the expedition had caused anxiety and fear at Versailles that the terms of the cession would not be fulfilled. From time to time Choiseul exerted pressure on the Spanish ministry to act. As early as December, 1763, the French ambassador at Madrid inquired of the Spanish government regarding the plans for occupation and

37. Croix to Esquilache, May 11, May 15, and May 22, 1765, all *ibid.* Actually Piernas was a well-trained officer, having graduated from the Royal Academy of Science in Barcelona with distinction in mathematics and having served in the regiment for over nineteen years.

38. Croix to Esquilache, June 5, June 15, July 10, August 14, September 7, 1765, and Esquilache to Croix, June 27, 1765, all *ibid.*

was assured that "suitable measures were being taken." Choiseul's tender of French soldiers was meant to facilitate the handling of the military problem.[39] When Spain had failed by the summer of 1765 to take over the colony, Choiseul wrote indignantly to Paul Chevalier, the marquis d'Ossun, who was the French ambassador at Madrid, to find out what arrangements had been made for the occupation. "His Majesty will await with impatience your reply, so that he may decide what aid will have to be sent to the colony and the orders to be drafted for the commandant in Louisiana for the maintenance of government during the time that remains." Grimaldi defended the seeming inactivity of the Spanish crown on the grounds that "it was necessary to consider many things so as not to take an imprudent step, to inform ourselves of the condition of the colony, its needs, and the type of goods to be given as presents to the savages."[40] There seems little doubt that Grimaldi after the winter of 1764–1765 had urged the speedy marshaling and dispatch of the expedition. Ironically, special circumstances in France were chiefly responsible for the repeated postponement of occupation.

Although the frigate had sailed the first week in September, it did not anchor opposite El Morro fortress in the harbor of Havana until November 20. A scarcity of fresh water had meanwhile compelled the ship to put into the port of Sto. Domingo, where desertions among the soldiers extended the stay. After the troops had disembarked in Havana and had passed in review, Ulloa concluded that the personnel and equipment conformed to the high standards of His Majesty's army.[41] Despite the approach of winter, the Spanish governor sought to complete as quickly as possible all preparations for the last leg of the

39. D'Ossun to Choiseul, December 5, 1763, quoted in Villiers, *Les dernières années*, 224, and Choiseul to d'Ossun, April 25, 1765, in Leg. 174A, Papeles de Cuba, AGI.

40. Choiseul to d'Ossun, July 31, 1765, enclosure in letter from d'Ossun to Grimaldi, August 20, 1765, and Grimaldi to d'Ossun, August 25, 1765, both in Leg. 2542, Audiencia de Sto. Domingo, AGI.

41. His favorable impressions vanished in a short time. See Ulloa to Croix, November 27, 1765, in Leg. 2357, *ibid.*

journey. The shallowness of the channel at the mouth of the Mississippi and the damage sustained by the frigate in crossing the Atlantic induced him to commandeer two smaller vessels, a frigate or packet called the *Volante* and a brig presently in the harbor, to convey the party. On January 17 the ships set out for New Orleans. Louis de Villemont, a French nobleman who had lived in Louisiana and who had advised Grimaldi on forming the expedition, commanded the smaller vessel. Inclement weather held up the passage. Curiously enough, the brig reached its destination, the French outpost of Balize, first on February 12.[42] Almost two weeks later the *Volante* joined its companion at anchor. The Spanish expeditionary force, two years in its organization, was ready to put foot on the soil of Louisiana.

42. Rodríguez, *Primeros años*, 99; Riu to Ulloa, February 12, 1766, in Leg. 109, Papeles de Cuba, AGI.

II

The Colony That France Almost Forgot

The vast territory that Spain received in 1762 embraced mainly the region to the west of the Mississippi River as far as the Rocky Mountains and included the Isle of Orleans. For France, Louisiana had been considered an adjunct to the more valuable colony of Canada. In the middle of the eighteenth century French statesmen believed that an additional opportunity for their country in the struggle for overseas wealth lay in expansion into the wilderness to the south of the Great Lakes. Exploration and settlement of this region would have concrete advantages. It would confine France's major rival and competitor Britain to the east and south of an important tributary of the Mississippi, the Ohio. Contact could be made also with the rich silver-producing Spanish colony of New Spain, bringing an opportunity for smuggling with its inhabitants. Besides, the region to the south of the lakes had natural resources that might be tapped to increase the wealth and prosperity of the homeland. The forests of this huge, uncharted domain contained beaver and other animals whose pelts were highly prized in Europe, timber suitable for shipbuilding, and perhaps other commodities for export.

Unfortunately, from the standpoint of priority in exploration, France had no valid right to territory along the northern coast of the Gulf of Mexico. Spain had already claimed the region as a result of several earlier expeditions. None of these had led to significant centers of expansion. The discouraging results gave Spaniards little appetite for more forays, and they concentrated on exploiting the mineral wealth of Peru and Mexico. Spain did not, however, retreat completely from the region, for St. Augustine, founded in 1565, became a powerful fortress for the defense of the lifeline between the West Indies and the Iberian Peninsula.

Despite the well-proved claims of Spain, Jean Colbert, the ambitious and tireless minister of commerce for Louis XIV, resolved to add the area to the French colonial empire. In February, 1682, Robert Cavelier, the sieur de La Salle, at the bidding of Colbert began a voyage down the Mississippi from Canada with a group of Frenchmen and Indians. On April 6, after numerous encounters with the Indian tribes, he reached the mouth of the river, and three days later he claimed the territory for Louis XIV by erecting a post and a cross. His force being limited, he was compelled to return to France and organize an expedition to effect a settlement by the sea near the mouth of the river. Not only did his navigator on the return trip miss the mouth of the Mississippi, but the settlement that he later established on the Texas coast disappeared and he himself was murdered by his own men on the march to Canada for help.

It was left to Pierre Le Moyne, Sieur d'Iberville, to realize the dream of the French empire builder. With the full support of Jérôme de Maurepas, the comte de Pontchartrain, who was French minister of marine, the Canadian-born Iberville organized in 1698 an expedition at La Rochelle, which managed to cross the Atlantic safely and anchor near Pensacola. The hostility of the Spanish induced him to move westward, and the tiny fleet dropped anchor again near Ship Island, while Iberville and his men set out in small boats along the coast to locate a suitable spot for a settlement. On March 2, 1699, he discovered the entrance of the Mississippi and then with his men moved up the river, reconnoitering the banks and countryside as far north as present-day West Feliciana Parish. Turning back to the south, he decided to found a settlement on the Gulf coast rather than on the banks of the river because of the hazardous navigation for ships and danger from the British, who were close to the Mississippi. Hence Fort Maurepas, the first French settlement, was founded on a point of land on the eastern side of Biloxi Bay.[1]

The failure of Fort Maurepas to develop into a thriving center caused Iberville to seek another location. In 1702, after a voyage to France to obtain additional support, he constructed a new fort on the Mobile River, called Fort St. Louis de la Mobile, with an enclosed area of some 375 square feet and defended by 4 batteries of 6 cannons each.[2] This became a permanent settlement, replacing Fort Maurepas as the focus of French colonial activity in the region. Despite Iberville's strenuous efforts, the new colony grew little. France's involvement in the War of the Spanish Succession spelled neglect and inattention. The few emigrants from France were mostly from the lower classes, in general an undesirable lot, who lacked the energy and initiative to leave off the search for quick wealth and turn to agriculture as a sound basis for the economy. Indian raids, unfavorable climate, a sandy soil, and absence of women contributed to the unhappiness of the first settlers. Four years after the founding, the colonists numbered only 85; in 1710 the population had increased to 178, omitting the military men and a contingent of Canadians. The following year the location of the fort was again changed, this time to a spot eight leagues from the mouth of the bay, where the city of Mobile now stands.

As a royal colony directly under the crown, Louisiana had made relatively little progress. Its greatest economic and social advance resulted from the establishment of proprietary rule. In 1712 Louis XIV, following the successful example of England,

---

1. Marcel Giraud, professor of history at the Collège de France in Paris, is the outstanding authority on the history of Louisiana under France. He has published four volumes of his *Histoire de la Louisiane française*, which, based on an exhaustive study of archival records, promises to be the definitive work on this subject. Louisiana State University Press in 1974 published the English translation of the first volume of Giraud's *A History of Louisiana*, encompassing the reign of Louis XV, 1698–1715. See also Richebourg Gaillard McWilliams, "Iberville at the Birdfoot Subdelta: Final Discovery of the Mississippi River," in John Francis McDermott (ed.), *Frenchmen and French Ways in the Mississippi Valley* (Urbana, 1969), 127–40, and Edwin A. Davis, *Louisiana: A Narrative History* (3rd ed.; Baton Rouge, 1971), 37–41.

2. Davis, *Louisiana*, 43.

Louisiana Territory, detail of 1764 French map. Courtesy New York
Public Library

granted Louisiana by letters of patent to Antoine Crozat, a wealthy French merchant and nobleman.[3] In return for the right to exploit the agricultural and commercial potentialities, the proprietor was obliged to set up the government under the laws of France and with the crown controlling any military or naval units stationed in Louisiana.

For the first time in its history energetic efforts were made to promote the well-being of the colony. Under Antoine de la Mothe Cadillac the government was reorganized with the establishment of the Superior Council, destined to be a permanent feature of administration, and with the proclamation of the laws of France and the custom of Paris. Immigration was encouraged, particularly wives for the settlers, although with no conspicuous success initially. Agriculture replaced hunting and trapping as an important feature of economic life. The governor urged the planting of maize instead of tobacco and indigo and the raising of cattle to provide sufficient food and to make the colony self-sufficient; and, additionally, to increase the labor supply he imported several thousand Negro slaves. Attempts were made to expand commercial activity by treaties with the Indians to purchase furs and by contacts with the English and Spanish colonies to exchange goods. Unfortunately, these efforts met with less success than had been hoped for owing to the indifference or open hostility of the settlers to the innovations, the financial reverses of the proprietor, and the brusque personality of Cadillac. The replacements for Cadillac, Jean Baptiste Le Moyne, the sieur de Bienville, and Jean Michiele, the seigneur de Lépinay, were unable to place the colony on a better economic foundation, and in 1717 the first proprietor relinquished his right to the province.

Under the new proprietorship, that of the Company of the West, later the Company of the Indies, which was headed by a Scottish businessman and financier John Law, Louisiana took its great stride forward. In September, 1717, Louis XV conceded a charter to the joint stock company, with the same authority and

3. *Ibid.,* 46.

powers exercised by Crozat. The need for a new capital was finally recognized, and in 1717 Bienville, then governor, informed the directors of the company of his intention to locate a city in a crescent bend of the Mississippi at the closest point to Lake Pontchartrain. In 1718, with the approval of the company, actual work was begun on the building of the capital to be known as New Orleans. A reorganization of the provincial administration resulted in the division of the territory into nine districts: New Orleans, Biloxi, Mobile, Alibamons, Natchez, Yazoo, Arkansas, Natchitoches, and Illinois.[4] In 1722 at the conclusion of a treaty of peace between France and Spain, the Perdido River became the generally recognized boundary for the rival colonies.

Having greater financial resources, the Company of the West was able to promote many activities for the development of the colony. Increasing the population was of first importance. In the beginning the company endeavored to procure settlers by emptying jails and houses of correction and by rounding up vagrants in the ports and packing them off to America. To secure more substantial citizens, the company made land grants to prospective immigrants, even opening up the region to foreigners. Consequently, several thousand Germans and Swiss took up land along the banks of the Mississippi, with the chief area of concentration, known as La Côte des Allemands, being a short distance above New Orleans. The presence of the new nationalities, with their industry and thrift, was a steadying influence on the volatile, carefree French, giving more purpose and permanence to the colony.[5] A large number of slaves came in company ships to increase the labor supply.[6] By 1724 so numerous were the slaves, free Negroes, and mulattoes that Bienville issued the Black Code based mainly on the slave code enforced in St. Domingue.

On the whole, the colony made less progress after 1722. With

4. *Ibid.*, 54.
5. For an account of the German immigration, see René Le Conte, "The Germans in Louisiana in the Eighteenth Century," trans. and ed. Glenn Conrad, *Louisiana History*, VIII (Winter, 1967), 67–84.
6. N. M. Miller Surrey, *The Commerce of Louisiana During the French Regime, 1699–1763*, Columbia University Studies in History, Economics, and Public Law, LXXI, 1 (New York, 1916), 231, 232.

protection from the river and swamp by levees, New Orleans attained a population of over one thousand by 1729. The gradual spreading out of the settlers created posts at Baton Rouge, Natchitoches, and Rapides and plantations and farms above and below New Orleans on the Mississippi and along Bayou Lafourche. In 1729 the colony was faced with a serious Indian rebellion. The Natchez Indians suddenly went on the warpath, killing settlers and destroying villages before being finally suppressed and forced across the river by French troops.[7] The news of the Indian war persuaded the company of the futility of trying to transform Louisiana into a prosperous, paying enterprise. Inextricably enmeshed also in the finances of the French government, the company in 1731 appealed to the crown to withdraw the charter. The king's consent to the petition meant the reestablishment of Louisiana as a royal colony, a status preserved until the transfer to Spain in 1762.

For three decades the crown attempted to raise the level of Louisiana to that of St. Domingue, an increasingly valuable jewel in the colonial empire. Results of the efforts were meager. Two governors, Bienville, a member of the illustrious Canadian family, and Louis Billouart, Chevalier de Kerlérec, a former captain of the royal navy, were men of more than average resolve and courage. Indian wars, especially the attacks of the Chickasaws, brought on in part by the machinations of the British, were a major preoccupation that hindered the normal development that might otherwise have taken place.[8] During Kerlérec's tenure, 1753–1763, the Seven Years' War sapped the resources of the colony and, because of the superiority of the British fleet,

7. A somewhat romanticized account of Louis Juchereau de St. Denis, the French explorer and trader who had much to do with the securing of the Franco-Spanish frontier and the defeat of the Natchez, is to be found in Ross Phares, *Cavalier in the Wilderness: The Story of the Explorer and Trader Louis Juchereau de St. Denis* (Gloucester, Mass., 1970).

8. Gayarré, *History of Louisiana*, II, 67–88, 90. Governor Kerlérec complained bitterly of the lack of presents for the Indians and the consequent threat to French security in the province. Although his complaints about the nature of goods for distribution to the Indians were soundly based, France's position vis-à-vis the tribes in the lower Mississippi Valley was still strong. See Davis, *Louisiana,* 82.

spelled virtual isolation from the homeland. Not only did the conflict impoverish the colony, but it encouraged self-assertiveness and disregard for authority. For the people of Louisiana it was a period of neglect, and one that could hardly be termed salutary.

Although some men of ability occupied the governorship, the administration of the colony was inefficient, often venal, and generally inferior to that of other French possessions. Chief power was vested in a governor appointed by the minister of marine and receiving orders from him. Lower in the administrative echelon was the *commissaire ordonnateur,* or commissary general, whose authority was extended in 1729 to cover finance, commerce, agriculture, and justice. The obviously overlapping duties of the governor and this official led to numerous controversies, intensified by the conflicting reports sent back to France by each party. It was the greatest single cause of political discord.[9] The supreme judicial body was the Superior Council, established in 1712.[10] As the colony grew, membership in the council expanded to include by 1748 "the governor, commissary general, procurator-general, a counselor," and a number of minor officials.[11] The list of lesser officials revealed judges, syndics, sheriffs from the larger settlements, notaries, and

9. Kerlérec and Vincent de Rochemore, the commissary general who had a reputation as a spendthrift and a cheat, feuded for several years over the finances of the colony. The governor's indictment resulted in Rochemore's recall, but his successor Foucault took up his predecessor's cause, writing letters impugning Kerlérec's honesty and integrity. See Charles Gayarré, *History of Louisiana* (5th ed., 4 vols.; New Orleans, 1965), II, 90, 91. The upshot was that Kerlérec, though generally honest and certainly tireless in his efforts to defend the colony, on his return to France was thrown into the Bastille for graft, whence he was finally liberated at his friends' solicitation. See François-Xavier Martin, *The History of Louisiana from the Earliest Period* (New Orleans, 1963), 190, 191. For an excellent discussion of the commissary's role in Louisiana history, see Donald Lemieux, "The Office of Commissaire Ordonnateur in French Louisiana, 1731–1763: A Study in French Colonial Administration" (Ph.D. dissertation, Louisiana State University, 1972).

10. A favorable attitude toward the council's judicial activities, especially in cases arising out of civil law, is taken by Professor James Hardy, who concludes for a number of reasons that "the quality of both civil and criminal justice was better in Louisiana than in France." See James D. Hardy, Jr., "The Superior Council in Colonial Louisiana," in McDermott (ed.), *Frenchmen and French Ways in the Mississippi Valley,* 101.

11. Davis, *Louisiana,* 77.

clerks. These offices were filled by appointment from the king or governor or by payment of money. The Superior Council required registration of all of these offices, whether appointive or obtained through purchase, a procedure prevailing in the Spanish colonies as well as in other French possessions.

It is hardly to be expected that this governmental system would attract able persons. Under Louis XV France was a nation declining in power and influence. In the view of a prominent French historian, "France had neither the material nor the moral resources, which had enabled her to conduct with comparative success the colonization of Canada and the West Indies."[12] The principle of vendibility of office generally deterred men of talent in both Louisiana and Spanish America, and, similarly, the tremendous areas to be governed with inadequate communication slowed the execution of good policies.

The lawgiving authority in the colony belonged theoretically to the governor. These ordinances were mostly police regulations involving local issues of administration to be enforced by commandants and judges. The great body of civil and criminal law derived from the edicts and decrees of the king, the orders of the Council of State, and after 1712 the custom of Paris. In the district, the military head or commandant was the central governing figure, and the soldiers carried out his orders. Cases of considerable import might be appealed to the Superior Council.[13] The military force in the colony, recruited by levy or by inducement of pay from the lower classes in France, was never numerous, scarcely over a thousand men at one time. It enjoyed an unsavory reputation for sloth, indiscipline, and unreliabili-

12. Marcel Giraud, "France and Louisiana in the Eighteenth Century," *Mississippi Valley Historical Review*, XXXVI (March, 1950), 657.

13. That this body played a consistently dominant role in the affairs of the colony is debatable. It had in my opinion few truly legislative functions. But, an administrator lacking in force of character or rendered insecure by controversy with the commissary might cater to the wishes of this group. For a view of the council as a potent factor in the regime, possessed of distinct legislative powers, see Jerry A. Micelle, "From Law Court to Local Government: Metamorphosis of the Superior Council of French Louisiana," *Louisiana History*, IX (Spring, 1968), 85–108.

ty.[14] Maintaining the military establishment was costly, the expenditures running annually from 600,000 to 1,000,000 livres.

To the empire builders of the eighteenth century the economy of Louisiana proved a grave disappointment. From the first the colony had difficulty maintaining even a subsistence existence. In the swamps and bayous of lower Louisiana and in the forests of the hilly country to the north there were neither rich mines nor sedentary Indians. The future of the colony depended on agriculture and commerce. Using land first cleared by the Indians and later by their own efforts, the settlers established farms and plantations. In the early days, farming owed more to the Germans than to any other group. Corn, rice, vegetables, and wheat were the major sources of food, but these did not supply all the needs of the colonists. When the food supply was more assured, the settlers turned to crops for income, such as myrtle wax, silk, cotton, indigo, and tobacco. Both cotton and sugar were unimportant during the French period, the former owing to the dampness of the soil in southern Louisiana and the latter owing to the absence of a good method for granulating sugar. The raising of livestock grew slowly, with cattle, hogs, and sheep furnishing the chief supply of meat. In spite of the favorable attitude of the proprietors and royal governors, the colonists in 1763 were still dependent on imported food for subsistence.[15]

Without commerce the colony could not exist. Manufacturing was limited to a few items, usually for domestic use. The distribution of these goods and articles of foreign make and the flow of commodities to New Orleans resulted in a considerable internal trade. The numerous waterways provided the avenue by which the colony supplied itself. In time, the fur traders organized pack trains, using old animal traces and Indian trails.[16] The perils of ambush and the hardships associated with trekking through the snake-infested swamps and dense underbrush and

14. Lemieux, "The Office of Commissaire Ordonnateur," 89–92.
15. Davis, *Louisiana*, 71; *ibid.*, 130–34.
16. Davis, *Louisiana*, 75; Surrey, *The Commerce of Louisiana*, 82–96.

of rowing upstream against the strong current of the great river impeded any easy exchange of goods.

The economic life of the colony greatly hinged on the exchange of domestic commodities for foreign manufactures. From the first, contact with France was irregular because of a lack of merchant ships, the dangers of the long voyage, and the hostility of the British. From the homeland came cargoes of spices, cloth, cutlery, flour, wines, and some luxury items, and to the motherland the colonists dispatched tobacco, indigo, pitch, tar, lumber, furs, hides, and sundry commodities. After 1720 trade with the French West Indies was significant, with Louisiana shipping lumber, beef, tar, and pitch to this market and getting in return sugar, coffee, rum, drugs, and spices.[17]

During the eighteenth century, contraband trade with the Spanish and English was likewise expanded. In time of war the governor frequently legalized this commerce because of the interruption of normal contact between Europe and the Caribbean. As a regular practice, the Spanish government prohibited such trade in accord with mercantilism but could not altogether eliminate an overland trade with Mexico and Florida. Among the merchants of New Orleans the feeling existed that trade with the Spanish possessions offered the best return because of the payment for commodities in specie. But from the British the colonists procured scarce manufactured articles and occasionally flour. Dodges of all sorts were used to evade legal obstruction.[18] The isolation of the colony during European wars in which France was involved made it imperative for the colonists to disregard homeland regulations and set up their own commercial relations with neighboring foreign colonies.[19]

17. Lemieux, "The Office of Commissaire Ordonnateur," 129, 136, 137. One may gain some idea of the luxuries imported from France in a description of the decor of a mansion constructed by Chevalier Jean de Pradel near New Orleans. See A. Baillardel and A. Priolt, *Le chevalier de Pradel: Vie d'un colon français en Louisiane au XVIIIe siècle d'après sa correspondance et celle de sa famille* (Paris, 1928), 220, 221.

18. Surrey, *The Commerce of Louisiana*, 388–430, 451; Lemieux, "The Office of Commissaire Ordonnateur," 149–51.

19. Lemieux, "The Office of Commissaire Ordonnateur," 153, 154, aptly sums up the causes for Louisiana's failure to establish a prosperous commerce: "There was always

Commercial transactions of every type were constantly hindered by the lack of a sound currency. Coins, whether of gold, silver, or copper, were always scarce, a deficiency which the colonial administration attempted to remedy by issuing quantities of paper money. Over twenty-five million livres of paper money were put out by the Company of the Indies by 1719. It was inevitable that depreciation would take place, so that by 1746 it took twenty-two livres of paper money to equal one livre of specie. In addition to paper money, the colonists used bills of exchange, French treasury notes, storehouse receipts, and contracts in a desperate effort to fill the gap. Issuing unsupported paper currency unavoidably led to speculation and concomitant inflation. With this makeshift system, many transactions were naturally on a barter basis. To the French colonist in 1763 the dual issues of commerce and currency were intertwined and their solution could not be interminably postponed.[20]

This was the situation facing the settlers of Louisiana toward the end of the Seven Years' War when the territory was ceded by France to Spain. Misgoverned, suffering from neglect and privation, economically depressed, the colony needed a strong hand, whether that of France or some other power, to put it on its feet.[21]

Why did France agree to transfer to Spain this huge and potentially rich agricultural region stretching from the Gulf to Canada? As with many historical phenomena, no single reason, motive, or theory offers an adequate, fully satisfying explanation. To frame an answer that will better clarify the issue, the historian must be cognizant of the closely knit relations between

---

an ingredient lacking for the realization of stable commercial activities. When ships from France and the Spanish colonies were available there were either no products or not enough to trade. Conversely, when Louisiana products were available, war or commercial restrictions hampered trade. But at all times there was the financial problem: lack of silver and inflation."

20. *Ibid.*, 175–81, 182. Had the French treasury been well managed, the government might have lent a helping hand. But heavy indebtedness due to wars and unwise policies at home drained financial resources.

21. *Ibid.*, 153.

France and Spain in the middle of the eighteenth century, the traditional attitude of Louis XV's ministers toward the colony, the languishing state of colonial economy, and finally the strategic requirements of the Spanish crown in its imperialistic rivalry with England.

In the background was the seemingly perpetual competition of the Great Powers with stakes on the continent and in colonial empires. At the outset of the Seven Years' War, Spain was the principal neutral, courted by France and England. As the balance tipped on the scales in favor of the British, the French ministry appealed to Charles III of Spain to bolster the fortunes of his Bourbon cousin. The haughty attitude of the British ministry coupled with fear of its aggressive designs had already inclined the Spanish ruler to favor France. In 1761 Choiseul, the chief promoter of the new policy, prevailed on the marqués de Grimaldi, Spanish ambassador at Versailles, to recommend to his court close diplomatic ties with France. Already a strong Francophile, Grimaldi convinced Charles III of the necessity of this move for the safety of the Spanish Empire.[22] The resultant Family Compact consisted of three conventions, the first being a general alliance based on the bonds of kinship uniting the reigning monarchs of Spain and France, the second a secret agreement for military assistance in the war, and the third a commercial arrangement.[23] When the nature of the alliance was revealed in London by the conde de Fuentes on December 6, 1761,

---

22. The biographer of the Bourbons in Spain characterizes Grimaldi "as a person of illustrious descent, accustomed to the polished society of courts, elegant in his manners, magnificent, generous, and hospitable in his mode of life. He was averse to application, yet sedulous when application was necessary; he transacted business with an ease, dispatch, and accuracy highly agreeable to his sovereign; fond of amusement, yet never suffering amusement to interrupt the course of serious occupations. In political principles he was devoted to France, proud of that devotion, and guided in his operations by the Duke of Choiseul, but dreading the effect of the national prejudice against France and French alliances, and adroitly flattering his sovereign by an affectation of zeal for the independence and honour of his crown." See William Coxe, *Memoirs of the Kings of Spain of the House of Bourbon from the Accession of Philip V to the Death of Charles III, 1700 to 1788* (5 vols.; London, 1815), IV, 338, 339.

23. Rodríguez, *Primeros años*, 35.

relations between Britain and Spain were broken off, and in January, 1762, war became a reality. As the tide of victory ebbed against France in Europe, owing to the defection of Russia and the faintheartedness of Austria, Louis XV realized the need for peace. On the other hand, Charles III, with more resources to call on, sought to continue the war. To persuade the Spanish ruler to agree to a peace treaty and to accept the permanent loss of territory, particularly Florida, which had been conquered by the British, Choiseul offered to Spain the immense territory of Louisiana. It was essential for the immediate termination of hostilities.[24]

Simultaneously, Choiseul, an eminently practical statesman, could find no good reason for retaining the colony, now that Canada had been lost to Great Britain. To many historians of Louisiana, the so-called white elephant theory has credibility. Without Canada, which had always merited the first attention of the court, Louisiana could not be defended. Moreover, "the colony was notorious as a financial liability."[25] Crozat and Law, both men of finance, had speculated and lost millions of livres in the colony. In its last years as a royal colony Louisiana had absorbed more than 800,000 livres annually from the Versailles treasury. With a mounting public debt that culminated in the bankruptcy of the government in 1789 and with little prospect of the colony ever being put on a paying basis, Choiseul indeed had

---

24. See Ronald D. Smith, "French Interest in Louisiana from Choiseul to Napoleon" (Ph.D. dissertation, University of Michigan, 1964); John F. Ramsey, *Anglo-French Relations, 1763–1770: A Study of Choiseul's Foreign Policy,* University of California Publications in History (Berkeley, 1939); and E. Wilson Lyon, *Louisiana in French History, 1759–1804* (Norman, Okla., 1934). It is unrealistic to believe that Louis XV acted primarily out of generosity or by virtue of "Gallic impulsiveness." See William R. Shepherd, "The Cession of Louisiana to Spain," *Political Science Quarterly,* XIX (September, 1904), 451. Pierre Boulle, "Some Eighteenth-Century French Views of Louisiana," in McDermott (ed.), *Frenchmen and French Ways in the Mississippi Valley,* 27, argues with some plausibility that Choiseul was reluctant to yield Louisiana.

25. John W. Caughey, *Bernardo de Gálvez in Louisiana, 1776–1783* (Berkeley, 1934), 4. Davis, *Louisiana,* 69, 70, regards the white elephant theory as the most likely one. In general, I lean toward Caughey's view of Spanish motivation, which emphasizes the value of the province as a buffer between the English colonies and Mexico.

little reason from this standpoint for keeping it. Yet, despite supposition and conjecture, French motivation for the cession is still obscure.

Was Spain conscious of the financial obligations to be incurred in assuming ownership of the colony? There is little doubt that she knew already of the paucity of resources and the unprofitable history of the province. The Treaty of Fontainebleau, November 3, 1762, stipulated that "His Most Christian Majesty cedes in full ownership, purely, simply, without contradiction to His Catholic Majesty and his successors in perpetuity all the country known under the name of Louisiana, including New Orleans and the Island on which it is situated."[26]

Charles III's advisers were not in full agreement on whether to accept the treaty. Richard Wall, the Irish-born secretary of state, in general an advocate of neutrality in foreign policy, saw in Choiseul's offer a noose binding Spain to France in the future. If France were already an ally, it would make little difference whether the colony was French or Spanish.[27] On the other hand, the conde de Aranda, Pedro Pablo Abarca de Bolea, leader of the powerful Aragonese faction in court intrigue, viewed the acquisition as a new line of strategy, a means of establishing the Mississippi as a frontier between the French and Spanish possessions, "a recognized barrier and a long way from the populated centers of New Mexico. If France retains it, our commerce will suffer through smuggling and she will in the first crisis cede it as a jewel to the English, who desire it very much."[28] The king supported Grimaldi and Aranda. Significantly, he had already indicated a wish to take over the province. In an interview with the French ambassador at Madrid in 1760, he had declared: "I must arrange with France after the peace for Louisiana by means

26. Quoted in Rodríguez, *Primeros años*, 42. See also Frances G. Davenport, *European Treaties Bearing on the History of the United States and Its Dependencies* (3 vols.; Washington, D.C., 1917–34).

27. In 1754, Wall, along with Sir Richard Keene, the brilliant but unscrupulous British ambassador at Madrid, had manipulated the overthrow of the marqués de Ensenada, a friend of France and a rebuilder of the Spanish navy.

28. Quoted in Rodríguez, *Primeros años*, 43, 44.

of some exchange." On July 30, 1761, Choiseul, faced with French defeats, gave d'Ossun authority to exchange the region for an immediate declaration of war by Spain on England. This was rejected by the Spanish court, but seven weeks later the crown concluded the Family Compact. Although Grimaldi sought all of Louisiana, including Mobile, he had to be content with the territory west of the Mississippi and the Isle of Orleans. From Madrid d'Ossun reported that the Spanish court liked the cession: "The demarche, dictated by a dexterous policy, will justify to the Spanish nation the part taken by His Catholic Majesty in coming to the aid of France."[29] On November 13, Wall dispatched the note of acceptance to Grimaldi in Paris to be transmitted to the French court. It does not conceal the lukewarmness of the secretary of state to this territorial expansion.[30]

Although the agreement was sealed in November, more than a year passed before the Spanish crown undertook to organize an expedition for the occupation. What motivated this policy of inaction? One cannot speak with complete assurance on a point that has for so long been a mystery to historians. From an examination of the records one may adduce a number of factors and circumstances. The reluctance of Spain to act should be attributed in part to the negative policy of Richard Wall, a long-time opponent of French influence at the court. Not until he had resigned were circumstances more propitious for closer ties with France. The elevation of Grimaldi, an architect of the Treaty of Fontainebleau, to this post meant immediate implementation of a plan to incorporate Louisiana into the empire.[31] It is therefore no coincidence that concrete proposals

---

29. Arthur S. Aiton, "The Diplomacy of the Louisiana Cession," *American Historical Review,* XXXVI (July, 1931), 702, 703, 706, 719.

30. Wall to Grimaldi, November 13, 1762, in Leg. 3889, Estado, AHN.

31. The Spanish ambassador recounted an interview with the French minister over the matter of the belated occupation: "In conversation with the duc de Choiseul about Louisiana, he told me that he was writing to the marquis d'Ossun that we had delayed a year in assuming authority in the colony; he added immediately with a good deal of emotion that he did not understand the procrastination, which was truly a source of great

were offered in February, 1764, shortly after his nomination. The secretary of state himself assumed chief responsibility for what he regarded as his pet project.

But there were other factors to account for this lack of haste in assuming control of Louisiana. Recovery and rehabilitation after the Seven Years' War loomed large as an objective for the ministry of state. Spain had suffered losses in territory and resources. Costs of the brief participation in the fighting had been heavy. It was essential to rebuild in the West Indies the navy and the fortifications dismantled after their siege and capture. Moreover, Louisiana was a minor colony compared to Mexico, Peru, and even the Philippines. Finally, there is the traditional penchant for vacillation and procrastination, familiar to all students of the Spanish Empire. In 1763 the wheels of the bureaucratic machinery were turning slowly despite the lubricant furnished by the energy and intelligence of Charles III, assisted by a series of able ministers.[32] As has been seen, the organization of the expedition at La Coruña had required far more time than Grimaldi had contemplated.

Meanwhile, the colony was being haphazardly governed without the strong direction and aid from France necessary for its progress. The departure of Kerlérec in 1763 led to the appointment of Jean Jacques Blaise d'Abbadie, the commissary general and marine official, as governor and Charles Philippe Aubry as second in command of the military in the colony. The difficulties facing the new administration were enormous. The Indian question posed a greater problem now than in the past, for it was necessary to make peace between the Choctaws and the Alabamas. The arrival of the British garrison at Mobile, which had been ceded to England in the general settlement in 1763, complicated the negotiations and led to British participation in

---

embarrassment. I answered that I also was ignorant of it, but I did not doubt that there was some inevitable cause of the delay." See Fernando Magallón to the ministry, December 23, 1763, *ibid.*

32. Lyon, *Louisiana in French History,* 40, regards the slowness to act as normal: "Delay was not an unusual feature of Spanish colonial administration; there is no evidence that Spain desired to withdraw from her agreement with France."

the outcome. The finances of the colony were also in a miserable condition because of the expenses of the war and the inability of the French government to send funds.[33] The successors to Kerlérec soon discovered a more serious problem in the general attitude of the colonists toward the enforcement of law and order. The wartime years with almost complete separation from France had generated an individualism or self-reliance that bordered on lawlessness. In a letter of June 7, 1764, to the French ministry, d'Abbadie commented extensively on the tendency to flout authority and resort to violence. In retrospect, his recommendation that restoration of order was essential to the success of the colony would have stood the Spanish governor Ulloa in good stead.[34]

To augment the natural unrest in the colony came the news of its cession to Spain. Choiseul had wished to inform the people of the fact at once, but agreed to hold the notice at the request of the

---

33. Villiers, *Les dernières années,* 167, 168, 171–75, 176, 189.

34. Since this letter is a good exposé of the temper and the mores of the people of the colony, it is given *in extenso:*

> I have the honor to submit my observations on the character and dispositions of the inhabitants of Louisiana. The disorder long existing in the colony, and particularly in its finances, proceeds from the spirit of jobbing [speculation] which has been prevalent here at all times, and which has engrossed the attention and faculties of the colonists. It began in 1737, not only on the currency of the country, but also on the bills of exchange, on the merchandise in the King's warehouses, and on everything which was susceptible of it. It is to this pursuit that the inhabitants have been addicted in preference to cultivating their lands, and to any other occupation, but which the prosperity of the colony would have been promoted.... If the inhabitants of Louisiana had turned their industry to anything else beyond jobbing on the King's paper and merchandise, they would have found great resources in the fertility of the land and the mildness of the climate. But the facility offered by the country to live on its natural productions has created habits of laziness. The immoderate use of taffia [a kind of rum] has stupified the whole population. The vice of drunkenness had even crept into the highest ranks of society, from which, however, it has lately disappeared.
>
> Hence the spirit of insubordination and independence which has manifested itself under several administrations. I will not relate the excesses and outrages which occurred under Rochemore and Kerlérec. Notwithstanding the present tranquillity, the same spirit of sedition does not the less exist in the colony. It reappears in the thoughtless expressions of some madcaps, and in the anonymous writings scattered among the public. The uncertainty in which I am, with regard to the ultimate fate of the colony, has prevented me from resorting to extreme measures to repress such license; but it will be necessary to come to it at last, to re-establish the good order which has been destroyed, and to regulate the conduct and morals of the inhabitants. To reach this object, what is first to be done is, to make a thorough reform of the Superior Council.

D'Abbadie to the French ministry, June 7, 1764, quoted in Gayarré, *History of Louisiana,* II, 104–106.

Spanish crown. A letter from the French court, dated February 10, 1763, to the governor did carry the news of the transfer of the eastern part of Louisiana to Great Britain, thereby giving the impression that New Orleans and the territory west of the Mississippi would remain in French hands.[35] As the secret could not be withheld indefinitely—particularly in view of the Spanish efforts to organize an expedition—Choiseul finally announced the cession in a letter of April 21, 1764, to d'Abbadie. The reaction in the colony was one of regret and apprehension. In January, 1765, a mass meeting, attended by delegates from various parishes, voiced protests and resolutions urging Louis XV to revoke the transfer. Merchants and traders spoke out against the loss of business if Spain enforced the exclusive features of her monopolistic system. Other groups feared changes in governmental, legal, and social institutions. It is noteworthy that one of the speakers at the assembly was Nicolas Chauvin de La Frenière, the attorney general of the province, who already had a reputation for oratory and popular appeal. It was resolved that Jean Milhet, the wealthiest merchant in the city, should hasten to France to make a personal entreaty to Louis XV on behalf of the colonists. Milhet reached Paris safely, conferred with Bienville, a former governor and a friend of the settlers, and with Choiseul, but was not able to see the king. His mission a failure, he returned to New Orleans to report the outcome. Although there was little doubt in his mind concerning the future of Louisiana, the people were still unwilling to accept his words at full value.[36]

D'Abbadie's untimely death on February 4, 1765, placed the government of the colony in the hands of Charles Aubry, the ranking military officer. According to one of his detractors, Jean Bochart, the chevalier de Champigny, Aubry was "a small man, dry in manner, ugly, without nobility and dignity and without proper bearing. His physiognomy would have given the impression of a hypocrite, but this vice came from an excess of goodwill that led him to consent to anything out of fear of arousing displeasure."[37] Although this portrayal is too severe, he nevertheless lacked judgment and decisiveness on occasion. To his credit he was cooperative, conscientious, and loyal to the French crown. Like his predecessor, he was impressed with the desperate condition of the economy and "the inconceivable spirit of insubordination that has reigned in the country for the last ten years." The demands of the Indians and the presence of the British on the frontier also required much attention. Besides, he had an implacable rival for power in the person of Nicolas Foucault, the commissary, with the possibility of a recrudescence of the feud that had brought about Kerlérec's downfall. To Aubry the salvation of the colony lay in the prompt appearance of the Spanish. "Until the arrival of the Spaniards," he wrote to Paris, "I shall do everything I can to maintain the peace and tranquillity between the French, the savages, and the English, which is not easy to do."[38] The uncertainty of the date of the Spanish occupation exasperated Aubry and, unquestionably, for the popular mind constituted additional evidence of the indefiniteness and obscurity of Spanish intentions. The three-year delay was itself a serious obstacle to the establishment of a firm, viable regime.

37. Quoted in Villiers, *Les dernières années*, 204.
38. Clarence W. Alvord and Clarence E. Carter (eds.), *The Critical Period, 1763–1765,* Collections of the Illinois State Historical Library, X (Springfield, Ill., 1915), 436, 434. General Thomas Gage, commander-in-chief of British forces in America, received two letters from Aubry in the fall of 1765, in both of which the French governor stated that "he expected Don Antonio de Ulloa in a few days from Havana." See Gage to Conway, secretary of state, December 21, 1765, in Clarence Carter (ed.), *The Correspondence of General Thomas Gage with the Secretaries of State, and with the War Office and the Treasury, 1763–1775* (2 vols.; New Haven, 1931–33), I, 76.

III

A Government with Two Heads

Pragmatism was the overriding element in the rationale of the bizarre government established by the Spanish governor in 1766. In omitting the formal claim to Louisiana on his arrival in New Orleans (much to the bewilderment of the colonists), Antonio de Ulloa recognized the anomaly of his position. Until the red and yellow banner of Spain flew from the staff in New Orleans and over the outposts in place of the fleur-de-lis, the colony legally had two executives, the new Spanish governor and the French governor Charles Aubry. Custom and procedure in international law stipulated this formality. Before stepping ashore Ulloa sensed the indifference or latent aversion of the citizenry to the transfer. With a small contingent of approximately ninety soldiers, he lacked the force to impose his will. He was cognizant of the vast territory embracing the new acquisition, with its Indian tribes and with the English already on the frontier. Economic problems of large proportions faced the colonists. In this situation expediency and tactful diplomacy were of prime importance. It was logical, therefore, for the governor to advocate a policy of coordination with the existing French regime.

Ulloa's commission, signed by Charles III on May 1, 1765, set forth the guiding principles of the government:

> Don Antonio de Ulloa, captain of my royal navy, in view of your intelligence, zeal, and conduct, I have decided to appoint you as governor of the province of Louisiana, which has been ceded to me by His Most Christian

42

King my cousin and in consequence added to my crown. . . . I have resolved that in this new acquisition no innovation will be made in the government and no law or custom prevailing in the Indies will be applied, it being considered as a separate colony which may enjoy commerce with them [other Spanish colonies]; it is my will that with complete independence of the minister of the Indies, the council, and other associated tribunals all matters be referred to the minister of state, who alone will keep me informed of whatever occurs relative to your commission, and by this route you will receive your orders, instructions pertaining to the government and policy of that new, independent domain; I assign to you 6,000 pesos annually, which will be paid you from the amount provided for that province and paid against a draft on the treasurer or other agent connected with the royal treasury.[1]

It would appear that the Francophile Grimaldi from the first had promoted conciliation and the maintenance of the status quo. As early as December, 1763, after a memorable conference with the minister of state, the French ambassador had reported that Louisiana "with regard to its internal administration and commerce would be put on a different basis from that of other Spanish colonies."[2]

Taking his cue from Grimaldi, Choiseul sought to settle the qualms of the colonists over the transfer in his letter of April 21, 1764, to d'Abbadie:

I promise myself in consequence of the friendship and love of His Catholic Majesty that he will wish to give orders to his governor and to every other officer employed in his service in the said colony and city of New Orleans, so that the clergy and the religious houses that provide the curés and the missions continue in their duties and enjoy the rights, privileges, and exemptions with which they have been endowed by their establishments; that the regular judges, such as the Superior Council, continue to render justice according to the laws, forms, and usages of the colony, that the inhabitants be confirmed in the possession of their property, in accord with the concessions made by the governors and commissaries of the colony, and that the said land grants be registered and confirmed by His Catholic Majesty, even though they have not yet been sanctioned by me.[3]

1. Royal order, May 1, 1765, in Leg. 2543, Audiencia de Sto. Domingo, AGI.
2. Quoted in Villiers, *Les dernières années,* 224.
3. Choiseul to d'Abbadie, April 21, 1764, quoted *ibid.,* 196.

The regime to be created in Louisiana enjoyed a uniqueness in the framework of the Spanish colonial empire. Contrary to the usual method of dealing with newly acquired subjects, the crown did not insist on immediate incorporation into the imperial system under the Laws of the Indies and the minister of the Indies. Louisiana would be governed according to its former laws and institutions through directives from the secretary of state. It was obviously a concession to France and to Choiseul, another measure to give strength to the Family Compact so ardently espoused by the pro-French faction in Madrid. It is likewise evidence of a certain flexibility in the organization and functioning of the colonial system.

Did the Spanish crown regard this singular governmental arrangement for Louisiana as permanent? Evidence points instead to the temporary nature of the settlement. Although Louisiana was an agricultural colony, a financial liability, having little importance save as a dike to check the flood of British imperialism, it is most unlikely that its unique status would persist. Uniformity and centralization were paramount in the reformation of the colonial empire under Charles III. After a period of reconciliation, the enforcement of administrative conformity according to the absolutist concepts of the sovereign was inevitable. In announcing to the Council of the Indies the nomination of the new governor, Charles III hinted at the provisional character of the regime: "I have resolved that in this new acquisition no changes in its government will be made *for the moment.*"[4] In the interim the marqués de Grimaldi was responsible for formulating the policies for the colony. This did not augur well for the province, for, unfamiliar with colonial affairs and absorbed in questions of greater dimension in Europe, he could hardly give the territory the thoughtful attention that it needed to make the adjustment to a new ruler and a different culture.

---

4. Copy of an order of Charles III to the Council of the Indies, May 22, 1765, in Leg. 2594, Audiencia de Sto. Domingo, AGI. Italics mine.

Had the Spanish governor possessed a force sufficient to overawe the colonists, there would have been perhaps little need for a dual government. As it was, he counted on the quick incorporation of the French troops commanded by Aubry.[5] Foreseeing the advantages of experienced soldiers, Choiseul early in 1764 had offered to the Spanish the privilege of enlisting the officers and men of the French command remaining in the colony.[6] This was eagerly accepted by Grimaldi, who saw the opportunity not only to accelerate the occupation but to effect economies in recruitment and transportation. Consequently, the Spanish soldiers embarking on the *Liebre* in La Coruña in September, 1765, were to constitute a nucleus for a much larger force to be assembled in the colony.

In 1766, the French contingent under Aubry numbered close to three hundred men. This was the remnant of a more sizable force that France had maintained in the colony during the Seven Years' War. It was a motley aggregation, some elderly, others of ill health, having a reputation for desertion, unreliability, and general insubordination. French governors in the past had had low opinions of the forces stationed in the colony. Kerlérec had urged that Swiss soldiers replace them, because the French, "on account of the horrid acts of which they are known to be capable," had disgusted the population.[7]

Despite some knowledge of the character of the French contingent, Ulloa made overtures to incorporate it into his force. When his first proposal of keeping the customary pay schedule of the French soldiers and reducing the pay of the Spanish troops to the same rate was rejected, he then offered to them the

---

5. But the former governor Kerlérec, when consulted by Fuentes in Paris, averred that 1,800 soldiers would be necessary for full control of the province. See Lyon, *Louisiana in French History*, 41, 42.

6. Choiseul to d'Ossun, April 25, 1764, in Leg. 124A, Papeles de Cuba, AGI.

7. Gayarré, *History of Louisiana*, II, 71, 72. Governor Etienne Boucher Périer de Salvert confessed, undoubtedly with some exaggeration, "that his soldiers usually fled at the first flash of an Indian gun . . . that it would be much better to trust Negroes on the battle-field, and use them as soldiers were they not too valuable property, because they, at least, were brave men."

regular wages assigned to Spanish troops serving in the Indies.[8] Grimaldi approved this proposal in a dispatch to Ulloa of May 24, 1766.[9] Upon the announcement of equality in remuneration, some French soldiers hesitated but in the end all turned down the pay offer because they desired to return to France after long years abroad.[10] In writing to the captain general of Cuba, Ulloa averred that this was the principal cause of their opposition: "The French soldiers, despite the fact that they have been informed that His Majesty is placing those of this colony on the same scale of pay as all those in the Indies, insist that they be given their discharge because they have completed more than eight years since the time of their enlistment."[11] Even Aubry had no wish to enter the Spanish army. The French soldiers hence-

8. Actually, the initial offer to the French soldiers was better than it seemed, because the Spanish would pay in specie rather than in depreciated livres. See Clarence W. Alvord and Clarence E. Carter (eds.), *The New Regime, 1765–1767*, Collections of the Illinois State Historical Library, XI (Springfield, Ill., 1916), 182, 183.

9. Grimaldi to Ulloa, May 24, 1766, in Leg. 174, Papeles de Cuba, AGI.

10. A letter from Aubry to Choiseul makes clear that an offer by the Spanish governor was specifically made to the French troops: "I went at once to the barracks with the chief officers to give them the news and to explain to them in the strongest terms the advantages they would have in serving His Most Catholic Majesty, to which they responded with less vehemence, but they persisted in their request for leaves as soon as the act of possession occurred." See Aubry to Choiseul, September 1, 1766, in C13A46, Colonies, Archives Nationales, Paris, hereinafter cited as AN.

11. Ulloa to Bucareli, August 31, 1766, No. 7, in Dispatches of the Spanish Governors of Louisiana, I, W.P.A. Survey of Federal Archives in Louisiana, Louisiana State University Library, Baton Rouge. Antonio María Bucareli, like Ulloa, was from Seville, of noble family. Of approximately the same age, the two men were probably boyhood friends, but their paths had diverged sharply, Ulloa going into the navy, Bucareli into the army. Bucareli had distinguished himself as a field officer and inspector of fortifications prior to his American career. Appointed captain general of Cuba, he arrived in Havana on March 18, 1766, less than two weeks after Ulloa had landed in New Orleans. Bucareli was a newcomer to the Indies, and his preoccupation with learning the ropes in colonial administration, together with his innate sense of caution and a lack of initiative, may have prevented him from giving sound counsel to his friend in Louisiana. In 1771, because of good management of the island's affairs, he received the most coveted office in the region, that of viceroy of New Spain. His intimacy with Ulloa is evident from their personal letters during 1777 and 1778 when Ulloa was in command of the fleet transporting treasure from Mexico to Spain. Bucareli was also a close friend of Alexander O'Reilly's, with whom he corresponded extensively. A recent biographer extols his personal traits: "A kindly, courteous, considerate person, a Spanish aristocrat with a strong sense of *noblesse oblige.* His dominant motivation in life was to serve his nation and his King well." See Bernard E. Bobb, *The Viceregency of Antonio María Bucareli in New Spain, 1771–1779* (Austin, 1962), 268.

forth composed a separate military unit, taking their orders from Aubry. Their dissatisfaction was not so great that it prevented some of the soldiers and militia from voluntarily donning Spanish uniforms. But to enforce law and order and to quell riots or demonstrations would be difficult.

A stable regime depended therefore on strong reinforcements from Spain or from the empire for the miniscule garrison. "There is no other recourse than to bring the troops from Spain," the governor declared in a communication to Antonio María Bucareli, captain general of Cuba.[12] But to organize and transport a battalion from Spain in a reasonable period of time turned out to be an insurmountable task. In December, 1766, he outlined to Grimaldi the size and nature of the contingent needed, some seven hundred men with pieces of artillery. Over the next year and a half, Ulloa repeatedly petitioned the crown for the immediate dispatch of soldiers. "Your Lordship will understand," he wrote to Bucareli in March, 1767, "that it is virtually impossible to accomplish anything over here, or to handle this government with regularity without any troops to maintain respect and to contain so much freedom."[13]

Had Grimaldi solved the problem of troop logistics within a year, the Spanish regime in Louisiana might have run its course without interruption. It was not, however, until June 8, 1768, that he notified the minister of the Indies that some elements of the foreign companies had already set out from La Coruña to Havana, where they were to await the arrival of the Spanish troops to form the battalion of Louisiana. Perhaps he had some presentiment of the crisis developing in the colony, for he urged the minister to "hasten the embarkation from Cádiz of the Spanish contingent."[14] In a lengthy communication of June 25, 1768, he described the battalion of Louisiana as it was being

---

12. Ulloa to Bucareli, August 31, 1766, in Dispatches of the Spanish Governors of Louisiana, I.
13. Ulloa to Bucareli, March 25, 1767, *ibid.*
14. Grimaldi to Arriaga, June 8, 1768, in Leg. 2542, Audiencia de Sto. Domingo, AGI.

organized. It was to consist of mercenaries, chiefly French, and a large Spanish company, which was embarking from Cádiz with such speed that several officers presently in Madrid would be forced to take a later ship. Should any of the French soldiers under Aubry change their minds, this would be permissible, "as in any event they will be less costly than those sent from here." He concluded with expressions of regret for the loss of time in recruiting and dispatching the troops, "but greater promptness has been impossible because the expulsion of the Jesuits, the transfer of troops, the sending of some to Mexico, and other contingencies, which have arisen, have absolutely prevented it."[15] Before receipt of this reassuring letter, Ulloa dictated once more his great concern over the need for the Spanish troops, for "each day there is evident new signs of dissatisfaction and restlessness, proceeding from this mixed government."[16] The news of the withdrawal of the British from posts along the frontier led the Spanish governor to suggest that the number of reinforcements might be curtailed. "There are needed only enough to prevent attacks by the Indians and to keep the people in order," he advised.[17] But the timetable for the transfer of the Spanish troops from Havana was already set, with little chance of modification without inconveniences.

Meanwhile it was necessary to institute formalities that would signify the extension of Spanish sovereignty over the territory. The result was the celebrated *toma de posesión* at Balize. Without a sufficient force and unsure of the attitude of the French population, Ulloa entered into a type of condominium, or joint rule, with Governor Charles Aubry. It was an arrangement without precedent in the Spanish Empire of the eighteenth century. Although unique then, it became a familiar practice, with the same temporary features, among the imperialistic powers in the

15. Quoted in Lawrence Kinnaird (ed.), *Spain in the Mississippi Valley, 1765–1794*, American Historical Association Annual Report for 1945, II–IV (Washington, D.C., 1946–49), II, 54, 55.
16. Ulloa to Grimaldi, July [?], 1768, quoted *ibid.*
17. Ulloa to Grimaldi, October 6, 1768, quoted *ibid.*, 71.

last quarter of the nineteenth century. At Balize, on January 20, 1767, Ulloa signed with the French governor a tentative agreement for division of authority in the colony until the arrival of enough troops to ensure Spanish control. The terms of the contract were as follows:

> I, Don Antonio de Ulloa, will take possession of this post [Balize] today; and I, Charles Philippe Aubry, will turn it over in the name of the king, my master, in order that it may be evident that the entire colony and the Island of New Orleans, as is specified in the treaty of peace and in later transactions, belong to His Catholic Majesty, in the same form and manner in which it was ceded. But, as the Spanish troops that are necessary for the defense of the capital and the more important towns have not come as yet, I, Don Antonio de Ulloa, request in the name of the king, my lord, that Monsieur Aubry continue with the civil and military government of the capital and the French forts established earlier where there are many Indians and where the said troops are still a garrison; and I, Charles Philippe Aubry, having in mind the intentions of the two governments and especially to carry out the orders of the king, my lord, accept and assume charge of the civil and military government until the arrival of the first Spanish force, and for the well-being of the administration, we agree to act in concert and with reciprocal knowledge of the orders that must be given.[18]

As a symbol of the transfer, the French flag at Balize was lowered and the Spanish standard raised in its place in a ceremony marked by salvos of artillery and rounds of musketry. The ensign with the fleur-de-lis of the older branch of the Bourbon family continued to fly over New Orleans and the outposts. The failure to take possession of the capital did, in fact, prevent the *de jure* establishment of Spanish sovereignty, as the act of territorial cession in international law required a formal proclamation in New Orleans. On the other hand, one cannot challenge the validity of the claims of a *de facto* transfer. A letter from Choiseul to d'Abbadie, announcing the cession, and the later acceptance of Spanish funds by the colonists were tacit acknowledgments of the rights of the new monarch.

Did the dual concept in government work satisfactorily? To

---

18. In Leg. 20,854, Consejo de Indias, AHN.

the Spanish governor it was an empirical solution to a vexing problem of administration. As soon as troops could be sent in large numbers from Spain to occupy the capital and the distant posts on the frontier, the arrangement would be terminated. In his communications with Ulloa, Grimaldi, who had the power to veto the agreement, gave no signs of adverse reaction to what he must have considered to be a practical approach to the eventual imposition of authority. On the scene in the colony, success depended on cooperation and understanding between the two men and the willingness of the population to accept the accord. Sympathetic to the settlers, Aubry had prior to the agreement ventured to suggest suspension or modification of unpopular decrees and orders.[19] If he were unhappy with Ulloa's refusal to accept full responsibility for the administration in 1766, he had no impelling reason to change his mind after signing the *toma de posesión*.[20] There is little evidence that Aubry was disloyal or deliberately withheld information from the Spanish authorities. However, he was a man of moderate talents and could not at crucial moments control the officers and soldiers under him. In addition to the obvious misunderstandings arising from linguistic differences and lack of communications, there was another disadvantage. The employment of two flags confused the inhabitants, creating doubt about the permanence of Spanish rule.

To the English command in North America the nature of the

19. When the proclamation of the commercial decree of September 6, 1766, caused the disturbances in New Orleans, he wrote to Ulloa, urging that "he suspend the enforcement of the ordinance in order to avoid the bad results that a popular outcry might produce." See Aubry to Ulloa, in Leg. 187, Papeles de Cuba, AGI.

20. In response to a letter from Governor George Johnstone of British West Florida, Aubry admitted his dissatisfaction with the refusal of the Spaniards to take possession of the colony: "I flattered myself, monsieur, that I could leave for France shortly after the arrival of the Spaniards, but as Monsieur de Ulloa does not wish to take possession of the country until he has made a careful reconnaissance, I have been compelled to remain here longer than I thought for. Since I have commanded this colony, I have not had a respite from trouble and embarrassment, but I can assure Your Excellency that I have more now than I have ever had in my life." See Aubry to Johnstone, June 3, 1766, enclosure in Johnstone's dispatches to Thomas Pownall, July 19, 1766, in Correspondence of the British Governors of West Florida, DXCV, 33, 34, Public Record Office, London, hereinafter cited as PRO.

regime in Louisiana was mystifying but a source of gratification. In a December, 1766, dispatch to William Petty Fitzmaurice, the earl of Shelburne, English secretary of state for the Southern Department, General Thomas Gage commented on the problems of the Spanish: "Don Antonio de Ulloa still declines to take Possession of the Government of Louisiana. . . . The French and the Spaniards are far from agreeing in New Orleans and it's to be hoped that the King's Subjects may receive some Benefit from their Discussion."[21] Writing again in April, 1768, he alluded gleefully to the confusion in the provisional government: "It is difficult to ascertain by the stile [*sic*] of the . . . letters of Don Ulloa and Mons. Aubry whether the Province of Louisiana belongs to Spain or France."[22] There is another reference to this puzzling administration in a letter to Wills Hill, Lord Hillsborough, secretary of state for the colonies: "Some Advices lately received from Fort Chartres Give Information of a Strange Mixture of French and Spanish Government on the opposite side of the Mississippi, so that there is no way of knowing to whom the Country belongs."[23] English hopes of profiting by the disunity and confusion in New Orleans and elsewhere were not to be realized.

In handling administrative and judicial matters, the Spanish governor felt from time to time the opposition of the Superior Council. In 1766, this body consisted of nine members: the

21. Gage to Shelburne, December 23, 1766, in Carter (ed.), *The Correspondence of General Thomas Gage,* I, 116.
22. Gage to Shelburne, April 24, 1768, in Clarence W. Alvord and Clarence E. Carter (eds.), *Trade and Politics, 1767–1769,* Collections of the Illinois State Historical Library, XVI (Springfield, Ill., 1921), 266.
23. Gage to Hillsborough, October 9, 1768, in Carter (ed.), *The Correspondence of General Thomas Gage,* VI, 119. The letter explains the confusion in the administration of the outposts: "A French officer, Mon. St. Ange commands on the Mississippi, and receives Orders both from Don Ulloa and Mon. Aubry. Don Rius [Riu] a Spanish Captain, is appointed Governor of the Missouri. These two commanders are said to be entirely independent of each other, and expressly forbid to consult together, on any Publick Matter." Governor Johnstone remarked jokingly to the secretary of the Board of Trade anent the situation in the Spanish colony: "The fate of New Orleans is nevertheless still uncertain. Mr. Aubry wishes to deliver it & Mr. Ulloa will not accept of it or at least they play this Game with the Public." Quoted in Clinton N. Howard, *The British Development of West Florida, 1763–1769* (Berkeley, 1917), 127.

governor, commissary, attorney general, three regular councilors, and three assessors, or assistant judges. Usually the governor presided over the council but, as Aubry was primarily a
soldier, the commissary Foucault occupied this position. The
three councilors were chosen by the colonists. Although this
group had, in the opinion of some present-day historians, a kind
of lawmaking power, it was, without doubt, the supreme judicial
body. Like the Parlement de Paris, it claimed the right of registering all edicts and appointments. In exercising its functions it
might challenge the authority of the governor.

The inevitable reorganization of the colonial regime according to Spanish forms required the abolition of the Superior
Council as a court of law. In January, 1767, Ulloa drew up a
memorandum for the king, urging the dissolution of the council
for a number of reasons. There was evident injustice and in-
equity in judicial decisions, for "none of the councilors has studied anything, nor has he any knowledge of law," with perhaps the
exception of the attorney general. Furthermore, the councilors
resided as a rule outside the city and were remiss in attending its
sessions. Even the French government, according to an *informe*
from Aubry, had hoped to reform the council by designating
trained judges for the posts, but had been prevented from intro-
ducing this change by the outbreak of the Seven Years' War. (In
a letter of June, 1764, to the French ministry, d'Abbadie had
urged a complete reformation of the council in the interest of
good government.) "It does not appear," Ulloa stated, "that
there is any necessity for a court of this species, since we do not
have one in the Indies in places infinitely more important, such
as Havana."[24]

At Ulloa's recommendation, Grimaldi, in a royal edict of

24. Memo to Grimaldi, January, 1767, in Leg. 2542, Audiencia de Sto. Domingo,
AGI. Ulloa in his later postrevolutionary account of events was highly critical of the legal
qualifications of the councilors. They had no knowledge of law "other than that affecting
their normal occupations and everyday jobs"; the body was made up of "citizens who
possessed no more learning than that of any other citizen." See "Noticia de los
acaecimientos de la Luisiana en el año de 1768: Demonstrando por la serie de sucesos
experimentados el verdadero origen de la conspiración que se declaro en 29 de octubre
de aquel año, y de los autores que desde luego se conoclleron en ella" (Ms. 2827 in
Miscelánea de Ayala, XIII, Manuscritos de América, BP).

March 22, 1767, stipulated the suppression of the Superior Council. When the formal act of possession took place, the council would simply cease to exist. The attorney general and the councilors would, however, continue to receive salaries "as if they were in the exercise of their former duties." The governor would become the chief judge with power to give sentences according to law on all cases involving Spaniards and foreigners. In handling civil and criminal suits the chief magistrate would be assisted by an *asesor letrado*, or trained lawyer. All criminal suits were to be judged by the custom of the land; if the circumstances were not covered by precedents, recourse could be had to the Laws of the Indies. Naturally, any legal dispute between Spaniards would be resolved by the above code. The Superior Council was to have jurisdiction over cases pending at the time of the assumption of power by the Spanish government; but, if it neglected its functions or prolonged unnecessarily the consideration of cases, it would draw no pay. Litigants had the right of appeal from sentences of the governor to the king through the intermediation of the secretary of state. Under no condition should the commissary of war and the treasury interfere in matters of justice and administration, "notwithstanding any instructions that he may have or what has been practiced up to this time in the said colony."[25]

The decree, thus carefully drafted, was not executed during Ulloa's governorship because the formal act of sovereignty in the colony did not take place. Its intent was to concentrate political and judicial authority in the hands of the royal appointee, a principle already being applied in Cuba in the establishment of the intendancy. It is noteworthy that there is no reference to the formation of a local council, or cabildo, for the city of New Orleans, with alcaldes who customarily enjoyed original jurisdiction in many areas of law in the Spanish colonial municipality.[26] In late spring, 1767, Grimaldi ordered Bucareli to aid Ulloa in

---

25. Decree of March 22, 1767, in Leg. 2542, Audiencia de Sto. Domingo, AGI.

26. O'Reilly, who restored Spanish authority in 1769, designated a cabildo for New Orleans. Although Ulloa never mentioned this innovation, perhaps he would have adopted it if the occupation had been peaceably implemented. See Epilogue, herein.

the search for a "wise and honorable man" to fill the position of *asesor*.[27] The Spanish governor, fearful of its effect on the already low popularity of the regime, apparently did not disclose the terms of the edict to Aubry or to the colonists. But ominous rumors of planned reforms in government did leak out and contributed to the subsequent dissatisfaction with Spanish policies among all groups.

To reform the *policía,* or general administration, of the capital was likewise an aim of the indefatigable Spanish governor. At his instigation, a code or set of ordinances was compiled in May, 1766, to deal with all aspects of civic life, except for the establishment of municipal government.[28] The framers of the ordinances drew from previous regulations of the council, from the custom of Paris, and from Spanish theory and practice. Thus many laws appear to simply reissue or restate regulations dictated earlier by the French governors and the Superior Council and actually in force. The code is, however, more than a compilation of existing legislation. In spirit, tenor, and organization the ordinances reflect the Spanish tradition and practice of paternalism. From the issuance of special cedulas by Philip II in 1573, the Spanish crown had sought to mold civic life in America and to foster the material well-being of the citizenry through regulations embodied in a code known as the Laws of the Indies.[29] As governor of the mining city of Huancavelica, Ulloa had been responsible for the promulgation of special ordinances prohibiting or limiting practices considered unwholesome for the people. Although the New Orleans code shows the influence of

27. Bucareli to Grimaldi, August 17, 1767, in Leg. 1194, Audiencia de Sto. Domingo, AGI.

28. As far as I can determine, the code exists only in manuscript with the date May, 1766 (*faites en mai, 1766*), which raises doubts as to its general promulgation in the community. Repeated references to Ulloa's tyranny in later memorials of the Superior Council and of the citizens to the French crown suggest, however, that some of the ordinances may have been in force. See De la police, in Leg. 187, Papeles de Cuba, AGI.

29. There is nothing comparable to the Laws of the Indies in the colonial legislation of England and France. See J. Preston Moore, *The Cabildo in Peru Under the Hapsburgs: A Study in the Origins and Powers of the Town Council in the Viceroyalty of Peru, 1530–1700* (Durham, N.C., 1954), 43–47.

Ulloa's personal views, the pervasiveness of religion and the undue emphasis on morality are characteristic of Spanish legal thinking in the eighteenth century. Also, the imposition of excessive penalties for the infraction of laws is typical of European attitudes then toward crime and punishment. It is worthwhile to summarize the code of 1766 because it discloses Spanish thinking during this age and because it sheds light on the peculiar social and economic conditions existing in the largest city of the province.

The municipal code, drafted in the French language, consisted of five *titres,* or sections, entitled "Religion," "Manners," "Provisions," "Public Health," and "Public Safety," with a varying number of chapters and articles under each heading. One may gain an idea of the extent of the code from the fact that there are ninety-two specific ordinances in all.

Like the Laws of the Indies, which might have served in part as a model, the foremost aim of all law should be the inculcation of divine worship. "Religion is then the first and chief purpose of administration. . . . It is therefore as important for the happiness of man as it is for the permanence of states that religion be practiced and respected, because every religion reduced to its essence is idealism, and the best guaranty that we have of the probity of man is religion."[30] Every act or custom that interferes with worship at high mass on Sundays and feast days should be prohibited. No one should perform any work during the entire day for the celebration of Epiphany, Easter, Pentecost, Assumption, All Saints, and Christmas under penalty of reprimand and fines.

The second *titre,* concerning manners, embraced the suppression of all acts likely to cause public scandal, for "it is by the corruption of manners that the fall of states is prepared, through the support that this gives to vice and through indifference to virtue."[31] Heavy penalties of fines and imprisonment were to be

30. Six articles refer to the preservation of Catholicism.
31. Similarly, there are six articles in this section.

imposed on those who took part in indecent plays, promoted games of chance, and maintained houses of prostitution. *Filles de joie* who continued to practice their profession would be expelled from the city and even from the colony.

The third section, concerning provisions, with forty-one separate articles is the longest in the code. It bespeaks the meticulous attention of the framers to the protection of the individual citizen from illness and discomfort brought on by the consumption of bad food and wine. No advocate of pure food laws would disagree with this objective: "The choice and quality of food that one utilizes for his nourishment requires thus on the part of public officials a special inspection so that the ordinary person may consume only what is sound and fitting for the preservation of health." These regulations, in a sense replacing rules established ordinarily by guilds, which did not exist in the city, covered the activities of bakers, butchers, purveyors of meat and fish, sellers of berries and vegetables, operators of wineshops, innkeepers, and owners of wine cellars and warehouses. An apprenticeship was necessary for those who wished to obtain licenses to enter certain trades. Strict control should be exercised over the owners of cabarets, as these establishments could easily turn into centers of disorders that might affect the peace and security of the city. Proprietorship in this line of business was limited to twelve individuals who must hold licenses from the governor as chief magistrate and be recognized as men of good standing. To discourage drunkenness and debauchery, the proprietors of the shops should close their doors at 10 P.M. No liquor should be served to soldiers and sailors who had their own canteens or to Indians, Negroes, and mulattoes, under penalty of imprisonment and fine. Vagabonds, idlers, and women "of bad life" should be denied entrance. Evidence of Spanish zealousness in questions of religious propriety was an ordinance that obliged owners to summon the police to arrest persons guilty of swearing or blasphemy.[32]

32. Sec. 3, Chap. 8, Articles 1, 10, De la police, in Leg. 187, Papeles de Cuba, AGI.

Protecting the health of the inhabitants by additional measures was the aim of the fourth *titre*. Ordinances forbade unneces-
sary pollution of the environment by improper location of lat-
rines, disposal of garbage in the streets, and burning of straw
and refuse in public places. To combat sickness, which was
rampant during the summer, fully qualified surgeons and doc-
tors were essential for the municipality. A number of measures
regulated the licensing and practice of those in the professions so
that, in the interest of health and well-being, charlatans and
mountebanks could be excluded from living in the city.[33]

The last section, devoted to the maintenance of law and order,
was one of the most important and concerned everyone in the
city. Ordinances protected the citizens from exposure to the
hazards associated with the construction of dwellings and public
buildings. Masons and carpenters were ordered to take special
pains when engaged in building to see that no piece of the
structure constituted a danger to life and limb of passersby.
Horses and cattle should not roam through the streets. To avoid
accidents in narrow lanes, reckless riding or driving was expressly forbidden: "It is prohibited for any reason of whatever
quality or condition to gallop through the streets, whether with
one or more horses, or to drive a carriage with three or more;
corporal punishment will be meted out to those responsible for
injury to anyone."[34] Obviously, of greater import for the ordinary citizen were the ordinances concerning personal assault and
robbery. No one should carry a knife customarily employed for
fighting or should fire a musket indiscriminately in the settlement. Given the frequency of thefts, a curfew was to be imposed
on private homes at 11 P.M. in the summer and at 10 P.M. in the
winter. Soldiers, sailors, and vagabonds were not to be allowed to
walk the streets after 11 P.M. Since household slaves often posed
a threat to life and possessions, their freedom of movement and
attire was limited by four specific articles. A slave apprehended

---

33. Twelve ordinances compose this section.
34. Sec. 5, Chap. 2, Art. 8, De la police, in Leg. 187, Papeles de Cuba, AGI.

in the street after 8 P.M. in the winter and after 9 P.M. in the summer without permission of his master was to be imprisoned and possibly flogged. No slave might carry a knife or a large club. It was strictly prohibited for slaves to congregate, since these assemblies could lead to uprisings, and both masters and slaves were to be subjected to the penalties contained in the Black Code of 1724.

Provincial government involved the appointment and supervision of commandants at the various outlying posts. Ulloa wisely retained the former French officials in the Indian territory because of their acquaintance with the chiefs and knowledge of tribal customs and, from a practical viewpoint, because of the few Spanish officers. In strategic spots, where secrecy and complete loyalty were prerequisites, Spaniards assumed full control. The retention of French officials gave Aubry, who knew the agents and the special problems of their districts, additional opportunity to exercise authority.

Ulloa's approach to creating a Spanish regime evinced prudent judgment. Having few troops, he could not formally claim possession of the colony, and he was supported in this view by Grimaldi and the king. To avoid controversy with the French-speaking colonists that might lead to riots or clashes, he perforce set up a unique government with two executives. It was intended only as a stopgap until Spanish troops in sufficient numbers could reach Louisiana. The Superior Council he wished to abolish because it threatened his administrative power and malfunctioned as a court of law. As a sincere, well-intentioned, perspicacious reformer, he realized the need to issue a comprehensive municipal code that would provide health, sanitation, and security for the citizenry of New Orleans. But surely many in the city objected to the severity of the regulations affecting old customs and personal habits—in short to the austere, puritanical outlook of the governor. In the distant areas of the frontier there was no alternative to using French personnel who preferred naturally to communicate with Aubry rather than with the Spanish. The nature of this government might check the development of firm policies toward the English east of the Mississippi and toward the Indian tribes residing within the territory claimed by Spain. Among British officials, the seeming impermanence of the mixed regime gave satisfaction, and in the minds of the Indians it could hardly promote trust and security.

IV

The English Threat

As a naval officer and a civil engineer acquainted with construction of fortresses, Captain Antonio de Ulloa envisioned a vast improvement in the defenses of the colony.[1] Louisiana had been acquired by Charles III largely as a barrier against English encroachment on Mexico with its fabulously rich silver mines. Ulloa's wish to fulfill this objective must have been reinforced by his sojourn in Havana, which had suffered capture by the British fleet and been held for several months during the Seven Years' War. It was Spain's good fortune to recover her most important port and naval base in the Caribbean, but it would be a good many years before proud El Morro castle, dismantled by enemy engineers, would be fully restored.

Reports reaching Havana from West Florida after the Treaty of Paris concerning British military and naval activities along the Gulf coast must have been far from reassuring. On August 6, 1763, Colonel Augustine Prevost with a contingent of troops arrived at Pensacola and on October 20 Major Robert Farmar, with elements of the 22nd and 34th regiments, took possession of Mobile.[2] Energetic army officers repossessed French and Spanish forts nearby and opened negotiations with the Indians hoping to win their allegiance before the arrival of the Spanish. The British commanders soon realized the flaw in their system

---

1. See Chapter I, herein, for Ulloa's experience in the construction of fortifications in Peru and the inspection of naval facilities in Spain and certain other European countries at the orders of the marqués de la Ensenada.
2. Cecil Johnson, *British West Florida, 1763–1783* (New Haven, 1943), 8, 9.

of defense based on Fort Panmure at Natchez and Fort Chartres in the Illinois country. The enemy's retention of New Orleans either put reinforcements and supplies going up the river at his mercy or forced the use of an exceedingly costly and circuitous route across the Alleghenies and down the Ohio. Moreover, Indian tribes hostile to the British proved another deterrent to the speedy occupation of territory on the left bank of the Mississippi.[3] Thus, to many ambitious officers the key to British economic prosperity and military security in the region acquired by the treaty was the possession of New Orleans.[4]

Governor George Johnstone's arrival at Pensacola in October, 1764, meant the partial subordination of military control in West Florida to civilian authority. Developing the colony's economy entailed expansion of commerce with the Spanish colonies, in particular with the new regime in Louisiana. In a letter to the Board of Trade shortly after his assumption of office, he rhapsodized on the advantages of Spanish sovereignty to British merchants:

> Nature seems to have intended to place the seat of Commerce on this Bay within a few days sail of the Richest Cities in the World (the Havannah, Merida, Campeche, La Vera Cruz and Mexico). Penzacola bids fair for a considerable Share in their Commerce and now the New Orleans is ceded to the Spaniards, it must further serve as a means to introduce Commodities to the Spanish Dominions without a Rival, and so in a manner deliver to us the Keys to the Wealth of Mexico.

3. John R. Alden, *General Gage in America: Being Principally a History of His Role in the American Revolution* (Baton Rouge, 1948), 95, 101, 102.

4. As Governor Montfort Browne of West Florida wrote to Lord Hillsborough, "How happy a Circumstance, My Lord, would it Prove was New Orleans allied to His Majesty's Dominion, could an Event so Desirable take place, what an Everlasting Honor must Redound to that man who could be the means of so Valuable an Acquisition." Browne to Hillsborough, February 28, 1769, in Correspondence of the British Governors of West Florida, DLXXVII, PRO. After a trip down the Mississippi and on to Mobile, Lieutenant George Phyn in 1768 reported to Sir William Johnson on the commercial advantages of the city to England: "Were we in possession of New Orleans we would have a fine harbour in the Bay of Mexico, and secure to ourselves the produce of a large & Extensive Country, happy in a Luxurient Soil and which would not fail to be cultivated from the River Illinois to the Sea and by the cultivation of the Fertile lands of the Mississippi, the sea coast of this province would be of consequence and the Ports of Pensacola and Mobile would become I do believe flourishing places of trade." Phyn to Johnson, April 15, 1768, in Alvord and Carter (eds.), *Trade and Politics, 1767–1769*, 244.

Another advantage arising to this Colony from the Removal of the French from the Mississippi is that the Indian trade on its Banks from the Illinois downwards and even that of all the other Nations except the Cherokees, Catabaws and a few of the lower Creeks must center here; nor are disturbances now to be feared with those Nations; as no Rival Power remains to instigate them against us, we may depend upon Peace and Security.[5]

Even Sir William Johnson, English agent to the Iroquois, shared to a degree this view of the Spanish.[6]

To protect the new acquisitions, the British government felt obliged to build forts at strategic points along the Mississippi. At a meeting of the West Florida Council, Johnstone recommended the construction of a fort at the junction of the Iberville River (now Bayou Manchac) with the Mississippi to be called Fort Bute in honor of the British minister John Stuart, Lord Bute, who was Johnstone's patron. Johnstone argued that not only would it threaten the Spanish to the south and west but would guard a route to Mobile by way of Bayou Manchac and Lakes Maurepas and Pontchartrain to the Gulf. Thomas Pownall in London received a communication from Johnstone, dated February 19, 1765, pointing out the vital need for a fortified position at this site: "The Next Point could be the establishing of the Post at Point Iberville, on a large extended Place capable of containing a Regiment, at least:—There is no place of so much consequence to this Province as that Settlement, now the Iberville is opened, and which will command the whole Trade of the Mississippi, an Object of the highest Importance; since not less than seven hundred thousand Skins have been shipped from New Orleans, this year, in consequence of the Session [*sic*] of Canada by which most of the furs have come to Illinois, and so by the Mississippi."[7] With approval by the ministry the way was clear for construction.

There were many obstacles, however, to the realization of this

5. Johnstone to Board of Trade, November 9, 1764, in Correspondence of the British Governors of West Florida, DLXXV, 134, PRO.
6. Johnson to Cadwallader Colden, January 22, 1765, in Alvord and Carter (eds.), *The Critical Period, 1763–1765*, 417.
7. Howard, *The British Development of West Florida*, 27, 30.

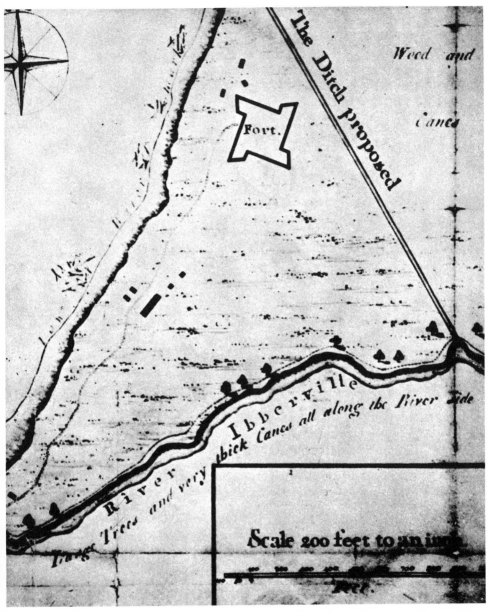

Wood and

Canes

The Ditch proposed

Fort.

Ibberville

River

Large Trees and very thick Canes all along the River side

Scale 200 feet to an inch

Feet.

British fort at Bayou Manchac (Iberville River). Undated map in British Museum, London

project on Bayou Manchac. Costs were high owing to the long transportation of materials from Mobile, and heat, fevers, and mosquitoes plagued the workmen, beset at the same time by shortages of supplies and provisions. In July, 1765, Major Farmar inspected the fort, finding it in a wretched condition. When the Alabama and Houma Indians raided in August of that year, the survival of the fort was put in doubt until the arrival eight months later of reinforcements from Mobile commanded by Captain James Chisholm. Nevertheless, the stockade at Fort Bute, or "the Manchac" as it was popularly labeled, developed into a center for a flourishing illegal trade.

In the British plan it was intended above all that Fort Bute should serve as a bulwark for the terminus of the waterway between the Mississippi and Lake Maurepas. Commercial and military intercourse with the interior was less liable to interruption by the enemy on Bayou Manchac than on the more direct route past New Orleans to the Gulf. In a letter of December 10, 1764, to Sir John Lindsay, commander of the squadron at Pensacola, Johnstone announced the opening of the bypass and requested the dispatch of a sloop of war to Point Iberville, the future site of Fort Bute. Lindsay promised to send the *Nautilus*, a frigate with a thirteen-foot draft, suitable for navigating the small stream.[8] High hopes entertained for the channel were doomed to disappointment. Despite toil, sweat, and expenditure of funds, it was too shallow for vessels of seagoing size from September to June and during the summer it was clogged with tree trunks and other debris brought in by high water. British colonial officials reluctantly relinquished a project that might have relieved some of their dependence on New Orleans.

About 140 miles north of Fort Bute on the east bank of the Mississippi was the second of the fortifications envisaged for the security of British territory in the west. Fort Panmure at Natchez, or "the Natches," erected on the site of the French Fort Rosalie, was to be both a formidable redoubt and a mart for trade

8. Johnstone to Lindsay, December 10, 1764, and Lindsay to Johnstone, January 7, 1765, enclosures in Johnstone to Lord Commissioners, February 19, 1765, in Correspondence of the British Governors of West Florida, DLXXV, PRO.

with the Indians and the settlers in the neighboring colony. Because of abundant fertile land and a healthful environment superior to that of Fort Bute, the settlement grew rapidly. With the end of British expansionism in the summer of 1768, the fort was denuded of troops and left as a trading post.[9]

Fort Chartres, strategically located above the junction of the Ohio and the Mississippi and below that of the Illinois and Mississippi rivers, was the third link in the chain of defensive strongpoints. General Gage had difficulty occupying the fort owing to the hostility of the Indians in the Illinois country. Fort Chartres remained an outpost of the British against the Spanish and the Indians until 1772, when it suffered the same fate as other British strongpoints on the Mississippi in being abandoned and having its garrison shifted to bases on the Atlantic seaboard.[10]

Such was the British military posture on the Mississippi in the spring of 1766. British troops considerably outnumbered the combined French and Spanish contingents, with Pensacola and Mobile as fortified points on the Gulf and with Forts Bute and Panmure under construction. Her vessels, both commercial and naval, plied the river above and below New Orleans. There was, however, an Achilles' heel in the system—the vulnerability of the major line of communication and trade up and down the river to attack from enemy-held New Orleans.

To what extent did the Spanish governor regard the British position as an imminent threat to Louisiana? His actions and his communications with his superiors implied a sense of urgency. His immediate response, after making contact with the French officials and unloading supplies, was a thorough inspection of the province. It was also customary for Spanish officials in any part of the Indies to familiarize themselves with the people and the land of the region which they were to govern.[11] A reduction

9. Johnson, *British West Florida,* 157, 67.
10. Alden, *General Gage in America,* 100–102, 144.
11. See J. Preston Moore, *The Cabildo in Peru Under the Bourbons: A Study in the Decline and Resurgence of Local Government in the Audiencia of Lima, 1700–1824* (Durham, N.C., 1966), Chaps. 2, 8.

in salary from that enjoyed in Peru apparently did not lessen his ardor to look over the new domain.[12] Accompanied by Aubry, Ulloa during the spring of 1766 visited most of the posts and settlements in the lower part of the colony. Starting from the capital, they journeyed up the river and overland to Natchitoches.[13] Perhaps his reason for visiting this outpost was that it was the closest to Spanish settlements in the viceroyalty of Mexico and therefore might figure in the opening or closing of trade between the two colonies. He had hoped to extend his itinerary to the Illinois country, but the distance and the time that would be consumed in ascending the river against the current compelled him to change his plans. On May 17 he was back in New Orleans. His diligent inspection of the region made a strong impression on Governor Johnstone.[14]

British military and naval activities on the Mississippi and in the territory adjoining Louisiana created, Ulloa concluded, a menace to Spanish occupation. In a report to the captain general in Cuba, written soon after his inspection, he commented on the vigorous efforts of the enemy and on the inadequacy of the Spanish defenses: "They [the British] maintain in those places two small armadas which point to the importance that they attach to that frontier, since they had hardly set foot on the soil

12. His salary at first amounted to six thousand pesos annually, somewhat less than he had received when serving as provincial governor in Peru. Grimaldi justified the lower figure on the grounds that the cost of living was higher in the viceroyalty. Ulloa's complaints about the shortage of personal funds were common among officials, for the Spanish government usually made inadequate remuneration and was frequently dilatory in payment, apparently secretly confident that the officials would connive or engage in graft anyway, which in the end would make them well rewarded. To my knowledge, Ulloa was never indicted for embezzlement or smuggling. See Grimaldi to Arriaga, November 4, 1765, in Leg. 775, Audiencia de Lima, AGI. But Grimaldi's order, dated July 23, 1766, augmented Ulloa's pay to eight thousand pesos, beginning the day of his arrival in Louisiana. In addition, the crown assumed the rent for the governor's quarters until a government house could be built. See Loyola to Ulloa, December 2, 1766, in Leg. 109, Papeles de Cuba, AGI.

13. It would seem that he got as far as this settlement. See Johnstone to Ulloa, June 19, 1766, in Leg. 109, Papeles de Cuba, AGI, and Alvord and Carter (eds.), *The New Regime, 1765–1767,* 304.

14. Caughey, *Gálvez in Louisiana,* 12; Howard, *The British Development of West Florida,* 127.

when frigates were brought in so that close contact could be kept up with Pensacola, Mobile, and Balize; others [vessels] in the anchorage or near the forts at Manchac, and, in contrast, on the Spanish side, even the old forts are in ruins and wholly lacking in munitions of war."[15]

Despite traditional suspicion and enmity, the diplomacy of the frontier required an early exchange of civilities and visits. Common problems of Indians, trade, and other matters that could not wait for solution made imperative the opening of formal relations. The Spanish governor took the lead in announcing his arrival in Louisiana in a letter to General Gage, commander-in-chief of British forces in New York.[16] This was followed by a friendly message to Lieutenant Colonel Ralph Walsh in Pensacola, whom Ulloa had been advised was in charge of the government of West Florida.[17] In doing so he stirred up a veritable hornets' nest. Unfortunately, his letter ignored Gover-

15. Ulloa to Bucareli, May 28, 1766, in Dispatches of the Spanish Governors of Louisiana, I.

16. The conciliatory tone of this communication is striking:

> Your Excellency may be Assured that You'll always find my offers sincere, and that I shall be ready to do everything to Serve you as far as is consistent with my Employment; Of which I shall Endeavor to give Your Excellency, and all His Britannick Majesty's Governors the most Convincing proof; and you may rest persuaded that my wishes are that Concord, Quietness and good Harmony may reign, and a happy Union Subsist betwixt the two Nations. It is in this Spirit that I shall contribute everything Conducive thereto, on my part, and promise Myself that Your Excellency corresponds with me in the same intentions, as I am well Acquainted with the Excellent Qualities of your Nation, and those which Your Excellency possesses in person; the Governor and French General Mon. d'Aubry has by his wise Conduct put everything for the present in such good Order, that there remains nothing for me to do, for His Britannick Majesty's Service, or Your Excellency's, or that of your Nation in general, he having facilitated before my Arrival the difficulties which presented themselves, with respect to the taking possession of the Illinois, in such manner, that the Savages Submitted without Opposition; tho I have had no Opportunity of Contributing to this, yet I hope for the future to be able to Establish good Order and Discipline, to which You will always find Me ready to Contribute.

See Ulloa to Gage, April 1, 1766, in Alvord and Carter (eds.), *The New Regime, 1765–1767*, 208, 209. For a detailed exposition of the role of colonial officials in the development of frontier policy, see J. Preston Moore, "Anglo-Spanish Rivalry on the Louisiana Frontier, 1763–68," in J. F. McDermott (ed.), *The Spanish in the Mississippi Valley, 1762–1804* (Urbana, 1974), 72–86.

17. Walsh's reply praised Ulloa's letter, "which is wrote with the Ease and Elegancy of Stile, so conspicuous in the inestimable Account of your travels which you have so greatly obliged the learned World." See Walsh to Ulloa, May 3, 1766, in Leg. 109, Papeles de Cuba, AGI.

nor Johnstone, then engaged in a bitter controversy with the military officers for supremacy in the colony's affairs.[18] Johnstone was infuriated at this official slight. Soon realizing his error, Ulloa apologized, and relations were eventually smoothed out. To make amends, Governor Ulloa dispatched an agent to carry his greetings in person to the governor of West Florida. According to Johnstone who was given to hyperbole, Don Antonio Felix Reisch, Ulloa's secretary and envoy, "has made the most Brilliant Appearance which Pensacola has Yet Seen." Not to be outdone, the English governor selected "Mr. Jones, the most respectable man among us to make my compliments in return which I am told is a ceremony that the Spanish Punctilio could not dispense with."[19]

Although the two governors did not meet, they kept up a lively correspondence during the summer of 1766. The style of the letters is flowery and overly polite, in short, typical of the belles lettres of the eighteenth century. As a man of some erudition and literary pretense, Johnstone expatiated in a letter of June 19 on the discovery of the poetry of Ossian, then the rage in the British Isles, with some philosophical interpolations.[20] Ulloa's letter, written in reply, covered several subjects:

> What I have expressed to you in my first letter I wish to repeat. I shall always look to the harmony, union, and association of the two nations, and as much as I can I will contribute to the contentment of Your Excellency, not just as an act of politeness and courtesy, but as a duty residing in all men, and especially in those who hold office and represent the persons of sovereigns,

18. The story of Johnstone's feud with the military is almost as intriguing as Ulloa's with Foucault and La Frenière. A former naval officer, owing his appointment to high family connections, Johnstone was unduly touchy over his authority. For some months the administration of West Florida was in turmoil. Because Walsh failed to turn over the keys of the fort and pay special honors to the governor, Johnstone ordered his arrest and court-martial. For a few hours Walsh was in jail but was released. George Montagu Dunk, the earl of Halifax, finally intervened, sending an order explicit enough to delimit the areas of military and civilian jurisdiction. This did not entirely end the dispute. The upshot was Johnstone's recall. See Johnson, *British West Florida*, 24–57.

19. Johnstone to Pownall, July 19, 1766, in Correspondence of the British Governors of West Florida, DXCV, PRO.

20. Scholars proved later that the poetry of Ossian dated from the eighteenth century and hence was spurious.

to look to the maintenance of Peace by means of concord among vassals. I
regard your intentions and those of other leaders of the colony the same as
mine. . . .

It gives me pleasure to hear of the success of my secretary Don Felix
Reisch, which was to extend our greetings, and it affords me delight to read
of the praise that you have for his spirit and conduct, and it has pleased me
to hear his account of your person and your talents. . . .

Since his arrival I have received three fine presents with which you have
honored me and I hope that we shall continue the exchange of gifts and
courtesies. . . .

I have begun to read it [the volume of Ossian's poetry] but have not
finished it. My duties here have not given me time for it. But I shall continue
to the end. Your reflections on the poetry please me as revealing your depth
of mind and knowledge.

Referring to other matters, the Spanish governor noted that the
colony would need flour and other foods in the future. The
merchants recommended by Johnstone would receive special
consideration in the procurement of these supplies, but no contract could be signed until the court in Madrid made a decision.[21]
Aside from practical matters, the discussion of literary trends
was an amateurish exercise. Probably Johnstone's vanity impelled him to try to impress the distinguished Spanish scientist.
Yet Ulloa, who had encountered few persons of learning in
Louisiana and whose range of interests was boundless, may well
have enjoyed the opportunity to reflect on the latest topics in
English literature.

The apparent cordiality in correspondence did not lull the
Spanish governor into a false sense of security. The protracted
itinerary having revealed the necessity of restoring and extending the French system of defense, he resolved to start as soon as
possible on the construction of forts at strategic points in the
colony. When the defensive concept had finally crystallized, it
was to embrace the building of forts at the mouth of the Mississippi, at the junction of the Missouri and the Mississippi, across
Bayou Manchac from Fort Bute, and in the vicinity of Natchez

21. Ulloa to Johnstone, July 28, 1766, in Leg. 109, Papeles de Cuba, AGI.

on the west bank. Minor posts, largely for Indian contacts, would be restored and strengthened. It was a program requiring heavy expenditures and, in time, vastly more military personnel. In emergencies the crown might supplement the regular troops with levies from the able-bodied among the French settlers. A census, taken in 1768, reveals that the colony had approximately 1,890 persons capable of bearing arms.[22] It is a small figure indeed for such an extensive area, but hopes were held for increasing the number through immigration of Acadians and perhaps Spaniards.

Of all the forts, Governor Ulloa gave more thought and attention to the one built on a small island in the Mississippi near the old French settlement of Balize. To a great degree the work was done under his personal direction. Known as Real Católica de San Carlos, it was ideally situated to dominate the entrance to the river. Primarily with this in mind, he made Balize his headquarters in September, 1766, and remained there for over nine months, much to the chagrin and dismay of many of the citizens of New Orleans, who felt offended at being ignored by the highest magistrate in the colony. Among some groups his policies had already caused resentment.[23]

Familiar with fortresses in Spain and Peru, Ulloa himself drew the plan for Fort Real Católica. Its dimensions were considerable. Since skilled workmen would be needed for the final stages of masonry and carpentry, he requested aid from Havana. His old friend Captain General Bucareli promised to dispatch men and money for its completion. In February, 1767, the Cuban official notified the minister of the Indies that fifty-three men, "who were not presently employed in similar jobs in the capital, would

22. Of the estimated total population of 5,556 for the province, the capital had 1,589 persons, 525 of which were men. See Padron de avidores de la colonia, in Leg. 2542, Audiencia de Sto. Domingo, AGI.

23. Not only was he engaged in the planning and construction of the fort, but he had the time to make scientific observations and to carry on extensive correspondence with learned friends in Europe. The British credited his long sojourn at Balize to the great dislike for him in New Orleans brought on by the proclamation of the ordinance of September 6. See Alvord and Carter (eds.), *The New Regime, 1765–1767*, 305.

be sent."[24] On March 12, the *Postillon,* a mail boat, put in at Balize "with the laborers and the funds." Some of the men, having been hastily recruited in the island, lacked a knowledge of their trade and were returned to Havana.[25] The rest apparently stayed on until the project was completed. It is not altogether clear when the work on the new post was terminated. Obviously, the major portion had been finished by May, 1767, for Aubry congratulated Ulloa on the plan and location of the fort, "advantageously situated, so it is seen by vessels coming from the open sea and who follow nearly always the northern route to be able to enter more easily into the river." Aubry wrote, "All these advantages make me conclude that you could not have placed it in a better spot to aid vessels and to be observed from afar off." Grimaldi also highly approved its construction.[26] There was no doubt that the fort on the Isla Real Católica was Ulloa's pride and joy.

Equally significant for the Spanish hold on the colony's seagoing commerce were navigational aids and the designation of a channel or channels for vessels. Shipwrecks were not infrequent near the mouth of the river because of shifting sandbars and the collection of logs and brush washed down during floods. As a naval officer, Ulloa saw the benefits of a single channel joining the river and the Gulf and having sufficient depth to accommodate all types of ships. Not only would it reduce navigational hazards, but it would facilitate the inspection of shipping to and from the great river. Toward the middle of March, 1767, he informed Bucareli of the completion of a channel and a signal pile to guide vessels through this dangerous area:

> This is to let Your Worship know that a new channel has been opened at the northern part of the mouth of the river. It is deeper than the one on the east, which previously was the only entrance. Near the channel there has been built a pyramid, with posts forty varas [yards] in height. This pyramid

24. Bucareli to Arriaga, February 25, 1767, in Leg. 2542, Audiencia de Sto. Domingo, AGI.
25. Ulloa to Bucareli, March 20, 1767, and June 17, 1767, both in Dispatches of the Spanish Governors of Louisiana, I.
26. Aubry to Ulloa, May 23, 1767, in Leg. 187A, Papeles de Cuba, AGI; Grimaldi to Arriaga, June 8, 1768, in Leg. 2542, Audiencia de Sto. Domingo, AGI.

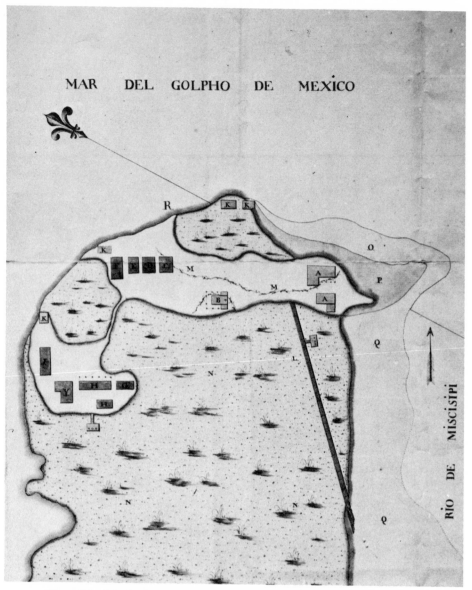

Plan of the Isla Real Católica de San Carlos: (A) Dwelling and kitchen of the governor; (B) Chapel; (C) Warehouse; (D) Guardhouse for the stores; (F) Barracks; (G) Surgeon's quarters; (H) Hospital; (Y) Bakery; (J) Carpenter's shop; (K) Diverse structures; (L) Wooden bridge for the quay, approximately 325 yards long; (N) Marsh; (O), (P), (Q) Shifting sand. Courtesy Archivo General de Indias, Seville

will be used as a pharos, and I do not doubt that in fair weather it will be seen by vessels from a distance of four to five leagues at sea. I give you this information so that you may give it to the vessels sailing from your port for this destination, advising them that this pyramid will show them the entrance to the mouth of the river, no matter from which side they see it, because it is situated on a small island, erected at two musket shots farther north than the canal.[27]

Ulloa's detractors subsequently criticized limiting the traffic in the river to a single channel. They argued that the northeastern passage selected by the governor was the most difficult for ships owing to the direction of the prevailing winds and the shallow water.[28] Ulloa's retort to his critics revealed his knowledge of navigation as well as his understanding of the security arrangements that must be enforced:

> Ports that have two different entrances in no way can be satisfactory, because while in one place His Majesty's orders are obeyed, in the other they are disregarded with impunity. . . . The eastern channel, which was the one prohibited, lost depth considerably in the year '66, remaining from eight and one-half feet to fourteen and one-half after the fall of the river. With this occurrence, which is very frequent, the Spanish governor ordered the one of the northeast to be used and not the other, since it has the advantage of being so short that it could be traversed in seven or eight minutes, when on the contrary that of the east required nearly an hour and the dangers were in proportion to the time for the passage.[29]

In his insistence on a single passage for all commerce in the river, Ulloa had much in his favor.

Unfortunately, the Mississippi proved too strong to conquer. The terrain in the delta was too soggy to support the foundation of the fort on the island, and Ulloa had to recommend to Grimaldi that the settlement remain "a port without a regular garrison," to be the residence only of pilots who were to guide

---

27. Ulloa to Bucareli, March 11, 1767, in Dispatches of the Spanish Governors of Louisiana, I.

28. Rodríguez, *Primeros años*, 432, 433.

29. "Noticia de los acaecimientos de la Luisiana," fol. 78v. From the standpoint of mercantile restrictions, collecting customs and prohibiting smuggling were made far easier.

Mississippi River passes, detail of 1764 French map. Courtesy New York
Public Library

ships into the river. A captain, or commandant, of the port was necessary, nevertheless, for the recognition of Spanish authority. In September, 1767, José Melchor de Acosta was selected for this post.[30] In the matter of the fort, Ulloa disclosed a tendency to precipitate action without a thorough understanding of the nature of the soil and the strength of the currents. The channel that he chose was one that favored Spanish sailors, judging by the few shipwrecks or few undue delays that occurred. But his decision to close all channels except one crippled the flow of contraband and hence affected the pocketbooks and attitudes of New Orleans merchants.

During the winter of 1766–1767, extensive preparations were made in New Orleans for the proposed construction of other forts against the English or the Indians. Ulloa entrusted Juan José de Loyola, the commissary of war, with assigning men and gathering supplies for expeditions to the Illinois and Arkansas country and Bayou Manchac. On January 17, 1767, he had at hand an *estado,* or statement of preparations (Table 1). From an examination of the *estado* it is clear that the Spanish governor attached greatest importance to the expedition to the Illinois country. It comprised more than half the military personnel and considerable supplies of muskets and gunpowder.[31] Ostensibly, the force was simply to strengthen the French detachment at Ste. Genevieve under Louis St. Ange, the French commandant of the Illinois territory. However, to keep the English in the dark regarding the real purpose of the expedition, Ulloa drafted secret instructions to St. Ange, to be dispatched by separate means unknown to the Spanish soldiers, which indicated another destination. Upon arrival at the French post the Spanish were to proceed without delay to the mouth of the Missouri River. Not far from its junction with the Mississippi they were to erect forts on two designated sites. The larger one was to rise on the north bank, to be garrisoned with twenty-five

30. Grimaldi to Arriaga, May 22, 1767, and the marqués de la Victoria to Arriaga, September 29, 1767, both in Leg. 2542, Audiencia de Sto. Domingo, AGI.

31. *Estado* given by Loyola, January 16, 1767, in Leg. 109, Papeles de Cuba, AGI.

TABLE 1

ESTADO, OR STATEMENT OF
PREPARATIONS

List that includes the officials, troops, naval personnel, and others that should compose the three expeditions that are to be sent to the Illinois, Arkansas, and Iberville River [Bayou Manchac]. The boats, provisions, supplies, and other effects are also included:

	Troops				Navy			
	Officers	Sergeants	Corporals	Soldiers	Masters	Pilots	Sailors	Boats
Illinois	4	2	4	40	2	2	18	2
Arkansas	2	1	2	20	2	2	14	2
Iberville	2	1	2	14	2	2	34	2
	8	4	8	74	6	6	66	6

	Swivel Guns	Cannons	Cartridges	Muskets	Powder (lbs.)	Artillery
Illinois	4	8	—	22	1813	1
Arkansas	4	4	2	18	944	1
Iberville	4	2	6	38	1232	1
	12	14	8	78	3989	3

Notes: 1. Swivel guns to accompany supplies, with 20 rounds for each
2. Powder for the Illinois country to be distributed

	Food				
	(100 lbs.)			(Barrels)	
	Biscuits	Meat	Rice	Brandy	Medicine Chests
Illinois	121½	54	4½	10	1
Arkansas	39½	17½	1½	6	1
Iberville	39½	17½	1½	5	1
	200½	89	7½	21	3

Notes: 1. Provisions for 120 days for the first trip (Illinois country)—for 90 persons
2. Provisions for each of the two remaining expeditions for 50 days—for 70 persons
3. Oars, seats, ropes, and other supplies for each boat to be purchased
4. Gifts and supplies for the Indians not included

men; the smaller, on the south bank, with fifteen men. The forts were to serve as centers of population, which was to consist largely of Acadians, "a quiet people, docile, with good habits, and God-fearing."[32]

The plan for the establishment of the forts disclosed an audacious strategy. It was essential to prevent the English from crossing the Missouri, "which belongs to His Majesty completely according to the treaty," threatening New Mexico, and entering into trade agreements with the Indians.[33] In command of the Spanish detachment was Captain Riu y Morales, second in rank to Ulloa, accompanied by a French engineer Guido du Fossat. The instructions carried by Riu were explicit. Characteristically, Ulloa dictated the daily routine of the soldiers, including the saying of the rosary "to keep all the good Christian practices of Spain." To offset the monotony and harsh physical demands of the trek, the men might carry their own brandy, but it was to be included in the cargo purchased by the crown. Indian policy was to be chiefly in the hands of the French commandant.[34]

Regrettably, the erection of the forts did not unfold according to plan. The terrain on the north side of the Missouri, on which Fort Carlos Tercero del Rey was to be constructed, proved unsuitable, being frequently under water as much as nine feet during the spring flood. Du Fossat abandoned the project and devoted his energies to raising the second fort on the south bank, to be named Príncipe de Asturias, Señor Don Carlos. Thus in the end only the queen and the heir to the throne would defend the new colony in the south and in the north! When completed, the post formed a square, running eighty feet on each side with protruding bulwarks. It had two gates, each three or four feet wide. There were two buildings inside the stockade on opposite sides, a barracks for the men and quarters for the officers. Five

---

32. Instruccion segunda para el establecimiento de las dos fuertes que se han de hacer en la entradad del Rio Misuri cuyo Armamento se ha puesto al cargo del Capit. de Yfanteria Dn. Franco. Riu, Article 26, in Leg. 2357, Audiencia de Sto. Domingo, AGI.

33. Articles 1–11, *ibid.*

34. Louis Houck, *A History of Missouri* (2 vols.; Chicago, 1908), I, 289–93.

cannons, two sixpounders and three fourpounders, defended the fort.[35]

Handling the Indian problem and disciplining the soldiers proved too much for Captain Riu. Hardships and boredom led to insubordination in November, 1767, when about half the men fled down the river to the English settlement at Natchez. After receiving reports from Riu and St. Ange, Ulloa was convinced of the former's incapacity. In letter after letter he castigated his subordinate's methods and actions. In April, 1768, Riu finally informed the governor that the work was near completion.[36] Despite this accomplishment, Ulloa ordered Riu to give up his position and return to New Orleans for reassignment. His replacement was Pedro Piernas, a soldier who had proved his worth in Ulloa's eyes by the construction of Fort San Luis at Natchez.[37]

A feature of Spanish defensive strategy included counterbalancing the English fort on the high bluff at Natchez. By the middle of June, 1767, Piernas, directing a small band of soldiers and workmen, had begun to build a fort on the low ground of the west bank across the river from the English site. Detailed reports to his superior revealed slow progress. "The work continues," he wrote, "notwithstanding the fact that many of the men have become ill from the heat." Toward the end of July, work had to be temporarily halted, because it was imperative to put up shelters to protect the men from the downpours customary at this season. In September provisions ran low, but supplies arriving from the capital allowed work to continue. In August Piernas had contracted a fever and though much improved in October, he nevertheless asked to be transferred to another post in the colony.[38]

35. *Ibid.,* I, 294, 295.
36. Riu to Ulloa, April 15, 1768, in Leg. 109, Papeles de Cuba, AGI. The correspondence between Ulloa and Riu is bulky, comprising some sixty letters.
37. Houck, *A History of Missouri,* I, 295, 296. Riu, displeased and disappointed, had offered to resign several times.
38. Piernas to Ulloa, June 18, 24, September 7, 8, 21, and October 28, 1767, all in Leg. 109, Papeles de Cuba, AGI.

To solidify the fortified position at Fort San Luis, Ulloa intended to encourage the migration of Acadians to the surrounding territory. Under pressure from the governor a number of families came to the area to take up land assigned to them. Although the soil was extremely fertile, they said they preferred to reside near their kinsmen at Pointe Coupée to the south. Piernas, in charge of the settlement, registered a sharp complaint against their attitude: "I should wish to lead an army rather than members of these families." The real reason for the reluctance of the Acadians to live near Natchez became apparent when they declared that the fort was "so exposed to the menaces of the savages that their wives and children and they themselves would live in continual fear." Only threats by Piernas kept them from leaving at once.[39]

The fort at Bayou Manchac, the site of which is now in the bed of the Mississippi because of the shifting channel, was constructed apparently with less difficulty. Although the climate was as bad as that of Natchez, the post could be supplied more easily from New Orleans. An English report in the summer of 1767 described the new fortification as "within 500 yards of it [Fort Bute] . . . a square fort of four Bastions, and the curtains Eighty yards in length." It was armed with "Eight pieces of Canon, six, six-Pounders and two of Eight," manned by "one officer and 25 Soldiers, with a Number of Artifacts and Labourers."[40]

Although undoubtedly somewhat alarmed at the military activities of the Spanish, the English commanders in North America did not overreact to the threat. Their confidence reposed on a numerical superiority of men and ships and their

39. Piernas to Ulloa, March 27, May 8, and April 28, 1768, all *ibid.*
40. Gage to Shelburne, August 31, 1767, in Carter (ed.), *The Correspondence of General Thomas Gage,* I, 149. The West Florida Assembly in its representation to the Lords of Trade, November 22, 1766, pointed out that it was necessary to have "fortifications and protection against Indian raids and possible conquest by a European power. . . . To see the Fortifications, Churches, Hospitals, and Public Buildings, which are everywhere erecting on the Spanish Dominions since the arrival of Don Antonio de Ulloa, whilst nothing is undertaken on our part, is extremely mortifying to those who consider the changeful State of European Powers." Quoted in Howard, *The British Development of West Florida,* 44, 45.

prowess in the last war. Brigadier General Frederick Haldimand, in command of British forces in West Florida, put the best possible light on the situation when he informed Gage:

> I am persuaded, sir, that the posts, very far from causing jealousy, will contribute to the maintenance of good understanding on account of the ease with which the officers can clear up affairs at once, in case difficulties should arise. It does not seem that it would benefit the Spaniards ever to undertake anything against us on these banks; perhaps they only foresee what would happen to them at the first war. It is true, however, that our posts on the Mississippi, very badly constructed, perhaps badly situated and dependent on New Orleans for their subsistence, are in a very hazardous position today.[41]

The remoteness of the frontier dictated an occasional exchange of visits and gifts. Piernas related what he assumed to be a courtesy call by the lieutenant governor of West Florida, Montfort Browne, to Fort San Luis in the summer of 1767: "I did all the honors appropriate; he reviewed the troops, received an artillery salute, and remained to dine; in short he was treated with the greatest respect."[42] This is not to say that a few provocative incidents did not occur. When they arose out of traditional national rivalry and antipathy or from the enforcement of new policies, they were generally quietly settled by the military leaders on both sides, who were determined to avoid the issuance of menacing notes or the display of force.

Garrisoning the newly built forts in the wilderness was a perennial trial for Ulloa and the English commanders. Desertions were frequent. The loneliness of the outposts, the absence of women, poor and irregular pay, and the impossibility of maintaining strict discipline all created a strong temptation to go down the river at the first opportunity. For the Spanish and French deserters the havens were Pensacola, Mobile, and British forts on the Mississippi; for the British malcontents it was generally New Orleans.

Almost from the first the Spanish governor experienced trou-

41. Quoted in ALvord and Carter (eds.), *The New Regime, 1765–1767*, 575.
42. Piernas to Ulloa, June 5, 1767, in Leg. 109, Papeles de Cuba, AGI.

ble in preserving the loyalty of the Spanish and French soldiers. His dispatch of July 8, 1766, to the captain general of Cuba emphasizes the seriousness of the problem of "deserters, of which we have a great number owing to the opportunity of being so close to the border of the English colony." There are frequent references to this in later communications to Havana.[43] The most notorious instance of desertion occurred at the Missouri post when Lieutenant Fernando Gomez and about half the garrison set off down the river to seek safety at the British Fort Panmure. At Ulloa's urging, General Haldimand ordered the men turned over to the Spanish authorities at Fort San Luis across the river. To the Spanish governor the deserters were to be classed not only as traitors to the king but also as thieves. British officers were taken aback at the grave charges, which carried long prison sentences.[44] Whether Ulloa intended to make an example out of these deserters or whether this was typical of his views on ship discipline is not apparent.

British officials were more tolerant of desertion. Although they regarded it as almost inevitable in the wilderness, they nevertheless made every effort to discourage the practice. Before the coming of the Spanish, Major Farmar complained of the frequency of desertions to New Orleans. After the arrival of the force from Havana, despite contrary suggestions from fellow officers, General Gage would not give credence to the report that the Spanish and French governors encouraged the habit. In the early part of 1767 when desertions were more numerous than usual, the Spanish governor proposed a formal arrangement, or cartel, for the mutual return of those who had illegally left their posts. This was objected to by Gage, as it "might be construed to extend to settlers, which will by no means answer." However, an informal plan was worked out. To aid the British, Ulloa agreed, at Haldimand's suggestion, to an act of deception, namely the proclamation of a general pardon to all British deser-

43. Ulloa to Bucareli, July 8, December 22, 1766, March 25 and August 31, 1767, all in Dispatches of the Spanish Governors of Louisiana, I.
44. Alvord and Carter (eds.), *Trade and Politics, 1767–1769,* 272.

ters who would turn themselves in. In consequence, a number of English soldiers, who had counted on a secure hideout in New Orleans, surrendered and were immediately put under their officers.[45] Lord Hillsborough complimented Gage on his favorable negotiations with the Spanish: "The Recovery of so large a Number of Deserters from His Majesty's Troops, who had taken Shelter under the Spanish Government, is a very considerable Acquisition and under the Circumstances you mention of the Regiments in North America being complete, His Majesty very much approves your having sent these Deserters to Grenada, to be incorporated in the Corps stationed in the Ceded Islands."[46]

It might be concluded that Ulloa's policy of containing the British in the West had a measure of success. A meticulous inspection of the colony had convinced him of the weakness of the old French defenses and hence of the need to restore them or build new and stronger forts. In retrospect, his scheme was more grandiose than practical, failing to take into account the obstacles of the terrain, the paucity of the hinterland population, and the large expenditures that Spain could not well afford at the time. Redoubts were to be built opposite the two British forts on the Mississippi, at the mouth of Bayou Manchac and at Natchez, and, in addition, the northern and southern perimeters of the colony were to be protected by posts on the Missouri and at the entrance to the Mississippi. There were no significant overt acts of aggression by the English, albeit these were feared by the Spanish, particularly in the Illinois country because of the large contingents of British soldiers there. In general, relations between the representatives of the two countries were good. The exchange of visits and correspondence, the espionage reports of Spanish and British officers, and the ceaseless flow of rumors emanating from the *voyageurs* and the Indians kept both governors reasonably abreast of each other's movements. Working for peace were the British anticipation of profitable inroads into the

45. Robert Rea, "Military Deserters from British West Florida," *Louisiana History,* IX (Spring, 1968), 124, 129, 131–35.

46. Quoted in Alvord and Carter (eds.), *Trade and Politics, 1767–1769,* 298.

lucrative Spanish trade of Havana and Mexico and the plain realization on both sides of the futility of hostilities. To the ministries in Madrid and London, economy in governmental expenses in a huge region, apparently barren of minerals, could not be ignored. The handling of deserters exhibited a degree of cooperation. Even in the formulation and application of Indian policy by the Spanish, to be dealt with in the succeeding chapter, there was less friction than might have been conjectured considering the British dependence on the fur trade.

V

Beads and Furs

The extent and complexity of the Indian problems in the wilderness may explain in part the reluctance of the Spanish to occupy Louisiana. It was realized in Madrid that colonial officials, though familiar with a great diversity of tribes of nearly all shades of the cultural spectrum residing from southern Florida to Cape Horn, had no real understanding of the nomadic and seminomadic Indians of the Mississippi Valley. Complicating the situation were the lucrative fur trade long exploited by the French and the presence of the British to the east and north. To develop a policy too precipitously might stir up the tribes against Spain and imperil its future sovereignty through Indian alliances with the British. By extending the reenlistment offer to the French soldiers under the Spanish flag in the spring of 1764, Choiseul hoped to avoid disorders arising from mistakes by inexperienced Spanish officials. The reenlistments, of course, did not materialize. The unwillingness of the French troops under Aubry to become a part of the Spanish force did not, however, deter French officials, familiar with Indian affairs, from accepting Ulloa's offer to remain at their posts. For Spain's influence in the region, the wisdom of the proposal was well justified.

To have an accurate, trustworthy account of the native groups living in the former French colony was basic for the formation of Spanish policy. Therefore Grimaldi was highly pleased at receiving from Fuentes in Paris in March, 1764, a list of the tribes, their locations, and the presents customarily given them by the French authorities. Since the list had been compiled at Choiseul's orders, Grimaldi did not discount its value. Fourteen distinct groups were mentioned: Apalachees, Biloxis, Pascagoulas, Chitimachas, Colapissas, Bayogoulas, Avoyelles, Houmas, Chanaches, Vachas, Tomikas, Offogulas, Atakapas, and Arkansas.[1] With these facts at hand, Grimaldi believed that he could evolve a sound policy toward the natives. Its foundation would be conciliation through continuing to give gifts and to maintain the trade in furs and hides. For the moment this embraced the fundamentals of the French policy. Modification of the policy and formulation of details would be left to the Spanish governor on the scene, subject to final approval by the secretary of state.

Meanwhile, speculation on the nature of Spanish procedure was rife at New Orleans and among British officers. Aubry had dire forebodings of the employment by the Spanish of a harsh policy that had gained them unpopularity with the tribes of the Southwest. Not only would it mean the end of prosperity for the French traders, but with the support of the disaffected savages the British might even seize the silver mines of Mexico:

> It is to be feared that the arrival of the Spaniards which we are expecting every day will cause a revolution very favorable to the English. All the nations of the continent know by hearsay about the cruelties which the Spaniards have practiced elsewhere in America and detest them generally.... It is certain that if the Spaniards try to act in the same way in Louisiana all will be lost. In the first war, the English will have legions of savages at their orders who, with arms and munitions and joined to the old enemies of the Spaniards, will penetrate easily as far as the mines, which are not three hundred leagues from the Mississippi and will destroy the source of the Spanish riches on some future day.[2]

In a later communication to the French ministry, Aubry repeated his anxiety over the adverse effect on the Indians of the tardy arrival of the Spaniards. The English, it is true, had been held up in their advance up the Mississippi to the north, but the

---

1. Fuentes to Grimaldi, March 9, 1764, in Leg. 2542, Audiencia de Sto. Domingo, AGI.
2. Aubry to French ministry, February 4, 1765, in Alvord and Carter (eds.), *The Critical Period, 1763–1765*, 431, 432.

security of the region depended on the friendliness of the Illinois. A letter from St. Ange, the French commandant of the Illinois post, was enclosed, depicting his plight: "Judging solely by the temperament of the Illinois, who have as yet done nothing, I am persuaded that the English will not reach here this year, and that is what causes me, sir, to reiterate the demands [requests] I had the honor to make to you in the letter of the 31 of last month for help for this post because I am destitute."[3]

The English commander-in-chief was skeptical that the Spanish would break with the traditional French Indian policy. General Gage deprecated any abrupt volte-face, the introduction of a policy of enslavement or subjugation: "From what I have been able to learn, the Spaniards mean to adopt the Plan of the French with respect to Indian affairs and that the Agents employed by the latter will continue in the Service of the Spaniards to Manage and Negotiate with the Savages. It is reported that Don Ulloa has already engaged in the Trading Company of the Illinois, tho' said at the same time, that he is not to remain long in Louisiana, being only sent there to regulate affairs against the Arrival of another Governor."[4] English hearsay regarding the initial policy was correct. No sensible governor would jeopardize a relationship on which so much depended. It was not only a question of profits for the traders, but one of the virtual existence of the colony. Indians in the South, except for the Catawbas and the Chickasaws, had stood by the French during the Seven Years' War. They would be indispensable allies in the event of another conflict with Great Britain. If they were alienated or antagonized, they had it within their power to annihilate the fort garrisons and raze most of the settlements.

Bearing these factors in mind, the Spanish governor in the beginning pursued a policy of appeasement and goodwill, if not fraternization, toward the tribes. Aubry's apprehensions over the severity of treatment were groundless. There were, indeed,

3. St. Ange to d'Abbadie, April 7, 1765, *ibid.,* 469.
4. Gage to Conway, June 24, 1766, in Carter (ed.), *The Correspondence of General Thomas Gage,* I, 93.

sound reasons for success in the long run. Like the French, the
Spanish did not contemplate any huge immigration to the region,
although augmenting the population was to be desired. Hence
the aborigines were not soon to be pushed from their hunting
grounds, with forest cleared and game scarce, as had happened
on the frontier of the English colonies. Again, like the French,
the Spanish exhibited few racial prejudices. In the viceroyalty
of Mexico and elsewhere the crown had encouraged interracial
marriages, with the result that a large, steadily increasing mixed,
or mestizo, class was appearing. Despite the "black legend" that
had currency during the Enlightenment in northern Europe
concerning Spanish attitudes toward the natives, the Laws of the
Indies were humanitarian and well intentioned. In Spain's favor
for the moment was a plentiful supply of presents with which to
win over the natives. Moreover, in this administrative area as in
others, the crown permitted a certain accommodation to local
conditions. Unless he acted in direct contradiction to traditional
attitudes, Ulloa might expect the backing of Grimaldi in policy
adjustments.

With Aubry's support, the Spanish governor reaffirmed the
French policy of friendship with the Indians. Chiefs of some of
the tribes residing near New Orleans visited the capital in March
and April. During his tour of inspection in the country above the
city, Ulloa smoked the customary pipe of peace and distributed
gifts liberally to the braves. There was no evidence of hostility by
the Indians, who were already well disposed toward the new-
comers on the advice of the French commandants and fur traders. According to an English source, the reception was enviable:
"I learn'd from good Authority that the Spanish Governor had
brought many sorts of presents for the Indians, & since they had
Established two Posts upon the Mississippi received all that came
and gave them every sort of thing they would want & since their
arrival the late Capt. Rea of the 21st Regimt. who commanded at
the Natchez informed me that the Indians did not seem so
attentive to the English as they were before and many of the
presents he offer'd them they rejected with scorn and said they

woul'd go to their brethern the Spaniards who gave them much better presents than we did."[5] Typical perhaps were the articles distributed among the Atakapas, which included laced cloaks for the chieftains, long knives, brass objects, beads, and several flintlock muskets with a considerable quantity of powder and balls.[6]

At the outset there was little interference by the Spanish with the trade conducted by the agents of the mercantile houses in the native villages and at the posts. The goods destined for this commerce comprised "cloth, blankets, brass kettles, hatchets, guns, knives, flints, powder and bullets, colored ribbons, plumes, brandy, razors, beads, wines, tobacco, rum, ready-made clothing, hats, paints of assorted colors, all types of notions and other goods." For the natives the consumption of liquor was demoralizing and often produced quarrels ending in death or mutilation. The uncontrolled sale of firearms was likewise a potential source of violence, as it put into the hands of the natives a formidable weapon that could be used against traditional foes and erstwhile friends. Although the French crown had imposed restrictions on traffic in both of these articles, little effort had been made to enforce them. The trade was highly profitable and only occasional protests against the harmful results were made, usually by missionaries, to little avail. In 1750 a certain Father Louis Vivier had bitterly condemned the sale of strong drink to the natives: "The brandy sold by the French . . . has ruined this mission, and has caused the majority of them [Indians] to abandon our holy religion. The savages and especially the Illinois, who are the gentlest and most tractable of men, become, when intoxicated, mad men and wild beasts. Then they fall upon one another, stab with their knives, and tear one another. Many have lost their ears and some portion of their noses, in these tragic encounters."[7] His remonstrance, like those of others, had not

5. Alvord and Carter (eds.), *Trade and Politics, 1767–1769,* 115.
6. See enclosure in Fuentes to Grimaldi, March 9, 1764, in Leg. 2542, Audiencia de Sto. Domingo, AGI.
7. Davis, *Louisiana,* 81. Governor Ulloa extolled to his fellow scientists the virtues of bear grease as a curative for rheumatism and other ills of the flesh and joints. There is a reference to its application and anticipated results in a letter from the French mathemati-

changed this deplorable feature of the Indian trade. Whether the Spanish could reform this aspect of internal commerce remained to be seen.[8]

To what extent did Ulloa follow the policy familiar to the English and French of surreptitiously encouraging intertribal wars? It had undoubtedly been a means in the past of weakening general resistance to the advancing frontier settlements. Apparently, there are no proved instances of its use, but in some remote quarters conditions might have tempted the Spanish to resort to this nefarious game.

One must remember that, in this period when Spain was developing an Indian policy in the former French colony, England was taking a long look at its own policy in the West. Reexamination might lead to revamping the strategy. Because of the proximity of the two colonies and their similar problems, it may be expedient to scrutinize British policy from the vantage points of origins, possible mutual influences, and solutions. After 1763 the relations of the English with the various tribes followed an intricate pattern. It is possible therefore to indicate only the main lines of action, which were uneven and subject to change, with special consideration of the regulations issued in 1765 by John Stuart, the Indian agent, and George Johnstone, the governor of West Florida, for the supervision of the Indian trade. A comparison of these with the rules drawn up by Governor Ulloa for Captain Riu's expedition to the Illinois country will disclose likenesses and dissimilarities.

At the end of the French and Indian War the British govern-

---

cian and astronomer La Condamine: "My dear travel companion. Although I have answered your last letter, I do not wish to lose the opportunity that Monsieur de Mandeville's son affords as a bearer of this letter to thank you for all your presents. Eight days ago I began to rub the lower part of my spine with bear grease, mixed with brandy, or spirit of wine, in order for it to penetrate with greater ease, as the masters of the profession have told me. . . . You will be astonished that I don't rub my feet and hands with the oil that you sent me . . . the remedy must be applied to the base of the nerves. This is the reason why I apply it to the spine." See La Condamine to Ulloa, June 15, 1768, in MS 18182, Biblioteca Nacional, Madrid, hereinafter cited as BN.

8. British officials had a low opinion of the traders. In 1773 Major Henry Bassett at Detroit characterized them as "the outcasts of all Nations and the refuse of Mankind." See Jack Sosin, *Whitehall and the Wilderness: The Middle West in British Colonial Policy, 1760–1775* (Lincoln, 1961), 218.

ment resolved to improve relations with the Indians. The Proclamation of 1763, though severely limiting the sale of Indian lands to private persons and land companies, admitted concessions to traders with partial oversight of their activities by the colonial governments. The dissatisfaction of the Indian nations with this policy, leading to Pontiac's Rebellion and a resurgence of French influence, necessitated a reexamination. Imperial management replaced provincial oversight as the essence of the new approach. Matters of Indian policy would be in the hands of superintendents, in the South in the person of John Stuart, to be directly though not entirely responsible to London. In cooperation with the military commanders, the superintendents set out to achieve a general pacification through firm control of the tribes east of the Mississippi and a restriction on colonial expansion to the west. Stuart sought to implement these measures by safeguarding Indian lands from claims by settlers, by delicate diplomacy with tribes that were neutral or hostile to the English, and above all by putting order in the Indian trade. These ideas were embraced in the so-called Plan of 1764, in the end chiefly the work of George Montagu Dunk, the earl of Halifax, and Lord Hillsborough. For Stuart the heart of the reform was control over individual traders through a system of bonding and licensing by the superintendent. As might be expected, the opposition was intense, coming from traders, merchants, and colonial assemblies.[9]

Unfortunately, the experiment in imperial direction did not endure for long. The protests of vested interests in the colonies and the cry in governmental circles for economy in expenditures could not be ignored. With Shelburne in power in the latter part of 1767, the Board of Trade revised its program. Its report, issued in March, 1768, permitted the superintendent to main-

9. John R. Alden, *John Stuart and the Southern Colonial Frontier: A Study of Indian Relations, War, Trade, and Land Problems in the Southern Wilderness, 1754–1775* (Ann Arbor, 1944), 172, 335, 336. Stuart was a first-rate agent, concerned with the future livelihood of the Indians along the southern frontier and the maintenance of stout ties of friendship with the crown. Johnstone, his collaborator, said that he was "one of the most judicious and intelligent men I have conversed with."

tain authority in political dealings with the Indians but returned control over trade to the colonial assemblies. Stuart's power having been greatly reduced, the traders resumed their exploitations.[10]

During this interim period, 1764–1768, Stuart regularized the Indian trade with limited success. The rules that he issued, in conjunction with Governor Johnstone, should be borne in mind because of their similarity to the later Spanish regulations. The major articles of the nineteen composing this document are given below:

1. That no Indian trader by himself or substitute, or servant, shall sell or give to any Indian any spirituous liquor of any kind whatsoever.

. . . .

3. That no trader shall employ any person or clerk, packhorseman or factor in their service before any agreement is first entered into in writing between them specifying the time, and condition of service, and also his or their names indorsed on the back of the licence which may be given to such trader whereby the principal trader shall then be deem'd answerable for his or their conduct.

. . . .

5. That no Indian trader shall employ any Negro or Indian or half breed, who from his manner of life shall in the conscience of a jury be considered as living under the Indian government as a factor or deputy to trade in any town or village on account of the said trader.

. . . .

9. That no Indian trader by himself substitute or servant shall sell any swann shott or riffled guns to the Indians.

10. That all goods shall be sold according to the following tariff, and if any trader by himself or servant shall sell any goods cheaper or dearer than in the following tariff, then such fact is to be considered as a forfeiture of their bond and licence.

. . . .

13. That no Indian trader by himself substitute or servant shall propagate any false report or reports among the Indians, or convene any meetings with them or deliver any messages to them without the concurrence of the commissary first obtained in writing.

14. That no Indian trader shall refuse or neglect to appear at any general meeting of the Indians or congress when duly summoned by the gover-

10. *Ibid.*, 259–62.

nor of the province superintendant or his deputy except in the case of sickness. Then such refusal shall be considered as a forfeiture of their bond and licence.

. . . .

16. That no Indian clerk factor or packhorseman shall beat or abuse any Indians and that they shall pay a proper respect to the medal chiefs and captains bearing commissions.

17. That no trader by himself substitute or servant shall trade with any of the Indians in the woods under any pretence whatsoever.

. . . .

19. That no trader by himself substitute or servant shall barter or trade with any of the Indians in any place except at the home or store of such trader; neither shall any trader his substitute or servant forcibly take from any Indian any skins on any pretence whatsoever.[11]

From the foregoing it is obvious that the British government sought to impose severe restraints on the commercial activities and even the personal habits of the traders. High on the list was the prohibition of the sale of brandy and firearms. To keep the unscrupulous factors from taking undue advantage of their clients, the crown insisted that transactions take place in the trader's store or house rather than in the woods or the Indian village and that exchanges be based on a schedule of fixed prices for articles. Physical maltreatment of the natives was strictly forbidden. As a final measure of control, the traders must comply with a summons of the commissary to an assembly of the Indians or a congress of traders. For nonobservance or violation of the regulations, the penalty was forfeiture of bond and license.

While Stuart and Johnstone were busy with reforms in West Florida, the Spanish authorities were not idle. In surveying Indian relations, Governor Ulloa concluded that innovations were essential to pacify the tribes and to develop the colony. Discontent among the Indians, brought on by abuses by the traders, could lead to forays and impede the advance of the settlers up the river and into the interior. Ulloa probably had a genuine

11. *Ibid.,* 341–44.

compassion for the natives, judging by his severe criticism of the Indian agents, or *corregidores,* of the viceroyalty of Peru in his secret reports to the crown and by the storm that his presence in Huancavelica aroused among conniving Spanish officials.[12] To counter the activity of English agents was also a consideration. Nor could he lightly dismiss the expressions of concern by Governor Johnstone of West Florida.[13]

It was not until the winter of 1766–1767 that Ulloa's thoughts on Indian policy and, in particular, on the role of the trader crystallized. His instructions to Captain Riu, head of the Illinois expedition, spelled out in detail his ideas on the treatment of the natives. A major purpose of the northern advance was "to preserve the friendship and the alliance of the Indians in the colony." The Indians should be "treated as brothers, who should not be subjected to injury, mockery, or derision and whose wives should not be molested, for in this lies a danger as great as that with the more civilized nations." One should give presents to the chiefs when they come to parley, but should not make the mistake of being too generous, for the Indians would expect something on every visit. "A distinction must be made in the distribution of gifts and medals between the chiefs of tribes for a long time friendly to the French and those of tribes of recent alliance. In no way alter the treatment of the older tribes, for it is of great importance that the traditional policy be maintained." As to the nations siding with the English, the Spanish must "take care not to offend them when they enter our territory . . . for this reason traders or citizens of new settlements should not cross to the English bank to carry on business with the savages living there; if the natives come over to our side on their own volition, for a visit,

12. His denunciation of the oppressive acts of the *corregidores* was perhaps the most forthright among Spanish officials of the eighteenth century. See Moore, *The Cabildo in Peru Under the Bourbons,* 44.

13. In a letter to Ulloa, Johnstone stressed the importance of a satisfactory policy toward the Indians: "In a Word our own Happiness and the Peace of the different Provinces entrusted to our Care, seem to be to depend on a sincere Resolution cordially to Unite in mutual good offices and neither to become the Dupes of the Indians, nor the Indian traders, who are more savage than them." See Johnstone to Ulloa, May 3, 1766, in *Correspondence of the British Governors of West Florida,* DLXXV, 27, PRO.

or to move their residence, no obstacle should be put in their way."[14] It was important to keep all Indian nations at peace, those living in English as well as Spanish territory, because their intertribal wars could injure Spanish subjects. English traders could not enter Spanish dominions to do business with the natives. Special provision was to be made for the commandant of the fort to trade with one of the local tribes. When the arrangement was made, the governor was to be informed. Every effort should be made to deal fairly with the Indians in the exchange of goods. A tariff of prices must be adhered to. If Spanish measures and weights were employed, they must be adjusted to the French system so that cheating and deception be kept to a minimum.[15]

A very significant part of the instructions for Captain Riu had to do with limitations on the nature of articles sold or exchanged to the natives. These provisions are as follows:

> 60. No person is to be permitted to go among the Indians for the purpose of trading without a license signed by the governor.
>
> 61. The introduction of brandy is prohibited completely, not only among the Indians, but also to the settlement. Those who would transport it for indispensable uses must also be licensed.
>
> 62. It is not permitted for muskets, gunpowder, or munitions to be sold to Indian nations that have not been accustomed to receive them; nor should those nations accustomed to obtaining them receive more than is to be allotted in the trader's commission.[16]

The second or secret set of instructions given Riu by Governor Ulloa reiterated with varying emphasis the above features of policy. The sale of firearms was authorized, however, for tribes in the interior of the Missouri only on a limited basis, "because they are not used to the musket."[17]

These regulations embodying Ulloa's sentiments on Indian policy disclose much similarity with British policy of the pre-Shelburne era, from 1764–1768. The concept of centralized

---

14. Instrucción para la expedición a la parte de Yllinueses, Articles 44, 45, 47–49, in Leg. 2357, Audiencia de Sto. Domingo, AGI.
15. Articles 50, 54, 56, 58, 59, *ibid.*
16. Articles 60–62, *ibid.*
17. Instrucción segunda para la expedición a la parte de Yllinueses, Article 23, *ibid.*

control of traders through bonding and licensing as a means of lessening the causes for unrest among the tribes on the frontier and in the interior was common to both. Restricting the sale of brandy and guns was necessary in the territory claimed by the British and the Spanish. Trading should be conducted at the posts or at the homes of traders in accordance with a tariff of prices established by the commissary or governor. It is obvious that the sale of Indian lands was not of immediate concern to the Spanish in view of the sparse population of Louisiana. There is no evidence that Ulloa was influenced directly by Stuart's policy, though he must have known the nature of many regulations. After studying conditions on the frontier he could well have reached identical conclusions. Avoiding Indian hostilities meant more economic progress and less expenditures for the garrisoned posts.

To enforce these regulations in the hinterland of Louisiana, where the traders had had almost complete liberty, was another matter. The Spanish governor counted on St. Ange, French commandant at St. Louis, and on Captain Riu on the Missouri as the principal instruments of supervision. Ulloa had corresponded with St. Ange from the first days of his arrival. On March 6, 1766, he had requested St. Ange to summon the chiefs of the neighboring tribes and inform them of his presence in New Orleans. In reply St. Ange mentioned the need for supplies and the difficulty of prohibiting the sale of brandy by the traders. Ulloa commended him on his efforts to forestall the consumption of liquor by the Indians through an understanding with British officers and promised to pass on to the court in Madrid other pertinent matters for its deliberation and decision.[18] Subsequent communications from this northern post stressed the difficulties of cooperating with the British, who clandestinely sought to win over the Indians and who invaded Spanish territory to capture deserters. The Sioux had arrived at

18. St. Ange to Ulloa, June 16, 1766, and Ulloa to St. Ange, July 15, 1766, both in Leg. 2357, Audiencia de Sto. Domingo, AGI.

the post for parleys, St. Ange notified the governor in October, 1767. As with the other tribes, they were the objects of cunning diplomacy by the English. Supplies were running low, but he looked forward to receiving merchandise from New Orleans. In May, 1768, his letters had a desperate tone, the gifts for the Indians not having arrived. "They [the Indians] were more liberally provided for during the time of French rule. It is no longer a matter of wishing to attract other nations." During the spring and summer, the major problems were the depletion of supplies and the threatened status of the Indian trader.[19]

To the British commanders in the West, the suspected designs of the Spanish in fomenting Indian raids were a constant preoccupation. From time to time traders and warriors reported dangerous plots and intrigues engaged in by French and Spanish officers to lower English prestige. Gage credited these rumors to French officers and traders, who cherished an abiding jealousy and hatred for their victorious enemies. He took special pains to exonerate the French and Spanish governors. "I have never been able to discover that any Intrigues have been carried on with the Indians under the sanction of the French and Spanish Governors; or have I Reason to Suspect that either Don Ulloa or Mon. Aubry have had any Concern in them," he informed Lord Hillsborough.[20] In London Gage's vindication was not taken at face value.[21] There is no substantial proof that Ulloa deliberately incited the Indians to hostile acts or that he conspired to organize a league of tribes against the English. It is likely that he pursued a policy parallel to that of the British. In parleys with the chieftains and by his orders to his subordinates

19. St. Ange to Ulloa, June 27, 1767, October 19, 1767, May 18, 1768, and June 23, 1768, all *ibid.*

20. Gage to Hillsborough, February 4, 1769, in Carter (ed.), *The Correspondence of General Thomas Gage*, I, 217.

21. Hillsborough's attitude was probably typical of the ministry: "I never had the least doubt that accounts received from the Indian Country of the Intrigues and Machinations of the French and Spaniards were greatly exaggerated and that many idle Stories are propagated with the views and purposes you mention in your dispatch. Such reports are not however to be entirely discredited." See Hillsborough to Gage, March 24, 1769, in Alvord and Carter (eds.), *Trade and Politics, 1767–1769*, 515.

he did encourage the Indians to sever their trading ties with the English and, if necessary, to move to Spanish territory. English traders were enjoined from carrying on business on the west bank of the Mississippi. Modern business ethos would condone these measures as fair competition.

But on one aspect of Anglo-Spanish relations the British commander-in-chief felt that he had a just complaint. French traders roaming the wilderness frequently trespassed on English soil to sell goods and to hunt for game. This posed a disadvantage to the English fur trade. Not only did the English pelts go to New Orleans, where restrictions were imposed by the authorities, but their traders had to compete with the French on the east bank. The indiscriminate killing of deer and buffalo might also create a shortage of food for the natives. Reports of violations of territory were common.[22] In the early summer of 1768 Gage was impelled to protest directly to Aubry and to Ulloa the unwarranted and illegal operations of the traders. From both officials the response was favorable. Aubry, for his part, in New Orleans "published a Proclamation, forbidding the French traders from going on the East Side of the Mississippi." In a dispatch to Hillsborough, Gage expressed the hope that "the like Proclamation will be published in the Country above, amongst the Inhabitants opposite to the Illinois, if it will have an Effect upon People, almost as wild as the Savages themselves."[23] Ulloa's reply to Gage's remonstrance was to deny knowledge of such acts by men of his command, but, if it were true, he promised full compliance and punishment of offenders:

I do not doubt but that such things were done before my time, but since my coming here, I have not heard of any such thing, having given the Strictest Orders, to the Commanders of the different Posts, by no means permit the Spanish Subjects to pass to the English, nor to have any commerce with them, except in particular cases of necessity requiring any to go, and then to have passports directed to the English Commander of the Districts to which

22. See George Morgan to Bayston and Wharton, December 10, 1767, *ibid.,* 130.
23. Gage to Hillsborough, August 17, 1768, in Carter (ed.), *The Correspondence of General Thomas Gage,* I, 183.

they belong, under Penalty that if they be found without one, they shall be entirely deprived of the rights of the Nation, and shall be Chastised by the English Chiefs at their Pleasure as the Breakers of the Peace and the good Harmony that Subsists between the two Powers.[24]

It is unlikely that either Ulloa or Aubry could end this practice. Conditions were probably worse after the events of October and November, 1768, which temporarily destroyed any central authority in the province.

The activities of the French fur traders paradoxically caused friction between the Spanish officials in Louisiana and their counterparts in Texas. Under the devious commercial system in force in 1766, intercourse between these two regions was strictly forbidden. From the old French post at Natchitoches the aggressive merchants continued, however, the illicit trade that they had initiated decades earlier with the Indians of the Southwest. A particularly nefarious line of business was the exchange of firearms and *aguardiente,* or brandy, for pelts. In March, 1767, the Spanish commandant at Adaïes accused the French official in charge, Louis de Perier, of conniving with the French traders to sell gunpowder and other outlawed articles among the Indians of the mission and presidios of his jurisdiction. There was a halfhearted promise to rectify the abuse.[25] That it persisted notwithstanding is borne out by a dispatch from the marqués de Croix, now viceroy of Mexico, to Ulloa in January, 1768.[26] The obstacles to communication in the wilderness and the absence of Spanish troops impeded any real enforcement of ordinances on the traders in this sector of the colony.

A précis of Indian policy, with special stress on the conduct of trade and the distribution of gifts, is found in a letter from Ulloa to Grimaldi, composed toward the end of the critical summer of 1768:

24. Ulloa to Gage, August 29, 1768, in Alvord and Carter (eds.), *Trade and Politics, 1767–1769,* 386.
25. Angel Martos y Navarrete to Ulloa, March 8, 1767, and Ulloa to Martos, June 22, 1767, both in Leg. 109, Papeles de Cuba, AGI.
26. Croix to Ulloa, January 18, 1768, in Leg. 149A, *ibid.*

It is the purpose of the government to keep them in peace, friendship, and concord at the post, without increasing the burden of the presents and support that they go to collect frequently. I apply my major attention to this latter point, hoping that I can deliver them from a bad custom, which through undue generosity increases their begging. On the other hand, I have permitted a free hand to the commandants and others who deal with them to take advantage of their particular position; with this understanding I have labored to bring about at least a reduction of extraordinary expenses of the Indians and at the same time to prevent the commandants from acting despotically or yielding before the threats of insults of the natives if they do not satisfy them on every occasion that they present themselves at the forts. But this was not enough to reach the goal, revealing the principal difficulty, which consists in the fact that the same traders who deal with them, to realize greater profits, persuade them to go frequently to the forts, telling them that they will get splendid gifts, as they have in the past, and that the same Indian nations have been given to understand in the parleys that have occurred. To do away with the abuse that has been practiced for a long time, I have divided up the areas of the different nations into districts and assigned traders of better repute to each. He is given a license to enter it and do business for a year, being responsible for any untoward event that might take place. He is to persuade the Indians not to come to the forts more often than is necessary to receive the customary gifts; he is to hand out to them regularly the things that they are accustomed to receive, so that it will not be necessary for them to come to the forts to get their [presents] under pretense of extraordinary gifts, which would be disapproved. In this way I am of the opinion that incidents will be less serious and in time this vicious custom will disappear.[27]

This letter reveals the mind of the bureaucrat and the heart of the reformer. The costs of gifts were heavy. The lack of sufficient appropriations for the colony had already impressed the governor with the need to curtail expenditures. It was clear that a proposal to effect economies would not be lost on the secretary of state. At the same time the nomination of traders of "better repute" and their assignment to specific districts were forward steps in establishing central control. The quintessence of reform was, however, as John Stuart had always advocated, the licensing of the individual trader, the existence of whose occupation de-

27. Ulloa to Grimaldi, August 4, 1768, in Leg. 2542, Audiencia de Sto. Domingo, AGI.

pended on the Spanish governor. By eliminating certain desperate and malevolent characters, the welfare and contentment of the natives would be greatly enhanced.

The consequences of this policy on the colony might have been foreseen. Even though the long-term advantages, the growth of trade and the pacification of the Indians, were obvious, it interfered with the freedom of action by itinerant merchants and by the supply houses, in short, by well-intrenched local interests. Almost complete liberty in dealing with the Indians had been customary, despite regulations by the French governors. Could this restrictive policy be enforced in the wide area of Louisiana? Would the traders submit to licensing? Would they give up the sale of guns and brandy? Some of these obstacles might have been overcome if sufficient authority had existed at the posts. As long as the governor had few troops at his command it would be impossible to enforce the policy. In the North, chief responsibility for implementation lay with Captain Riu, assisted by St. Ange. In May, 1768, a number of traders assembled at St. Louis to protest the intent of the regulations.[28] Faced by this formidable opposition, Riu notified Ulloa of his modification and postponement for a year of the enforcement of the rules governing this group:

> No trader of whatsoever condition that he be shall be able to trade in any other post than that in which I have designated for him, under penalty of confiscation of all the goods that he brought, which will be distributed as it best appears to the chief governor of the colony. I permit them solely to take provisions in the posts where they passed if they had need of them.
>
> It is ordered that all those going now to the Missouri present themselves during the month of June of next year, if later than that, under a fine of 500 libras and two months' imprisonment. I permit every trader who is now among the nations of the Missouri, with license from Señor St. Ange or any other French commandant, to conduct trade in the place where he is, without being able to turn over to others the goods he had, and I prohibit him from buying other goods from any other trader, under any pretext, under penalty of confiscation of the value of the goods bought and of the

28. Representación de los comerciantes al Capt. Riu, January 15, 1769, in Leg. 2357, *ibid.*

disposition of them at the will of the governor, and whosoever should sell will pay 500 libras as a fine, the amount to be at the disposition of the governor.

The traders from the English side who might be among the nations of the Missouri will not enjoy the privilege of trade with the goods that they have with them, because they should not trade on the Spanish side, and immediately they will cease trading and depart from the post where they will return to the English dominions. Whoever fails to comply will be arrested, his goods confiscated, and notice sent to his superior. The other traders on this side may trade with the goods they have, and as soon as they have finished their work, they are obliged to appear before me, not later than the month of June of 1769. Whoever should not obey this order will suffer confiscation of his goods, which will be at the disposition of the governor of the colony.

I charge all the traders to preserve harmony with all nations, since on that depends the tranquillity of the colony. I urge that they do not exact too much in their dealings so as to avoid complaints and suspicions and that they treat them [the Indians] with all the respect that is due them. Whoever fails to obey these admonitions will be punished according to his crime and will no longer enjoy the right to trade.[29]

To develop an effective Indian policy was a prerequisite for permanent occupation of the colony. Grimaldi saw the wisdom of adhering to the lines already drawn by the French government. To Ulloa was left the task of formulating the details of the policy. It was not only a question of placating the aborigines but of fostering the fur trade. Naturally, English rights and interests had to be considered in view of their contiguous territory and the mutual use of the Mississippi. One observes, interestingly enough, that the Spanish governor and John Stuart believed in the necessity of imperial control of Indian affairs primarily through strict supervision of the traders as a means of expanding trade and winning and retaining the goodwill of the tribes. Ulloa's actions constituted a valuable precedent for later governors. Salutary for the natives and beneficial in the future for economic interests, his policies denoted constructive thought and humanitarian impulses.

29. Ordenes del Capt. Riu a los diversos tratantes, January 15, 1769, *ibid.* See also Ordenes del Capt. Riu, June 17, 1768, in Leg. 109, Papeles de Cuba, AGI.

Whether the regulation of the fur trade was feasible at this moment hinged on the strength of local resistance and the acquiescence of the crown to outlays for its enforcement. The dissatisfaction of the traders in 1768 added to the strain already imposed on the Spanish regime. The commerce with the natives of the hinterland was one of a number of threads in the economic fabric of the colony. Its expansion depended on the fundamental policies adopted by the Spanish government for foreign trade and for internal development.

VI

Commerce and
Currency

It was hardly less difficult for a camel to go through the eye of a needle than for Louisiana to become an integrated part of the Spanish mercantile system. To the colonial merchant-planter group in New Orleans, nothing short of a miracle could bring this to pass. This was the economic issue that hung over the colony and its solution was awaited with doubt and apprehension. In reality, there were alternative courses that faced the Spanish ministry in developing economic policies for Louisiana. It might leave unchanged the present system, propping up the economy with generous subsidies with no prospect of discontinuing them. This would not, however, fit in with the aggressive, reform-minded administration of Charles III and José Gálvez. The second alternative was the eventual assimilation of Louisiana into the imperial system despite the financial costs and the hardships to the colonists. The adoption of this latter approach was almost inevitable in view of the general tendencies toward centralization and uniformity in the empire in the eighteenth century. Moreover, if Louisiana was to serve as a bastion for the defense of Mexico—the *raison d'être* of its acquisition—its economy would have to be strengthened. An impoverished colony, dependent on large grants of funds from the Mexican treasury, with a meager population, could not provide the sinews for defense against the encroachment of the British Empire. Grimaldi himself was not unaware of the economic difficulties of Louisiana. Restrictive policies must be applied, but gradually.

Foreign trade was the lifeblood of the colony. During the Seven Years' War and in the subsequent three-year interim, Louisianians had not felt the impact of severe commercial decrees. To France the traders exported furs and hides and from New England the colony obtained clandestinely the flour that could not be produced in the warm climate of the South. Some lumber, pitch, and tar were sold to the French colonies in the West Indies, which in turn supplied New Orleans and other areas with sugar, rum, and additional items available in the tropics. Smuggling was normal, particularly with the English, who were close at hand in Mobile and Pensacola and to the north on the Mississippi above Bayou Manchac. The phrase, "going to little Manchac," bespoke the illegal commercial intercourse with the British merchants. This type of business the average citizen of New Orleans regarded as essential, regular, and profitable.[1] In sum, the colony had considerable freedom of trade. Without this wide scope of economic opportunity, it was believed, life would have a subsistence basis.

To what extent would Spain permit this species of commercial liberty? At the outset Grimaldi's instructions to Ulloa categorized Louisiana as a special dependency, which would not be immediately incorporated into one of the viceroyalties and hence would not be subjected to the commercial ordinances of the Indies. It was a concession calculated to curry favor with the French population. It was unthinkable, however, that in time the crown would not seek to enhance imperial unity and to secure simultaneously financial advantages from the new possession, as long as the regulations, essential for this purpose, did not undermine the economy of the colony and permanently alienate the inhabitants.

It was not long before the crown resolved to act. On May 6,

---

1. Caughey, *Gálvez in Louisiana*, 10, 11. John G. Clark, *New Orleans, 1718–1812: An Economic History* (Baton Rouge, 1970), 111, emphasizes the English role in the colony's trade: "Great Britain was more successful than France in penetrating the empire of other powers, thus establishing a vast informal empire and busily creating a broad industrial plant at home."

1766, it issued the first of a series of decrees affecting foreign commerce. For Louisiana the ordinance authorized a limited amount of direct trade with certain Spanish colonies and with the French West Indian dependencies. Beef and grain might be transported in Spanish vessels from certain ports designated for this purpose upon payment of a 5 percent export duty. To prevent fraud, the French government must appoint agents to reside in the ports to purchase the commodities. The colonists in Louisiana were permitted to export timber, rice, corn, and other agricultural products.[2]

Despite the closer trading ties with Spain and Cuba and the flow of some Spanish coins into the currency, the economy of the colony showed little improvement. At the end of the summer of 1766 many citizens complained that the prices for exports had fallen and the costs of imported articles had risen. As a result hard money, already scarce, was in even shorter supply, thus dimming the prospect for the expansion of business activities. Believing that it was necessary to stimulate legitimate commerce and also to quiet the complaints of the people over high prices, Governor Ulloa now issued tighter regulations to control foreign trade and, in particular, the sale of imports. On September 6, 1766, he authorized Aubry to promulgate a decree that was aimed at curtailing some of the freedom enjoyed by those engaged in foreign trade:

> His Catholic Majesty, desiring only the well-being and profit of his subjects in Louisiana, being informed by Captain Ulloa, sent to take possession of it, of all that concerns the provisioning of the colony and of the exportation of commodities and other products for export, has resolved to favor the inhabitants of this land by permitting the entrance of ships from the French colonies of St. Domingue and Martinique which will transport here wine,

2. Gayarré, *History of Louisiana*, II, 167. As a matter of fact the viceroy of Bogotá had acknowledged late in 1765 the receipt from Arriaga of an earlier order stipulating the exclusion of trade from his region with Louisiana. In July, 1766, Arriaga cautioned Bucareli not to encourage contacts between Louisiana and Mexico: "There must remain the prohibition between Louisiana and all the king's possessions in America as existed at the time of French sovereignty." See viceroy of Bogotá to Arriaga, November 17, 1765, and Arriaga to Bucareli, July 6, 1766, both in Leg. 2542, Audiencia de Sto. Domingo, AGI.

flour, and other provisions and will carry from this colony wood and other commodities, while efforts are being made to develop commerce with Spain; [he] has resolved to grant passports to shipowners from France who will carry provisions and other wares necessary for the colony. But as these concessions have been accorded only insofar as they are advantageous to the inhabitants of Louisiana, and because for some time the merchants have raised the price of articles, particularly that of wine . . . to the detriment of the people . . . it is ordered that all captains coming from St. Domingue as well as those from France be provided with passports from His Excellency the secretary of state for His Catholic Majesty—otherwise they will not be received—present themselves to Monsieur de Ulloa with their passports upon arrival and with an invoice of the cargo. It is forbidden to unload anything without his permission noted on the passport or the invoice. It is ordered also that the [French] commissioners present themselves similarly before Monsieur de Ulloa to give a list of the prices at which the merchandise is to be sold, so that they can be examined by fair and intelligent persons of the colony, and if the prices are too high, they will not be allowed to sell them. . . . The said merchants will be obliged to accept payment for these goods in the present currency. They will [also] obtain one-third of their outgoing cargo in timber and other produce of the colony.[3]

The decree represented the first real interference by the Spanish government in the commerce of the colony. Although one of its minor purposes was to protect the ordinary citizen from monopolistic prices charged by importers, its major thrust was to eliminate smuggling—the nightmare of Spain everywhere in the Gulf and Caribbean—by requiring the presentation of duly authenticated licenses or passports. Procedure of this sort was customary in the Spanish colonies. Whether the French merchants and their colonial counterparts who had operated with few regulations would obey the decree was problematical.

To Ulloa's consternation and wrath there was an almost immediate adverse reaction to the regulation from the commercial elements in the colony. On September 8, the merchants in New Orleans petitioned the Superior Council not to issue the decree until the attorney general could study its provisions. The impor-

3. Gayarré, *Histoire de la Louisiane,* II, 147, 148. See also Rodríguez, *Primeros años,* 120, 121.

ters objected to the requirement for posting the price list of the goods in the market, and the ship captains denounced the irksome obligation of obtaining passports and presenting them to the Spanish governor. A second memorial containing additional signatures was presented to the Superior Council. The commissary Foucault, closely associated with the mercantile interests, remonstrated vigorously with Ulloa, declaring that this order impinged upon his authority and that consequently he should have been consulted before its issuance. In a September 29 letter to the French ministry, Foucault criticized the decree on the grounds that "His Majesty [the king of France] did not intend to deprive his subjects, for the benefit of Spain, of privileges and exemptions which they have always enjoyed, when he made the cession" of the territory. According to the commissary, Aubry had, however, given assurances that the ordinance would not be fully enforced.[4]

Because of the hostile attitude of the importers and merchants, it is doubtful that the decree was enforced to any extent. There were undoubtedly some advantages for the consumers in the control of prices. But the public was inarticulate and politically impotent. From the first the mercantile interests looked upon the ordinance as an unwarranted step in the encroachment of the crown on their liberties. Their resentful stance may have been one of the motives that caused Ulloa to remove his residence from New Orleans to Balize for many months.[5] With Ulloa out of the city it was not difficult for the disgruntled shipowners and merchants to connive with Foucault and La Frenière to evade many of the restrictions placed on smuggling. In this clash over trade regulation is to be found a significant cause for the growing disillusionment with Spain among members of an influential and privileged group.

Ulloa's efforts to stamp out smuggling are well illustrated in the case of the Spanish schooner *Nuestra Señora de la Luz*. In

4. Gayarré, *Histoire de la Louisiane,* II, 148–50, 151.
5. Gage to Shelburne, January 17, 1767, in Carter (ed.,) *The Correspondence of General Thomas Gage,* I, 119.

October, 1766, the ship arrived at Balize from Campeche, with a cargo of *palo de Campeche*, or dyewood, under the pretext of needing timber for her masts and provisions to continue the voyage to Havana. Without a license to trade, the master of the vessel intended to anchor at New Orleans and dispose of his cargo, contrary to commercial regulations. In detaining the ship and ordering an investigation of the circumstances of her trip, Ulloa hoped, so he wrote Grimaldi, to make an example "so that no one else would follow this path." The minister of state at Ulloa's request took up the matter with the governor of Campeche, who denied any knowledge of the departure of the vessel for Louisiana. But, through connivance of the Superior Council, the master succeeded in disposing of his freight in the port and in obtaining sufficient provisions and wood for the repair of his vessel. In June, 1767, he sailed for Havana with a relatively empty hold.[6] Although the shipment of dyewood had been sold, impediments had been put in the way of this traffic in the detention of the vessel for seven months and in her departure without a cargo. As a result of this incident, the crown eventually brought pressure to bear on officials in Campeche to terminate "this laxity so injurious to the state and the royal treasury." Furthermore, the list of sailings from New Orleans for the year 1767 showed a marked decline in the number of vessels engaged in the exportation of dyewood.[7]

In acquiring West Florida, Great Britain had high hopes of expanding the lucrative illegal commerce with the Spanish and French colonies as a means of tightening its military grip on the northern shoreline of the Gulf of Mexico. To fulfill the latter aim the British navy for several years after the war still imposed some of the wartime regulations on foreign shipping, thus hampering contacts with Spanish traders. Governor Johnstone in his report

6. Ulloa to Grimaldi, October 23, 1766, Grimaldi to governor of Campeche, March 3, 1767, and Ulloa to Arriaga, March 4, 1768, all in Leg. 2542, Audiencia de Sto. Domingo, AGI.

7. Grimaldi to governor of Campeche, December 14, 1768, and enclosure in Ulloa's dispatch to Arriaga, March 4, 1768, both *ibid.*

to the Lords Commissioners, dated February 19, 1765, recommended removal of all restrictions on trade with the Spanish possessions:

Every Body here at the beginning [is] in high hopes of a Commerce with them [the Spanish]. But that has been entirely interrupted by His Majesty's Ships. I am persuaded from the letters I have received from Havannah, Merida, and Campeche, it might be carried on to any Extent, in Furniture, printed linens, Cheques, Sadlery & Bays in return for Bullion & Dyewood.

I think there is no Subject better worth their Lordships Consideration, both for the Benefit of Britain, and this Province. Above 200 people have left this country, who had come in hopes of that Correspondence, and, in case it is still resolved to be prohibited, we must certainly move to Point Iberville, for that Place must then be the Seat of Government, where the Land produces everything spontaneous, and the whole trade of the Mississippi will fall into our hands, also that of the Missouri & Arkansas. But if the Spanish Trade was open & our Dependence lay in Foreign Commerce, Penzacola is certainly the best adapted for it, because the Produce of all the colony round [now the Iberville is open] may be brought here in three days, at a medium by water carriage, so that we might enjoy both, with equal ease.

Another Cruel Disadvantage arising from excluding the Spaniards, is the Total Want of Cash, which it occasions and no Paper Money, that dangerous Expedient being yet established, we are in a deplorable Situation, in every Respect, whereas, if that Trade was opened, we should have dollars, as plenty as Half-pence in London.[8]

In answer to the appeal from officials of the colony, there was some relaxation of maritime restrictions by the admiralty. Limited communication was opened with Havana and New Orleans. The economy of West Florida took a turn for the better. Although British merchants at Pensacola and Mobile sold manufactured goods to the French and Spanish colonies around the central Gulf and the Caribbean, they were unable to tap the market of Mexico. The opening of the Iberville Canal was a fiasco. To the British traders in the North, on the Ohio River and the Great Lakes, the Mississippi was the predestined artery for

8. Johnstone to Lords Commissioners, February 19, 1765, in Correspondence of the British Governors of West Florida, DLXXV. This plea was reiterated by the West Florida Assembly in a representation to the Lords of Trade, quoted in Howard, *The British Development of West Florida,* 114.

export to the European market. New Orleans was a natural entrepôt for the sale of pelts and hides. Considering the narrow trails and almost impassable roads, the traders found it far cheaper and more convenient to send their catch downstream via canoes, rafts, and barges to the Spanish capital. Not even an offer by the British government of a bounty on skins shipped directly east could divert trade from its natural course southward to the Gulf. Great Britain might prevent its trappers and traders from crossing the great river, Gage informed Shelburne, but it would be virtually impossible to halt the shipment of pelts down the river.[9] To the bold military officers, the ineluctable deduction was to seize New Orleans.

Yet Great Britain occupied an enviable position in Louisiana. There was no gainsaying its dominance in trade. As John G. Clark says, its merchants filled a "vacuum" created by their French counterparts, who never assigned trade with Louisiana a high priority. Furthermore, "in the broad areas of money and credit, the French government did not demonstrate that sympathy and support for commercial interests so noticeable in Great Britain."[10] The unproductiveness of the economy prevented local merchants from providing sufficient credit to tide over planters and farmers in difficult times. In consequence, in the 1760s Great Britain had an unparalleled opportunity to play the chief role in colonial trade. Its trading establishments had the capital to extend credit, accepting payment in kind if necessary, and its merchant marine could perform the essential service of transporting commodities to markets in the outside world where there was a demand.

In spite of a continuation of smuggling, encouraged by the British, economic conditions in Louisiana grew worse in the fall and winter of 1766–1767. Flour in particular became meager. During the Seven Years' War and until the arrival of Ulloa, the colony had imported a considerable quantity of this staple from

9. Gage to Shelburne, January 17, 1767, in Carter (ed.), *The Correspondence of General Thomas Gage*, I, 119.
10. Clark, *New Orleans, 1718–1812*, 86, 108.

New England. The imposition of restrictive regulations had somewhat curtailed the supply. However, it was Ulloa's conviction that the dearth was in part due to the machinations of Foucault, who wished to discredit the new government.[11] The shortage existed until the arrival in April, 1767, of two thousand barrels from Cuba. Although the food supply improved in the spring of 1767, other features of the economy declined. Prices for exportable commodities sank. Timber, indigo, and pelts found less demand in the markets of St. Domingue and Martinique, where competition with produce from the English colonies was permitted. Since Louisiana was no longer a French possession, the colonial authorities in the islands were under no obligation to extend special privileges to the merchants of New Orleans.[12]

Through dispatches from Ulloa and other sources, the Spanish crown was aware of Louisiana's economic difficulties. To widen its opportunities for trade and to envelop the territory more readily in the mercantilistic web, Spain ordered the application to Louisiana of the royal ordinance of March 23, 1768, which extended to the population the advantages in trade already possessed by other Spanish colonies in the decree of 1765.[13] The general intent of the earlier decree had been to provide greater channels for foreign commerce by removing shackling ordinances devised in the sixteenth century for the establishment of mercantilism.

The preamble to the order of March 23 bespoke the crown's solicitude for the economic welfare of the newly acquired territory:

> Since the province of Louisiana came under my sovereignty, it has been my wish that my aforesaid subjects experience no loss in the change of ruler

11. In addition to the numerous letters and reports dispatched by Ulloa to Grimaldi, Bucareli, and Arriaga, the Spanish governor drew up after his departure from Louisiana a lengthy explanation of the causes and course of the rebellion of 1768. Although not without some bias, it presents a fairly trustworthy account of the events and personalities of the uprising. See "Noticia de los acaecimientos de la Luisiana," fols. 24, 25.

12. Rodríguez, *Primeros años*, 124, 125.

13. *Ibid.*, 132.

and that means be found of protecting them and enhancing their status as long as they add to their prosperity and are not contrary to the general interests of the monarchy. To this end I have ordered that commerce be established between Spain and the above province, and for the present, and until another order replaces it, this to be executed according to the qualities, circumstances, and method expressed in the following articles.[14]

To the Spanish government the order of 1768 was part and parcel of the policy of liberalization calculated to expand trade throughout the colonies and to augment the general well-being of the people of the empire.[15] It goes without saying that this policy would also augment the royal treasury! The order permitted trade by any merchant with the Spanish ports of Cádiz, Seville, Cartagena, Málaga, Barcelona, Santander, La Coruña, and Gijón, with the stipulation that an invoice of the cargo be presented to a customs official upon arrival of the ship in port. All vessels should be "of Spanish construction and owned by Spaniards or naturalized citizens of the kingdoms and two-thirds of the crew Spaniards or naturalized citizens." To prevent the abuse of these privileges, it was required that ships carrying cargoes from Spanish ports must proceed directly to Louisiana. Produce shipped from Louisiana must originate in the colony. No tax would be collected on goods and articles transported from Spanish ports to the province. Although no export duty was levied on products of the colony, these commodities upon reaching a Spanish port must pay a 4 percent import duty. In the event that the produce of Louisiana could find no market in Spain owing to its inferior quality or to competition with native products, exportation of the produce to foreign countries without payment of duty was allowed.[16]

It is doubtful whether the Spanish government could have

14. Quoted *ibid.*
15. A brief treatment of this decree along with other features of Ulloa's economic policies is to be found in Jack D. L. Holmes, "Some Economic Problems of the Spanish Governors of Louisiana," *Hispanic American Historical Review*, XLII (November, 1962), 523, 524.
16. Rodríguez, *Primeros años*, 133, 134, 135.

foreseen the unfavorable reaction to the decree in Louisiana. When the news of its publication in Spain reached the colony in May, Ulloa was confronted with a mounting tide of angry opposition.[17] To the objection that under Article 37 of the new order the Spanish merchants might take over all shipping, he replied that Louisianians henceforth were naturalized citizens and therefore had the right to participate fully in the trade of the Gulf and the Iberian Peninsula, owning ships and supplying crews.

Of graver import to the mercantile elements in the colony was the general direction of the order of March 23. Henceforth the colonial trade would be closely tied to Spain, which might eventually shut off commerce with France and especially with the French West Indies and thus cripple or destroy the lucrative trade in contraband. Already in straitened circumstances because of declining export prices and other adverse factors, the economy would experience, it was believed, a disaster of great proportions. The natural flow of trade necessitated outlets in Europe and in America outside the limits of the Spanish Empire. In an outburst of indignation, Jean Baptiste Noyan, the son-in-law of La Frenière, offered his house for sale, asserting that "in a little while it [the colony] would be uninhabitable."[18] His act symbolized the bitterness felt by the mercantile community.

Hampering the functioning of the economy was the lack of coins or specie. This was not a new development, but one which had existed from the earliest days of colonization. Specie, brought over by the colonists and government officials or introduced as the result of foreign trade, vanished in a short while to pay for imports. Consequently, merchants and traders relied almost entirely on paper money as currency. There was an almost endless list of paper serving this purpose: "bills of exchange, treasury notes, orders on the treasury, orders on the storehouse, contracts between individuals and with the Com-

---

17. *Ibid.*, 135.
18. "Noticia de los acaecimientos de la Luisiana," fol. 27v.

pany of the Indies, royal notes, and card money."[19] In order to
prevent depreciation and stabilize the currency, the crown by
1733 had initiated the practice of dispatching "silver and merchandise to meet the yearly expenses." This did not prove effective and in a relatively short time the government again turned to
issuing bills of credit to discharge debts, hoping in this way to
conserve silver in the colony. Unfortunately, the costs of administration increased steadily without the dispatch of sufficient
silver from the treasury. This could have only one outcome—the
downward drift of the livre, the major unit of currency. It could
lead also to a tendency to speculation in money, which, the
commissary general in 1745 asserted cynically, "was the only
occupation to which the inhabitants were really attached."[20]

Later French commissaries undertook without success to remedy the unhealthy situation. In 1758 Vincent de Rochemore
called in all forms of paper money and, not without lining his
own pockets, replaced them with bills of exchange amounting to
1,995,000 livres. The value of these diminished when the near-
bankrupt French government was unable to redeem them. In
the course of time, card money, treasury notes, and other forms
of paper came back into use. In 1761 the acting commissary
Foucault had estimated, perhaps with some exaggeration, the
total paper money in circulation at 10,000,000 livres. The following year the French crown made a final effort to restore order in
finances by instructing the commissary to draw 800,000 livres'
worth of bills of exchange from the treasury to meet current
expenses and to reduce the debt.[21] The cession of the province to
Spain augmented the instability of the livre by raising the questions of whether the old currency would be accepted and
whether the French government would redeem the currency.

The confusion in the monetary system, aggravated by the

19. Surrey, *The Commerce of Louisiana*, 115. For a more recent account of this see
Lemieux, "The Office of Commissaire Ordonnateur," 156–82.
20. Surrey, *The Commerce of Louisiana*, 123, 137.
21. *Ibid.*, 151, 152, 153. The vacillation in value of the monetary unit naturally made
ordinary business transactions more difficult.

rising indebtedness of the colonial administration, presented Ulloa with a weighty problem. On the day of his disembarkation at New Orleans, he received from Foucault, who had succeeded d'Abbadie as commissary, a pessimistic assessment of the colony's finances. The Spanish governor assured Foucault that the paper money then in circulation would constitute legal tender for all transactions, but at 75 percent of its theoretical value.[22] The unwillingness of the new regime to recognize the bills of exchange at par value antagonized the commissary, who held a considerable quantity of these notes, and, according to Ulloa, the denial of this opportunity to profit enormously converted Foucault into an inveterate enemy of the Spanish.[23]

To shore up the currency, Ulloa offered now to assume the expenses of the colony. Although Grimaldi had promised him 150,000 pesos in specie, Ulloa had in his possession in March, 1766, only slightly more than 30,000 pesos.[24] This sum was quickly expended and the coins soon disappeared in recognition of their value over paper money, with the condition of the currency in no way improved. In the summer and fall of 1766 the status of paper money was placed in jeopardy by two decrees from Versailles, both doubtless prompted by the precarious nature of the French treasury. The first of these, signed on May 4, suspended payment on bills of exchange issued by the French authorities for the years 1763, 1764, and 1765, amounting to more than 2,600,000 livres. A second decree stipulated the collection of the bills of exchange by the spring of 1767, with the promise that they would be replaced by notes signed by Foucault to be paid by 1777. Bills not presented within the specified period were considered null and void. It was plain that the Spanish governor did not feel obligated to assume the responsibility for redeeming a large amount of paper money, but out of

22. Rodríguez, *Primeros años*, 114.
23. "Noticia de los acaecimientos de la Luisiana," fols. 11, 11v.
24. During the summer of 1765, the viceroy of New Spain acknowledged receipt of a royal order of May 21, 1765, stipulating the annual remittance of 150,000 pesos to Havana for the expedition to Louisiana. See viceroy of New Spain to Arriaga, August 20, 1765, in Leg. 2542, Audiencia de Sto. Domingo, AGI.

sympathy for the colonists he recommended to Versailles that the second order be suspended and replaced by a decree entailing fewer hardships. Although the latter decree could have imperiled the wealth and prosperity of the colony, Foucault did not, according to Ulloa, wish its suspension, seeing in its enforcement a means of personal gain and likewise another way of discrediting the regime.[25] To relieve the French officials, Ulloa proffered Foucault a sum of money, which was eagerly accepted.

Before many months had passed, Ulloa realized the necessity for larger annual appropriations by the crown. "This colony is in great need of funds," he stated in a letter to Bucareli. "There is not even the necessary money for reparations." Scarcely a month later, he renewed the plea: "I cannot do anything but beg earnestly of Your Lordship that as soon as the money destined for us . . . [can be sent], please forward it without delay, taking into consideration that we do not have any resources from which to obtain funds, and that these people start insurrections, even without any cause, as has happened many times before."[26] Financial urgencies prompted another plea for the dispatch of funds. If 40,000 to 50,000 pesos could be sent at once from Havana, it would suffice to meet the current obligations that could not be postponed indefinitely. In greater detail than in previous communications, he elaborated on the reasons for the pressing nature of his request:

> It is more important to me to receive this amount right away than to receive the whole amount in May or June, even if I would receive twice the amount, because it is not spent all at once, and if I could only have the necessary funds to meet the most urgent needs, I would be satisfied. If we had a treasury, we would not be obliged to make loans and could wait for the funds sent by the king, but we have none and the money which comes to us leaves immediately for Europe and this leaves us completely destitute. . . .

25. "Noticia de los acaecimientos de la Luisiana," fol. 24.
26. Ulloa to Bucareli, December 12, 1766, and January 23, 1767, both in Dispatches of the Spanish Governors of Louisiana, I. The assumption of the colony's debts contracted since 1762 was the topic of a conversation between Choiseul and the Spanish ambassador Magallón. Because of the size of the debt and its complications, the issue was left hanging. See Magallón to Grimaldi, April 18, 1766, in Leg. 3883, Estado, AHN.

I am very sure that Your Lordship, in view of these circumstances, will act as quickly as your duties allow you and that you will help us in our present need, as you know better than anyone else the consequences of this situation, and also know the position in which this colony is, populated with foreigners and surrounded by all kinds of dangers.[27]

Two weeks later Ulloa reaffirmed his dire need for funds. To impress upon his superior the explosiveness of the situation, he announced his intention to send a schooner, the *Activa*, immediately to Havana to obtain the funds and convey them to the colony. The final paragraph of the letter was a woeful prophecy of what might happen unless financial assistance was forthcoming: "I hope that Your Lordship, with his great prudence and reflection, will not hesitate to help avoid the imminent danger which is threatening us; this is so great that I have not enough words with which to express myself. Many things happen, and I beg of Your Lordship to send me your help while there is yet time."[28]

What was the response of the Spanish crown to these urgent petitions from Ulloa for money? What was the priority assigned to the financial needs of Louisiana? The answers to these questions determined in part the outcome of Spain's initial efforts to establish a government in the former French colony.[29]

There seems little doubt that in the winter of 1766–1767 Grimaldi and Bucareli were convinced of the validity of Ulloa's appeals for funds. Why then was there an inadequate appropriation and less action? The explanation lies partly in the financial situation in Cuba, which like Louisiana depended on silver from Mexico, and partly in the state of the treasury of the viceroyalty

27. Ulloa to Bucareli, March 3, 1767, in Dispatches of the Spanish Governors of Louisiana, I.

28. Ulloa to Bucareli, March 15, 1767, *ibid.*

29. What TePaske says about Florida prior to 1763 might well be applied to Louisiana: "Despite its strategic importance, no name was more repugnant in Cuba or New Spain than 'La Florida.' Maintaining the outpost was a heavy burden, and for many Mexicans and Cuban officials the destitute province was not worth the expense. It was not surprising that the situado arrived sporadically or not at all and that shortages, poor quality, and high prices characterized the supplies delivered to Saint Augustine." See John TePaske, *The Governorship of Spanish Florida, 1700–1763* (Durham, N.C., 1964), 228.

itself. As Ulloa's superior, the captain general of Cuba received the shipments of treasure from Vera Cruz and allocated the sums to the two provinces. In a communication of April 4, 1767, Bucareli informed Arriaga that he had received a packet of letters from Louisiana in which Ulloa described the "deplorable situation of the region owing to the lack of money" and appealed for the immediate dispatch of 40,000 to 50,000 pesos. It was impossible to comply, Bucareli said, "as the allocation for that colony and for this place has not arrived." He went on to stress the paramount needs of Cuba, chief of which was the construction of fortifications for Havana, a vital matter since the capture of the city by the British during the Seven Years' War. "I find myself," he said, "in the same position of importunity. . . . You will understand the impossibility of remitting that sum, although it saddens me that I cannot satisfy the urgency because experience has shown me how much one who commands suffers in spirit."[30] A few weeks later Bucareli again called the attention of the minister of the Indies to Ulloa's plight.[31] Despite his sympathetic attentiveness it is not unlikely that the captain general was following an expedient familiar to the times of borrowing for his own jurisdiction sums marked for other colonies.[32]

Unfortunately, chance dealt Ulloa a blow in his hour of need. The Mexican treasury, the source of the *situado,* or allowance, for Cuba and Lousiana, did not have at the moment funds at its disposal. Ulloa's governorship coincided with the visit to the viceroyalty of José Gálvez, who instituted the investigation of high officials and introduced new methods of tax collecting and accounting.[33] For both provinces it signified delays in revenue

30. Bucareli to Arriaga, April 4, 1767, in Leg. 2542, Audiencia de Sto. Domingo, AGI. Moreover, to add to Bucareli's own financial problems, a strong earthquake struck the island in June, 1766, severely damaging the fortifications and cathedral at Santiago. See Cayetano Alcázar Molina, *Los virreinatos en el siglo XVIII,* ed. Antonio Ballesteros (Barcelona, 1945), 184.

31. To pay the debts of the colony, Ulloa had been compelled to borrow nine thousand pesos from the captain of a ship that had been wrecked on the coast. See Bucareli to Arriaga, April 20, 1767, in Leg. 2542, Audiencia de Sto. Domingo, AGI.

32. This is borne out in the correspondence between Arriaga and Bucareli. See also Holmes, "Economic Problems of the Spanish Governors," 522.

33. Bobb, *The Viceregency of Bucareli,* 14, 15.

collection and shipment of subsidies. Arriaga was thoroughly cognizant of the difficulties in Mexico. He sadly confessed to Bucareli the dismal outlook for future appropriations: "I look upon this evil of the lack of funds with the regret of not seeing a hopeful outcome for the ideas that the viceroy and the *visitador* expound in New Spain, being continual the expenses they entail and distant the realization of their aim of expanding the royal treasury. Not only do I have little confidence that the full *situados* will get there, but I have misgivings that one-half will be sent."[34] The duration of the inspection and reorganization of the Mexican treasury influenced the future of Louisiana.

Ulloa's moving pleas for additional funds did not fall on deaf ears in Madrid. Eventually, Grimaldi saw the need for increasing the annual subsidy. The tardiness of his response in part proceeded from the low priority enjoyed by Louisiana against Cuba and other regions of the empire.[35] His decision to act was no doubt brought on by an earnest appeal from the Spanish governor, dispatched in the winter of 1766–1767 and containing a statement of proposed expenditures for the colony. The expenses were of a dual character, ordinary and extraordinary. The former, including such items as costs of goods and gifts for the Indians and salaries for the Spanish and French officials, amounted to 179,678 pesos, or 29,678 pesos more than the entire allocation for the year. The extraordinary expenditures equated generally with the physical restoration of the colony, rebuilding government houses and constructing forts throughout the colony. In his report Ulloa declared that it was imperative to make up for the many years of neglect by France: "There is no building in the colony that does not need repair, and many new structures are required." Churches and chapels were falling down. For protection against the English and Indians, forts

---

34. Arriaga to Bucareli, May 19, 1767, in Leg. 1630, Indiferente, AGI.
35. The Spanish ambassador Magallón clearly expressed this view in 1766 to Choiseul, who had repeatedly criticized Spain for its reluctance to assume sovereignty: "The king of Spain accepted Louisiana, although knowing that we were doing nothing but acquiring an annual obligation of 300,000 piastres in exchange for the negative and remote advantage of having it so that no other country may possess it." Quoted in Rodríguez, *Primeros años*, 46, 47.

should be built at Balize, at Manchac, at New Orleans, and in the Illinois country on the Missouri. Not omitted was a request for more money to encourage the immigration of Acadians, perhaps as many as 10,000 families, provided their passage was paid and means of subsistence for a year ensured. No figure was given for the extent of this outlay.[36]

Grimaldi's resolve to aid Louisiana, approved by Arriaga and Miguel de Muzquiz, secretary of the treasury, meant a considerable increase in the *situado*. On May 13, 1767, he notified Arriaga of the king's decision to increase the annual sum by two-thirds, that is, by 100,000 pesos, with the stipulation that payment should begin as of July 1, so that the province would receive for 1767 one-half the amount, or an additional 50,000 pesos. Another reservation on the use of the money was that 25,000 pesos must be employed in the immigration plan for the Acadians. On May 20 the necessary orders went out from Arriaga to implement the royal will.[37] How substantially the needs would be satisfied hung on the amount of silver received in Havana from Croix, the viceroy in Mexico, and on the pecuniary requirements of Cuba.[38] In this connection it is worthwhile to point out again the semiindependent position assumed by Bucareli in the disbursement of funds: "I intend to fulfill it [Arriaga's order], in proportion as the sums arrive from New Spain, since, as I explained to Your Excellency in a letter of the 18 of that month [May], we are at the present time troubled by a dearth of funds in every branch of the government, with an insufficiency for very important obligations."[39]

Although handicapped by a shortage of funds, the Spanish governor embarked on a program to rehabilitate the colony. Adding to the normal costs of government were the outlays for

36. Expediente Luisiana, Nos. 6, 7, in Leg. 2542, Audiencia de Sto. Domingo, AGI.
37. Grimaldi to Arriaga, May 13, 1767, and Arriaga to Croix, Bucareli, Alterriva, and Ulloa, May 20, 1767, all *ibid.*
38. Carlos Francisco de Croix assumed the duties of viceroy on August 23, 1766, about five and a half months after Ulloa's arrival in New Orleans, and remained in office until he was replaced by Bucareli on September 22, 1771. See Alcázar, *Los virreinatos en el siglo XVIII,* 57.
39. Bucareli to Arriaga, July 4, 1767, in Leg. 2542, Audiencia de Sto. Domingo, AGI.

construction of the fort at Balize, for the three expeditions to the outposts north of New Orleans, for rebuilding religious structures, and finally for resettling the Acadian immigrants. No wonder the royal treasury at New Orleans was bare! The alternative was, however, a piecemeal reconstruction, taking a number of years, unpopular with the French inhabitants, and probably unacceptable to Grimaldi. The establishment of durable defenses for the empire required vigorous means, cost what they might.

It was not until almost the end of the summer that Ulloa's hopes for a solution to the colony's financial predicament were raised. Meantime he had addressed another poignant appeal to Bucareli for funds: "I have not words enough to explain to you the danger to which the colony is exposed, nor of the importance of receiving prompt succor to alleviate the most urgent needs and to quiet, in some way, the disturbances that we are now experiencing." But on August 24 he got word from Arriaga via Havana of the augmentation of the annual allowance for Louisiana to 250,000 pesos.[40] Four days later the two-masted schooner, *San Juan Bautista,* dropped anchor at New Orleans with 60,000 pesos aboard. Perhaps fortune was beginning to smile on this neglected bureaucrat in an outpost of the empire! There was one drawback—one that could upset well-laid plans—namely, the slowness of remittance from the strongboxes of Mexico. Perhaps, with some foreboding, Ulloa pled with the captain general "to intercede with your intendant in regard to this matter, so that I will not find myself again in the same conflict which I have just experienced."[41]

Despite temporary relief by the arrival of funds, the financial problem continued to haunt Ulloa. Toward the end of September he had to confess that the sum "has not been enough to entirely satisfy all our creditors, who expected to be paid in full

40. Ulloa to Bucareli, June 17, 1767, in Dispatches of the Spanish Governors of Louisiana, I; Ulloa to Bucareli, September 9, 1767, in Leg. 2542, Audiencia de Sto. Domingo, AGI.

41. Ulloa to Bucareli, August 28, 1767, in Dispatches of the Spanish Governors of Louisiana, I.

from the first remittance of money, as they were promised." In the offing there was, moreover, the additional expense for the military units to reinforce the Spanish troops already in the province. The tale of woe and distress continued. In December, a note of despair crept into a message to his friend in Havana: "If the said allowance is not sent with more regularity than it has in the past, I do not know what will happen, because, as I have already informed Your Lordship, when there is no money there are no friends and the king is the one who painfully suffers for the storing up of provisions which when bought out of season cost double or three times more than their own value when bought in time."[42]

Until the treasury in New Orleans had ample reserves, the Spanish governor had to resort to the customary expedient of loans. His chief creditors were the shipowners, either British or English colonials, who supplied flour and other food from New England, and French merchants in New Orleans. In time the Spanish commissary Loyola printed notes for the payment of debts, paper that declined in value almost 50 percent because of the uncooperative, even antagonistic, attitude of some officials of the old French regime, excluding Aubry, and because of the speculative mania gripping the commercial community. The gradual, but inevitable, results were the loss of public confidence in the treasury and the steep, inflationary prices for foodstuffs and necessities.[43]

Much of the internal opposition to Spanish financial policies centered on the French commissary Foucault. It was his responsibility to pay the salaries of the French officials employed in the administration of the colony. In February, 1767, he wrote to the Spanish governor that he was greatly in need of funds to pay his personnel. Ulloa replied that the Spanish commissary would advance a sum in anticipation of the arrival of silver from Havana in March or April.[44] Unable to obtain all that he wanted,

42. Ulloa to Bucareli, September 21, December 2, 1767, *ibid.*
43. Rodríguez, *Primeros años*, 127, 128.
44. Foucault to Ulloa, February 12, 1767, and Ulloa to Foucault, March 10, 1767, both in Leg. 187, Papeles de Cuba, AGI.

the French commissary complained to Aubry. The tone of Foucault's subsequent letters to Ulloa was bitter and resentful. Ulloa felt it necessary to point out that "every country that is obliged to get subsistence from the outside finds itself in that situation."[45] Foucault's attitude toward the governor was widely known throughout the colony.[46] In October, 1767, the commissary requested that Ulloa instruct Loyola to turn over additional funds. In desperation, Foucault appealed for a personal loan, since "there is not a sou in the treasury."[47] There was no letup in the tense relations of the two men.

In summary, the crown's commercial and financial policies failed to achieve the success hoped for. It was the government's intent to assimilate Louisiana as far and as fast as possible into the imperial system, with its legalistic exclusiveness. Weaning the colony from its old ways was almost impossible, for, even with force, trade would not flow in artificial channels. In hindsight, what the economy required for its development was the input of private or governmental capital. Because of this lack only a small number of slaves worked the plantations, although this was the era of the black flood from Africa. The colonists regarded the imminent loss of their economic liberties as a considerable grievance. Added to this was the shortage of specie. The need for funds was clearly perceived, but circumstances militated against the dispatch of silver in sufficient quantity and without protracted delays. Adequate subsidies might have constituted a sustaining prop for the first regime. In the persons of Foucault and La Frenière, the firebrands among the dissenters believed they had the leadership to compel the Spanish government to reverse its policies or face the consequences.

45. Foucault to Ulloa, May 12, 1767, and Ulloa to Foucault, May 18, 1767, both *ibid.*
46. Aubry apologized to Ulloa for the criticism that was current in the colony: "You know men too well not to realize that persons in high places of responsibility, however distinguished they may be, suffer reproaches and an angel on earth would even be subject to censure." See Aubry to Ulloa, March 30, 1767, *ibid.*
47. Foucault to Ulloa, October 31, November 2, 1767, both *ibid.*

VII

Clouds on the Horizon

Signs of discontent and dissatisfaction in the colony were more evident in the winter of 1767 and the spring of 1768. Tension between Spanish and French officials continued to grow. The unwholesome state of the economy and the increasing unpopularity of the governor constituted a potential danger. But these problems were not insurmountable, given the solid support of the Spanish officials in Madrid and the Caribbean. That they inaccurately gauged the storm warnings was not the fault of Governor Ulloa, who bombarded his superiors with requests for firmer backing. In retrospect, there would have been no "bloody O'Reilly" or "creole martyrs" in the annals of Louisiana if prompt remedial measures had been adopted.

At the bottom of the misery and unhappiness in the colony was the stagnation of the economy, with little prospect of amelioration. Partly to blame was the unresolved monetary crisis. The dearth of funds from the Spanish treasury still existed. This had a twofold crippling effect on the economy, for it was not only virtually impossible for the government to meet the contractual obligations of the officials, but it was difficult to carry on ordinary commercial transactions without a supply of coins. As fast as the specie was paid out by the commissary Loyola, it vanished from circulation, going mainly to the English and French merchants engaged in the colonial trade.

The financial policies of the French regime were both an asset and a liability to the solution of the monetary issue. From the outset Foucault had paid the bills of the French officials. Because of the limited amount of money from Cuba, he had arranged to meet some of the expenditures of the Spanish regime, with the tacit understanding that these would be repaid in time. It was the firm hope of the government in Paris that Spain would assume all costs of administration from the day of Ulloa's landing, on March 5, 1766.[1] One of the expenses that Foucault met in the early days of Spanish occupation was the outfitting of Ulloa's expedition to reconnoiter the colony.[2] Furthermore, owing to the straitened condition of the Spanish treasury and Foucault's sympathy for his compatriots, the expenditures for the subsistence and maintenance of the Acadian immigrants for almost a year and a half came from the French treasury. For months he sought unsuccessfully to shift this item of expense to the Spanish.[3] The financing was done through the issuance of letters of exchange, or drafts on the French treasury. For the first nine months the total reported by the commissary was approximately 235,000 livres, with a supplement of 41,000 livres to support the Acadians.[4] The minister of marine did not approve of provisional financing, but felt powerless to halt it, in view of the dire need of the colonists. Time and again César de Choiseul, duc de Praslin, urged the commissary to settle the accounts and arrange to transfer the officials and soldiers to France.[5] From a practical

1. The minister of the marine directed the commissary to draw up in triplicate a list of expenditures made by the French authorities from March 5, 1766, to the present for presentation to the Spanish court. See Praslin to Aubry and Foucault, February 23, 1767, in Colonies B, AN.

2. This involved not only provisions and supplies for sixty persons for two months, but also many presents for the Indian chiefs expected to greet the governor at the posts en route. See "Journal des dépenses de la colonie de la Nouvelle Orléans, année 1766" (MS in New York Public Library).

3. In November, 1766, Foucault informed Praslin of the arrival in September at New Orleans of some two hundred Acadians in an English ship from Halifax: "My plan was to refuse these miserable people any kind of assistance in order to compel M. Ulloa to provide it, but it has not been possible for me to resist the urgent requests that he and M. Aubry jointly made upon me, with their assurance that all expenditures contracted from the appearance of the Spaniards and thereafter be at the account of the king of Spain." See Foucault to Praslin, November 18, 1766, in C13A46, Colonies, AN.

4. Praslin to Foucault, February 23, 1767, *ibid.*

5. Apparently, the minister of the marine was uncertain about indemnification, for he had written to Foucault in June, 1766, to accelerate his activities, "so as to shorten your stay in Louisiana as far as possible, since it is an expense that is pure loss for His Majesty." See Praslin to Foucault, June 19, 1766, *ibid.*

standpoint the postponement of formal occupation required the retention of the French personnel.

On the other hand, the French government dealt a blow to the financial stability of the colony by ordering the paper money withdrawn from circulation. Foucault was instructed to force the colonists to turn in the *ancienne monnaie,* estimated at roughly 7,000,000 livres, for which receipts would be issued with the value of the notes to be fixed by the treasury when all the notes had been accounted for.[6] Considering the lag in the flow of Spanish money, Foucault, with the consent of Aubry, advised Praslin that it would be unwise to retire all of the French notes then in circulation. To do so would "plunge it [the colony] in extreme distress."[7] To stabilize the currency, he issued an order on January 1, 1767, stipulating that owners of notes report the amount they held, after which dates would be fixed for remittal and assignment of receipts.[8] By September, 1767, the redemption of the paper was far from complete, with the conversion of only slightly more than half the amount.[9] Adding to the fiscal confusion and uncertainty was an order from Paris, on May 4, 1766, suspending payment on letters of exchange issued in the years 1763, 1764, and 1765. Understandably, the crown wished to sever its involvement in Louisiana as rapidly as possible, but the order raised doubts as to the value of the drafts for 1766. Foucault appealed to Ulloa "to assemble all the merchants in your presence and assure them that you will write at once to the Spanish court to have it petition His Most Christian Majesty for the payment of the letters of exchange and all that will be drawn until the departure of the [French] officials from here."[10] The Spanish governor, cognizant of the plight of the French officials, agreed to refer this to Grimaldi, but he refused to underwrite in

6. Praslin to Aubry and Foucault, July 24, 1766, *ibid.*
7. Aubry and Foucault to Praslin, December 15, 1766, *ibid.*
8. This was approved by Praslin. See Praslin to Foucault, July 21, 1767, in Colonies B, IV, AN.
9. Foucault to Praslin, September 8, 1767, in C13A45, Colonies, AN.
10. The sum comprised the letters of exchange for the army from 1763 to the end of 1766. See Foucault to Ulloa, August 28, 1766, *ibid.*

any way a debt amounting to approximately 2,683,000 livres. Subsequently, Grimaldi acknowledged the validity of the bill for the pay and maintenance of French soldiers from March 5, 1766.[11] Meanwhile, Ulloa, to check the inflation brought on by the depreciation of the French currency, authorized the commissary to issue Spanish notes. This was only partly successful.

The only real cure for this monetary malady was to import large amounts of Spanish specie. In anticipation of the increased subsidy, Ulloa resolved to abolish the role played by Foucault in financing the administration. An order of December 14, 1767, to be in effect as of January 1, 1768, declared that Loyola would assume payment of French civil and military officials until the arrival of the Spanish troops.[12] This effectively reduced Foucault's functions to those of an executor and caretaker of governmental property, settling the accounts of the French administration and assembling an inventory of the properties to be taken over by the Spanish, for which indemnification was to be made.[13] It undoubtedly increased the enmity of the ambitious commissary toward the Spanish governor.[14] Aubry regarded this step as a favorable one in the final stage of the *prise de possession*. "A great tranquillity reigns at this moment in the midst of all the changes that this country has experienced," he wrote to the ministry in Paris.[15]

Like other well-conceived plans of the Spanish governor, the

11. Procedure for payment of the debt would be worked out by the two courts. See Grimaldi to Ulloa, June 24, 1768, in Leg. 174, Papeles de Cuba, AGI.

12. Ulloa to Foucault, December 14, 1767, in C13A45, Colonies, AN.

13. The appraisal of buildings and other real property, owned by the French crown in New Orleans and outside the city, was agreed upon by Ulloa, Aubry, and Foucault at the figure of 865,799 livres, 19 sous, and 8 deniers. O'Reilly subsequently reduced the amount by 262,609 livres, 18 sous, and 8 deniers, claiming that the first evaluation was made on figures presented by d'Abbadie in 1764 rather than in 1766 at the time of the Spanish occupation. See Relación que manifiesta los precios en que el año pasado de 1767 se estimaron los edificios que pertenecian a S. M. Christianissimo en esta villa, in MS 19246, BN.

14. Foucault declared that he would still have to draw letters of exchange on the French treasury to pay for transporting the officials and troops to France. See Aubry and Foucault to Praslin, January 19, 1768, in C13A48, Colonies, AN.

15. Aubry to Praslin, January 20, 1768, *ibid.*

execution of this move was premature. It was essential to have the funds from Mexico at hand. But this was not the case, as he soon discovered. Toward the end of December, 1767, he resumed his appeals to Bucareli for money, the only means of avoiding the development of a grave situation: "I want to reiterate to Your Lordship the poverty of this country due to the lack of funds, having used the last and being without even the necessary means for daily needs; nobody can be paid, the troops, the body of officers, clerks, and the providers." In February, Ulloa was reaching the limits of his patience. In a communication to the captain general, he was sharply critical of his superiors.[16]

As had been the case before, the appeal was futile. In spite of the growing hardships in the colony, there were no funds forthcoming. So hard put was one of the creditors, Captain William Moore, who was a supplier of flour, that he volunteered to sail his own ship to Havana to obtain payment for his cargo. In June, when no favorable answer had been received from Bucareli, Ulloa authorized Moore to take his brigantine *Africa* to Havana ostensibly to carry passengers and dispatches to the city, but secretly to receive payment for the commodities transported to New Orleans and to bring back word when the specie would be shipped to the colony.[17] This was handled successfully by the capable captain.

One senses occasionally the feeling of despair and resignation to the inevitable, as in a letter of June 22 from Governor Ulloa to Havana. There is, however, no expression of a desire to abandon his post because of the unwillingness or inability of the crown to fulfill his most urgent requests. Ulloa was still hoping against hope that somehow the situation would be righted:

> The lack of money, together with the abandoned condition of this colony, has come to a pitiful extreme....
> The situation is more to be noted and its consequences more deeply felt in a new domain like this, where at a time when a new sovereignty is being

16. Ulloa to Bucareli, December 29, 1767, February 2, 1768, both in Dispatches of the Spanish Governors of Louisiana, I.
17. Ulloa to Bucareli, February 2, June 22, 1768, both *ibid.*

established we lack even the things for the bare necessities of life. These facts make our new subjects, and those who furnish our provisions, predict a very dark future. We are not sure yet of the loyalty of these new subjects and our credit is not yet established either; all these facts are the cause of great discontent.[18]

Governor Ulloa's hopes for an ultimate solution to the financial distress of the colony were raised temporarily by the arrival of funds from Cuba. On July 12 the packet *Hermosa Limeña* dropped anchor at New Orleans with 100,000 pesos for the local treasury. The remainder, which amounted to less than one-half the annual allowance of 200,000 pesos, owing to deductions for the expenses of the troops being assembled at Havana for Louisiana, was to be dispatched later in a second vessel. This was to preclude the possibility of a loss of greater magnitude if the money had been aboard one ship and it had foundered at sea. In gratefully acknowledging receipt of part of the allowance, Ulloa nevertheless remarked that this sum did not suffice to pay the debts of the royal treasury, so that "we will remain more or less in the same situation in which we were at the time of the receipt of the 60,000 pesos that Your Excellency sent before."[19] This was the last shipment of funds from Havana during Ulloa's administration of the colony.

The final plea for funds came in a dispatch of August 1. In this lengthy communication to Bucareli, Ulloa depicted once more the economic tribulations of the people. All of this must have had a familiar ring to the captain general, who by now probably imagined that if the regime had survived so far it might continue another year, when the shipments of treasure from Mexico would be prompter and more extensive. Running through this letter is a quiet note of desperation:

> The dangerous situation is as bad as it was before. For this reason I so advised Don Andrés de Balderrama, and he ought to have acknowledged Your Excellency's orders, that is, on his way if he should meet a vessel

18. Ulloa to Bucareli, June 22, 1768, *ibid.*
19. Ulloa to Bucareli, July 20, 1768, No. 50, *ibid.*

conveying money, to find out the amount which she was carrying, and if it was not 150,000 pesos or more, not to interrupt his trip, but keep on his mission, because with less than this amount it would not be possible to help the situation of this country.

To quiet them and to stop the distrust created by rumors, I beg of Your Excellency to please make the necessary arrangements in order that Don Lucas Villaescusa bring on his return at least 50,000 pesos from the 100,000 that have been kept in your city. I believe that the balance of the money will be enough for the expenses of the troops already there and for those that you are expecting from Spain. I have promised this to all concerned in order to keep them quiet and to be satisfied with this hope, because not having been able to fulfill my word before, anything that I offer is met with distrust. They will subsist anyway; did they not subsist until the arrival of Captain Moore? There is nothing to do at the present but to keep on going ahead, because if there were anything here to which to recur, I would have done it, as I have already done with the new villages, having sent word to Nueva Inglaterra [probably British West Florida] to stop making trips down here at the present time, because we do not have any money to do any trading. I have also suspended all works already started; in all, I am in a terrible struggle without being able to pay salaries, wages, pensions to the clergy, and the daily salaries of the troops.[20]

How far the crown was in arrears in its dispatch of the *situado* for the newly established regime may be seen in Table 2, showing Ulloa's financial receipts for the approximately thirty-two months of his government. From these figures it is apparent that Ulloa received slightly more than two-thirds of the amount promised by the crown. Of this sum, 100,000 pesos were held in Havana. Hence, to pay salaries, construct forts and outposts, and restore governmental buildings and churches, he had had at his disposal by the end of October, 1768, approximately 280,000 pesos, or less than half the original appropriation.[21] It is obvious that these funds were insufficient for the conduct of government

---

20. Ulloa to Bucareli, August 1, 1768, *ibid.* Andrés de Balderrama was a naval lieutenant attached to the frigate *Volante*, at anchor in New Orleans, who accompanied Captain Moore in the *Africa* on his voyage to Havana in June and returned on July 30 on the same vessel. See Ulloa to Bucareli, July 20, 1768, No. 53, *ibid.*

21. Table given in Rodríguez, *Primeros años*, 125, 126. See also figures given by Croix in a report to Arriaga, July 29, 1776, in Correspondencia de los Virreyes, Ser. 1, Vol. XIII, Archivo General de la Nación, Mexico City, hereinafter cited as AGN.

TABLE 2
APPROPRIATIONS AND RECEIPTS OF
THE FIRST SPANISH REGIME
IN LOUISIANA

Sums appropriated by Grimaldi			
1766		150,000	pesos
1767		200,000	
1768		250,000	
	Total	600,000	pesos
Funds actually remitted to Ulloa			
December 20, 1765 (Havana)		40,000	pesos
June 14, 1766 (frigate *Jupiter*)		50,000	
December 14, 1766		174	
January 1, 1767 (*Corazón de Jesús y Santa Bárbara*)		59,886	
March 25, 1767 (lent by Don Juan Urcullo)		9,000	
September 9, 1767 (bark *Juan Bautista*)		60,000	
July 12, 1768 (packet *Limeña*)		100,000	
	Total	319,060	pesos
Funds retained in Havana for expenses of troops for Louisiana		100,000	
Total deposited in New Orleans and Havana		419,060	pesos
	Total appropriated	600,000	pesos
	Amount deposited	419,060	
	Amount still due Ulloa in October, 1768	180,940	pesos
	Total appropriated	600,000	pesos
	Amount deposited in New Orleans	319,060	
	Amount available for maintenance of the government	280,940	pesos

and for the ambitious program of public works that he conceived essential for the future of Louisiana. Solvency required an even larger *situado* and the curtailment of many projects.

The remissness of the Spanish government in dispatching the subsidies which immeasurably hurt the regime in Louisiana, was due partly to the extraordinary condition of the treasury after the Seven Years' War and the low priority given the colony's needs. The reorganization of the Mexican fiscal system by José Gálvez slowed down the flow of money from this important source.[22] Should any blame for the delays have been placed on Viceroy Croix, who directed the shipments of silver from Mexico City? Subsequently, Croix felt impelled to defend himself when intimations of inattention and inefficiency were made by Ulloa and Bucareli. "But as both accuse me of a scarcity of funds in the *situado* of that colony in whose remittance there was not the least fault on my part," he declared indignantly to Arriaga, "I cannot refrain from stating it again so that you will be well aware of it."[23] Taking into account his record as an able soldier and administrator, he was probably the victim of the slowly turning wheels of bureaucratic machinery.

One must scrutinize more closely the conduct and attitude of Ulloa's immediate superior, Captain General Bucareli, and of the top echelon of officials in Spain, the secretary of state Grimaldi and the minister of the Indies Arriaga. There is little doubt but that Bucareli was sympathetic to the plight of Louisiana. In July, 1768, he emphatically averred to Ulloa that he would facilitate all shipments of silver to New Orleans: "Your letter informing me of the sad condition of the colony through lack of money arrived yesterday. Notwithstanding that in the island of Cuba we are in the greatest misery that we have ever suffered, no deductions from the amount assigned to that colony [Louisiana] will be made." Undoubtedly, the dispatch of the entire sum from Havana at one time—if it had been there—would have been highly advisable as a quick way of relieving the tight financial bind, but conveying a sizable sum in a single vessel without an escort of a frigate or man-of-war would have been ruled out in Spain on the grounds of security.[24] In the middle of

22. As Bobb points out, the era of exceptional prosperity for the mining industry did not begin until the 1770s. See Bobb, *The Viceregency of Bucareli*, 172, 173.

23. Croix to Arriaga, December 4, 1769, in Correspondencia de los Virreyes, Ser. 1, Vol. XIII, AGN. See also Ulloa to Bucareli, August 28, 1767, in Dispatches of the Spanish Governors of Lousiana, I.

24. Bucareli to Ulloa, July 11, 1768, and Bucareli to Arriaga, June 28, 1768, both in Leg. 2542, Audiencia de Sto. Domingo, AGI.

October a hurricane, with the feminine appellation Santa Tere-
sa, struck Havana, and for the next few months Bucareli's energies were directed toward effecting a recovery from this natural
catastrophe.[25] In the fall and winter of 1768–1769 it is unlikely
that Ulloa would have received a loan or special gift from the
Cuban treasury.

Despite Bucareli's overt solicitude for the monetary troubles
of the colony, there is little evidence that Grimaldi and Arriaga
were unduly alarmed or apprehensive over the possible consequences of their policies. To these statesmen there were much
graver problems facing the empire in Europe and America.
Thus, contrary to Ulloa's repeated warnings, they envisaged no
dire emergency or the possibility of an insurrection. Because of
their failure to read correctly the symptoms of revolt, they must
bear a share of the onus for the events of October, 1768.

The decline in trade, legal and illegal, during the early months
of 1768 contributed to the debilitation of the economy. The
absence of specie was simultaneously a cause and a sign of
unfavorable conditions. Equally important in the slackening of
trade was the effect of the commercial regulation of March,
1768. Nearly all groups denounced it as contrary to their liberty
of trade, which, they believed, was essential for the prosperity of
the colony. It raised the specter of decreasing exports and imports, since no sound basis for trade between the province and
the metropolis existed. If tightly enforced, it would limit trade
with France and the French islands and abolish contraband transactions with the English. The anonymous author of a memoir
sent to Choiseul in 1766 declared that the right to trade with
France was in the best interests of Spain, the only way "to augment the population and make out of it [the colony] a strong base
to safeguard the rich possessions to which she must serve as a
barrier.... This liberty is indispensable in the present state of
affairs."[26] Only the future could reveal how severely Spain in-

---

25. Alcázar, *Los virreinatos en el siglo XVIII*, 185.
26. Mémoir au sujet du commerce français à la Louisiane, August 1, 1766, in
C13A46, Colonies, AN.

tended to implement the decree. Grimaldi notified Ulloa in June that some relaxation was needed, with passports to be given to French merchants to assure the arrival of "goods and provisions indispensable" for the colony.[27] Nevertheless, the grim prospect of mercantilism was responsible for a loss of commerce, with a concomitant rise in prices of commodities in short supply and an additional depreciation of the paper money. In the fall of 1768 the atmosphere was charged with uncertainty, distrust, and resentment.

Contributing to the economic ills of the colony in 1768 was Acadian migration and settlement. Having sold their land in Nova Scotia to pay for their passage to the French islands in the Caribbean and to Louisiana, they arrived virtually penniless and had to be supported by the government until they could clear the land, build their homes, and raise crops for their sustenance. If they dreamed of a bountiful Arcadia in a land of bayous, swamps, and forest, they were doomed to disappointment. Theirs would not be an easy life, with epidemics taking a toll and floods destroying their property. Foucault provided funds from the French treasury to maintain the Acadians for a period of time. By 1768 the expenses were borne largely by the Spanish governor, who had part of the yearly subsidy earmarked for this purpose. These hardy pioneers staked out farms and plantations on both sides of the Mississippi as far upstream as Baton Rouge and Pointe Coupée. As Ulloa glowingly informed Grimaldi, "This territory can supply Spain [with wheat] at reasonable prices, and it will be a source of income most useful for the monarchy and most fortunate for the citizens here."[28] Unfortunately, the climate proved too warm for the production of wheat,

27. Grimaldi to Ulloa, June 20, 1768, in Leg. 174, Papeles de Cuba, AGI. In March, 1768, prior to the enactment of the commercial decree, a small group of merchants, headed by Gilbert de St. Maxent, a friend of the Spanish, addressed a petition to the governor seeking special privileges for the products of Louisiana in Spanish trade. See Representación, March 10, 1768, in Leg. 187, Papeles de Cuba, AGI.

28. Alcée Fortier, *A History of Louisiana* (4 vols.; New York, 1904), I, 153; Ulloa to Grimaldi, July 20, 1768, in Leg. 2542, Audiencia de Sto. Domingo, AGI.

which had to be imported at much cost from New England or raised in the Illinois country.

In the summer of 1768 the Acadians had reason for satisfaction with their living conditions. They had land, tools, and security from Indian attack. Their comfortable situation encouraged Catholics residing in Maryland to seek asylum in Louisiana. Henry Jerningham, a Marylander, wrote to the Spanish governor for permission to send an agent to explore the possibilities, claiming, "We have seen many letters from the Acadians to their Countrymen, praying them to speed themselves to partake of their good fortune in that fruitfull region." Ulloa assented, noting that, if immigration took place, the entrants must comply with the Spanish conditions for naturalization.[29] There wasn't time during his administration for the plan to materialize. Some of the Acadians, however, were dissatisfied, usually because they had arrived later in the colony. Although these immigrants received food, clothing, and tools from the Spanish authorities, they were ordered to take up land near Natchez, at some distance beyond the early settlements near New Orleans. Ulloa's intention was to strengthen Spanish control across the river from Natchez to forestall English encroachment and at the same time to prevent a concentration of Acadians in one area, which might endanger Spanish influence. In April, 1768, the commandant posted an order on the chapel door at Pointe Coupée, threatening Acadian settlers who presumed to invite any of the recent immigrants to reside with them.[30] This threat had the desired effect, but it undoubtedly created enemies among the settlers, who realized that they had fled originally to escape sovereignty of a foreign power only to be forced again to live

29. Quoted in Kinnaird (ed.), *Spain in the Mississippi Valley,* II, 37–41.

30. "It is formally and expressly forbidden for all Acadians who have holdings dependent on the post at Pointe Coupée to shelter, even to receive in their homes, even if they are relatives or friends [newly arrived Acadians], under penalty of being deprived immediately of land granted them and in cultivation, it being His Majesty's design that the Acadians build their homes on the exact territory conceded to them." See enclosure in Duplessi to Ulloa, April 24, 1768, in Leg. 187, Papeles de Cuba, AGI.

under alien rule. Befriended by Foucault, they were open to anti-Spanish propaganda and rumors.

Far up the river in the Illinois country, opposition to Spanish regulation by the fur traders continued in the fall of 1768. St. Ange, with the approval of Captain Riu on the Missouri, suspended the requirement that all traders descend the river to New Orleans to confer with the governor and receive a special license to operate in a particular district. But grumbling persisted over efforts by the authorities to confine the activities of the vendors to the west bank of the river and to outlaw the sale of firearms and brandy among the braves.

There were likewise signs of discontent among the Indians hitherto friendly to the Spaniards. The lack of funds curtailed the distribution of presents to the chieftains. St. Ange reported in May, 1768, the dangerous effects of the paucity of gifts: "I have represented to you the smallness of the presents for the savages. I have had nothing else in mind but cherishing the hopes that you have given me of satisfying them. They were treated more liberally during the days of the French. It is not a question of wishing to attract new nations. I should like never to see any." A month later he noted the complaints among the tribes of the Missouri over the limitation on the activities of the fur traders. It was necessary for him to placate the chiefs, otherwise the tribes would have assembled at the post and there would have been nothing to give them.[31] In spite of the restlessness of the Indians over the scarcity of presents, there were no serious incidents and no signs of a transfer of allegiance to the British.

Besides having to solve questions of commerce and defense, the Spanish government had to formulate a church policy. On the surface this would appear to offer few difficulties, as both France and Spain were solidly Catholic. Complications might arise, however, from the introduction of elements associated with the church-state theory of Spain in its American colonies. It

---

31. St. Ange to Ulloa, May 16, June 23, 1768, both in Leg. 2357, Audiencia de Sto. Domingo, AGI.

was well known that the secular and ecclesiastical organizations were far more closely identified in the American viceroyalties than in the French colonial empire. If Spain insisted on uniformity in policy, it would mean the adoption of the mission system as the regular means of converting and controlling the Indians. Much depended, therefore, on the attitude of Ulloa, who, though a man of religious beliefs and devotion, was first of all a colonial administrator. Compromise and adaptation in these matters were basic.

In 1766 the provincial church, which had to look to Spain for direction, occupied an inferior status in the colony. It was ill organized, manned by a backward clergy, and lacking in wealth. From the founding of the colony until its acquisition by the Company of the Indies, priests and friars had made little real headway in spreading the faith.[32] Since then not much progress had taken place. Louisiana lagged far behind the Spanish colonies in the conversion of the natives and in the construction of churches and monasteries. True, the frontier missionaries had contributed to the pacification of the tribes. Also, though the church was less energetic than it should have been in propagating and maintaining Christianity, it had not pursued a policy of strict religious intolerance. Some French Protestants were allowed to enter, and it is estimated that 10 percent of the German population living on farms above New Orleans was also Protestant. In short, as the Jesuit historian Father Charles O'Neill puts it, "Religion for the Louisiana of Louis XIV and Louis XV was a pervading, tempering influence, but not a dynamic, decisive force."[33]

The responsibility for the spiritual life of the region had been largely in the hands of the religious orders. The bishop of Quebec had divided the Mississippi Valley among the Jesuits, Carmelites, and Capuchins, assigning to the last named the area of the Isle of Orleans, the region west of the Mississippi, and the

---

32. Davis, *Louisiana,* 90.
33. Charles E. O'Neill, *Church and State in French Colonial Louisiana: Policy and Politics to 1732* (New Haven, 1966), 280–82, 287.

land as far north as the Ohio River. Friction over jurisdiction developed between the Capuchins and the Jesuits, who had been given the area to the north of the Ohio. The loss of favor by the Jesuits at the French court and their forced departure from America in 1764 were triumphs for the Capuchins. It was with this knowledge in mind that the Spanish crown included three representatives of this order in Ulloa's expedition in 1766.

The laxness in the observance of religious rites and in the standards of morality among the people were criticized by the Spanish priests. One of these, Father Clemente Saldaña, has left us a graphic description of scenes in Father Dagobert de Longuory's church in New Orleans in 1766:

> The principal thing about them is their habit or manner of conducting themselves [in church], where not only reigns a libertinage and dissipation, which is admired here, but stuns us in Spain, at seeing women in a group, garments around their necks—all the rest bare, feet and arms, while the preachers deliver their homilies on sundry topics, but it would not be enough if the temple were free of such insults. The church is so filthy and unclean that it would be unsuitable even for beasts, and without denigrating the name it serves at times as a secular theater or scene for plays; from one side to the other it is full of benches, and in front the stools; on days of assemblies it is filled with women having no more respect than if they had been in their homes, wearing their dressing gowns, heads bare, but otherwise adorned like the devil. Who would not be horrified at seeing on Holy Thursday and Friday on those doleful occasions young women and young men jumping up and running around the church, and even peering into the corners asking alms for the poor? How poor they are in reality! On this basis everything is allowed and if you go to the mass or vespers where all sing, the priest intones, continues singing, the acolytes sing, those in the church sing, all sing, nobody is understood, so it is an infernal confusion but in the end they are entertained and they go there because there is no other place where they can be amused. . . . The saints of the church can be known only by the books, in no other way, but with our coming His Majesty has succeeded in getting a lighted lamp, with the basin of holy water an old tinplate bottle, so as to the rest, clear proof of their love for the temple.[34]

34. Quoted in Vicente Rodríguez Casado, "Costumbres de los habitantes de Nueva Orleans en el comienzo de la dominación española," *Miscelánea, Revista de Indias,* II (October–December, 1941), 176–79.

With these conditions in mind, the Capuchins sought to reform the tone and character of the provincial church. It was intended to institute dignity and seriousness in the services and to strengthen the moral fiber of the community. Education of the clergy was to be emphasized. Very wisely, the crown did not resort to the mission system because it was too costly and contrary to French traditions.

As one imbued with strong convictions, the Spanish governor abhorred the physical neglect of the house of God. Churches and buildings used for charitable or medical services badly needed repairs. Some had even disappeared. In his petition to Grimaldi in 1766 for an increase in the *situado*, Ulloa listed construction and repair of churches and chapels as a major item among the extraordinary capital expenditures of the colony: "It is necessary to repair the major religious edifice, which is so threatened with ruin that it was decided to remove the Holy Sacrament and place it in a guard house . . . to construct a church for the Ursuline nuns, who do not have one, and to rebuild the convent, since the present structure is so dilapidated that they have been forced to reside in private homes."[35] The outlay for material rehabilitation of the colony was one of the causes for the indebtedness of the regime in 1768.

Although beset by serious administrative problems, Ulloa found some solace in marriage. His long years of bachelorhood ended when he was fifty. Contrary to a long-standing creole myth concerning the circumstances of his marriage, he was wedded by proxy to the young Doña Francisca Ramírez de Lareda y Encalada, daughter of the affluent conde de San Xavier, citizen of Santiago de Chile, but related to the old families of Seville. In conformity with service regulations, Ulloa had petitioned Charles III for permission to marry, stating very frankly his wish for an heir and the need for preserving the family estate: "Being the second of my family, I am to inherit a

35. Expediente formado con motivo de la sublevación, in Leg. 2542, Audiencia de Sto. Domingo, AGI.

mayorasgo [entailed estate], located near Seville, which will by the laws of inheritance pass to others on my death through lack of succession, because out of five brothers none is married, four being in His Majesty's service and the fifth an ecclesiastic; and, if a suitable person can be found, I, having no funds, may obtain a sizable dowry that is not of common occurrence in those kingdoms [Spain]."[36] It was a marriage of convenience, common in the eighteenth century, and from this union there were seven children. Upon the arrival of his bride in June, 1767, the Spanish chaplain performed a second ceremony at Balize, after which the couple ascended the river to take up residence in the capital.

To the disappointment and dismay of the creole aristocracy, the entry of the governor and his bride was marked by little fanfare. In the old days of the French colony, an event of this nature would have been attended by balls, levees, public entertainment, and charitable donations. Of a retiring disposition, the governor preferred seclusion in his residence to public receptions and dinners.[37] Although Ulloa spoke French, his wife did not, a fact that accentuated her wish to avoid a public appearance. Their indifference to social function was interpreted as Castilian snobbery and hauteur. Since there was no royal palace in the capital, Ulloa arranged to rent two houses for their occupancy for 880 pesos annually. Additions to their quarters were made for their personal comfort, including "a gallery to serve as a bridge joining the two." Carpenters were employed to build furniture and shelves for the office.[38] The birth of their first child, a daughter, in New Orleans the following spring contributed to their happiness.

Ulloa's distaste for public display revealed itself also in his preference for private worship. Rather than attend services in

---

36. Representación de Antonio de Ulloa, October 30, 1764, in Leg. 26, Marina, AGS.
37. In congratulating the governor on the safe arrival of his bride at the Isla Real and anticipating with pleasure their sojourn in New Orleans, the faithful Loyola announced that no preparation had been made for a formal entry into the city because he knew of the governor's dislike for public ceremony. See Loyola to Ulloa, July 2, 1767, in Leg. 109, Papeles de Cuba, AGI.
38. Loyola to Ulloa, July 12, 1767, *ibid.*

the church, he had mass said in his home by the chaplain. Creoles assumed that this was another sign of the vanity and pride of a Spanish nobleman.[39] Nor did his liberal ideas on race relations appeal to the French population. He saw no harm in permitting a white man and a Negress to be married, by the man's personal confessor, contrary to the Black Code of 1724.[40] In justification he could have pointed to the humane Laws of the Indies, which encouraged racial intermarriage, particularly of Spaniards and Indians, as a means of amalgamating the social structure in America. His condemnation of gambling and tippling, favorite pastimes of the populace, did not enhance his reputation as a friend of the masses.

Thus, in the fall of 1768, conditions boded ill for the province. An economic crisis, brought on by the threatened enforcement of the regulations of September, 1766, and March 23, 1768, was in the offing. Trade, legal and contraband, had declined; prices had risen; and the confidence of the mercantile community, which dreaded assimilation into the Spanish commercial system, was waning. Restoration of church buildings added to the outlays. The cost of supporting the Acadians was not inconsiderable. Moreover, the newly arrived immigrants, though benefiting from Spanish policy, disliked forced settlement near Natchez, across the river from the English fort and at some distance from their kinsmen at Pointe Coupée. This was not, however, a morass from which one could not reach solid ground. Ulloa regarded the arrival of Spanish specie as the key to the improvement of the economy through payment of the debts, amounting in June to 100,000 pesos, and stabilization of the currency. His poignant

---

39. A British officer, who visited New Orleans, commented on this: "The Spanish Governor's personal behaviour to the French in general is rather severe, perticularly to those who are in the Character of Gentlemen which occasions great disgust among them; he seems determined to keep them as much under as possible and shows only to two or three Merchts. any countinance and those people it is thought when he takes possession he will give the Exclusive trade to." See Alvord and Carter (eds.), *Trade and Politics, 1767–1769*, 117.

40. See deposition of Father Dagobert, who was critical of Ulloa's conduct, in Gayarré, *History of Louisiana*, II, 219, 220.

appeals for sufficient funds were not answered owing to the prior demands of Cuba and the state of the Mexican treasury. But had Grimaldi and Arriaga foreseen the peril faced by the regime in Louisiana, extraordinary measures might have been adopted to save the situation.

Ulloa's personal influence was low. His idiosyncrasies, in particular his disapproval of public pastimes and customs, were more apparent than ever before. His marriage, instead of widening his prestige in social circles, had had the opposite effect. The French aristocracy conjured up the image of a haughty Spanish hidalgo, who looked down on all classes of society. Whether or not he realized it, the stage was being set for an event that determined his future in Louisiana. The storm that had slowly been gathering was about to break.

VIII

"The Good Wine of Bordeaux"

"For myself, I am of the opinion that at all times, one great portion of the events of the world are attributable to very general facts, and another to special influences. These two kinds of causes are always in operation, their proportion only varies."[1] Although Alexis de Tocqueville's dichotomy of causal relationships still has validity, a revolution, even though abortive or incomplete, is a far more complex and intricate phenomenon. It is rather the result of a totality of forces operating in the past, some more obvious than others. The revolt of the French colonists in October, 1768, was to a great degree the culmination of two clearly distinguishable elements: an adverse reaction by a majority of the population to unsatisfactory conditions and the activities of a small but determined group of merchant-planters.

The roots of popular disaffection were numerous. There was a malaise that the colony had developed in the process of adjustment to the sovereignty of another power. A sentimental attachment to France remained despite amiable overtures by the Spanish authorities. English observers in West Florida remarked on more than one occasion on the hostility of Frenchmen toward Spaniards.[2] This suspicion of foreigners was strengthened by

1. Alexis de Tocqueville, *Democracy in America,* abr., ed., and introd. Andrew Hacker (New York, 1964), 166.
2. "I found from the first Frenchman to the most inferior of them a Determined & fixed hatred to the Spanish Nation & Government also a Resolution formed by many of them Especially the Merchts, to quit the Country and settle in our Colonies were they sure of meeting with Protection & that desire proceeds as they saw from a Certainty that when Don Ulloa takes possession he means according to the Customs in the Spanish Colonies to

143

the natural individualism of the frontiersmen, accentuated by neglect by the French crown during the Seven Years' War.[3] The widespread unpopularity of the Spanish governor was another intangible factor in the situation, and the state of the economy contributed to the dissatisfaction. Trade declined owing to the uncertainties of foreign markets. Inflation, caused by shortages of consumer goods and an unsound currency, flourished unchecked. As in all periods of economic recession, these conditions bore most heavily on the lowest strata of society. The inability of the Spanish regime to meet its debts dimmed the prospect of a brighter future. In sum, a climate highly propitious to the formation of an anti-Spanish plot had developed in the colony.

But unfavorable political and economic conditions are generally not sufficient to bring about a revolution. Crane Brinton discards the theory of "spontaneous growth" as a complete explanation. His analogy of the garden and the gardener incorporates both the environment and the planner: We must "hold that revolutions do grow from seeds sown by men who want change, and that these men do a lot of skillful gardening, but that the gardeners are not working against Nature, but rather in a soil and climate propitious to their work; and that the final fruits represent a collaboration between men and Nature."[4]

In the uprising of 1768 the catalytic element was the stance of a powerful, discontented group of traders and landowners. Eventually, they reached the conclusion that their economic interests were imperiled by the assimilation of Louisiana into the Spanish

---

make a Monopoly of Whole Commerce and make the rest of the Merchts. trade with them, they say further that Spanish justice to Individuals will not be conducted with that impartiality that they had been used to under the French Government." See Marsh to Haldimand, November 20, 1767, in Alvord and Carter (eds.), *Trade and Politics, 1767–1769,* 114.

3. Ulloa emphasized this strongly in his account of the rebellion to Grimaldi: "The inhabitants of that colony live in an independence so general that once a man retires to his home he sees himself as absolute lord without subjection to any authority. From this is born the liberty that reigns among them to do whatever they wish and treat their superior with so little respect that he is governor in name only." See "Noticia de los acaecimientos de la Luisiana," fol. 27.

4. Crane Brinton, *The Anatomy of Revolution* (Rev. ed.; New York, 1952), 93.

mercantile system. The decrees of September, 1766, and March, 1768, foreshadowed a limitation on both legal and illegal trade. Although Louisiana received some exemptions, it would be difficult for the colony to sell its produce on the Spanish markets and to import from the mother country the manufactured articles necessary for existence. Governor Ulloa's efforts to put the lid on contraband were well known. From time to time members of this clique had protested against the decrees and acts of the Spanish regime. Convinced that their status was threatened, they favored force as a means of changing the direction of Spanish policy. Their program of action, basically economic in motivation, would be ostensibly defended on the respectable grounds of Spanish injustice and of flagrant violation of the laws and mores of the province.

The ringleaders of the cabal that might have charted a new destiny for Louisiana were two prominent colonial figures, the commissary Foucault and the attorney general La Frenière. It would be difficult to assess the proportionate contribution of each to the uprising. As a former French official, Foucault had considerable prestige among the officers of the old regime and among those engaged in commercial activities. Knowing the interests of the merchants, he worked to preserve their prosperity by retaining the ties to France and the French islands. Like previous French colonial officials, he had selfish interests which would suffer in the decline or collapse of the economy. If Spanish accusations were correct, he had profited by countenancing smuggling and by taking bribes in the purchase of supplies for French officials. He stood to gain greatly by the redemption of the paper currency at par value. Having luxurious tastes, he maintained a well-appointed establishment in the capital, but, since his income did not match his desires, his indebtedness was considerable at the time of O'Reilly's arrival in the colony.[5] Shrewd, energetic, but unprincipled, he was an indispensable part of the leadership.

5. Although discounting the traditional feud between the governor and the commissary, Aubry probably had good reason to complain of his rival's favored status. "I pay dear for the rent of a house," he wrote Choiseul, "while M. Foucault leads a happy,

Popular with the crowd because of his handsome appearance and his eloquence at public gatherings, La Frenière was likewise an essential element in the leadership. His personality, unlike that of Foucault, had a charismatic quality. Judging by his speeches and his actions, there was some idealism in his makeup. It is possible that some of the thinking of the Enlightenment directed his conduct. He had a sympathy for the rights of colonists, which, he believed, were threatened by the policies of the crown. But like his fellow conspirator, he had personal reasons for disliking the new regime. Rumors of the forthcoming suppression of the Superior Council by the Spanish, in which his position as attorney general would be abolished, had circulated widely throughout the colony. That he used his office to advance his own interests was probably true. According to Ulloa, the attorney general was especially embittered over the disapproval by the crown of a contract that he had proposed to import Negro slaves on exceedingly profitable terms for those involved.[6] His influence with the mass of the people and with the mercantile and landed groups made him a natural leader of the opposition.

It is believed that the initial scene of the conspiracy was the home of Madame Marie Louise de Pradel, the widow of Chevalier Jean de Pradel. The day was sometime during the summer of 1768. The garden of her mansion, near the city and adjoining the property of La Frenière, was ideally located for the secret meetings of the plotters. Involved in a clandestine affair with Madame Pradel, Foucault was accustomed to spend much

---

tranquil existence; he has Negroes, cattle, land, coaches and is lodged in a palace that the king has built for him and his employees. God forbid that I am a person of such low character to envy his fate, but I am angry that he wishes to give me only my expenses and that he refuses me the necessary money to maintain with dignity the position that I hold . . . so that I find myself obliged to borrow from and use the rest of my patrimony." See Aubry to Choiseul, April 24, 1765, in C13A45, Colonies, AN. An inventory of Foucault's personal papers in 1769 disclosed debts of 60,000 livres. A judgment against Foucault's property was instituted by the *procureur des biens vacans,* or purveyor of unclaimed property, who declared that Foucault had been compelled to turn over approximately 36,000 livres in old billets "to avoid being forced to resign his position." See Aubry to Praslin, October 6, 1769, and September 19, 1769, both in C13A49, Colonies, AN.

6. "Noticia de los acaecimientos de la Luisiana," fol. 23r.

time in her home.[7] Here he, La Frenière, and others hostile to Spanish policy hatched their scheme with consummate skill for the expulsion of the Spanish governor.

One of the first moves of the conspirators was to dispatch an undercover mission to Brigadier General Haldimand, who was in command at Pensacola, to seek support from the British in the effort to liberate the province. The British general, however, rejected their proposal for the moment, unwilling to be a party in an uprising against the Spanish and acknowledging insufficient military strength for the purpose.[8]

In retrospect, it is incredible that Ulloa had no inkling of the formation of a conspiracy until it was almost too late to act. In later defending his ignorance, he credited the secrecy to the family ties and connections of La Frenière, who was related by blood and marriage to many of the important families of the colony. Within this intimate circle, secrets could be kept.[9] Nevertheless, the fact that significant aspects of the plot did not get out until the last week before its occurrence points to the circumspection and intense concern of the participants for its success.

The timing of the revolt was the last days of October. It might have occurred earlier during May, when the general tenor of the

7. His relations with her were probably responsible for his refusal to compel the Superior Council to render a judgment in a suit brought by her daughters in France against family property in Louisiana. He ignored letters from Choiseul and Praslin, demanding that action be taken on claims of the Mademoiselles Pradel against their mother. See Choiseul to Foucault, January 5, 1766, and Praslin to Foucault, July 21, 1767, both in Lettres Envoyées, Colonies B, AN.

8. Rodríguez, *Primeros años,* 142, 143.

9. Our knowledge of the conspiracy is based to a considerable extent on the facts obtained from a cross-examination of the accused and witnesses and from the confessions of the accused in the trial initiated by O'Reilly in September, 1769. See Proceso incoado contra los sublevados, in Leg. 2543, Audiencia de Sto. Domingo, AGI. A copy of the essential documents is to be found in Leg. 20,854, Consejo de Indias, AHN. That the conspiracy in its inception was a kind of family affair seems plausible. La Frenière was married to the granddaughter of Charles Frederick d'Arensburg, a Swedish nobleman and military adventurer, who joined the Company of the Indies in 1721 and migrated to Louisiana. Arensburg's daughters married into the Noyan, Bienville, Masan, and Villeré families. In addition, the commandant of the post at Chapitula, François Chauvin de Léry, and the captain of a militia company, François Labarre, had married cousins of the attorney general. See Rodríguez, *Primeros años,* 140, 141, 147.

unpopular decree was known in the city. One is forced at this point to speculate on the reasons for the delay. Apparently, the idea did not really germinate until the mercantile community had ample evidence that Spain intended to merge the economy of Louisiana with that of the imperial system, with insufficient concessions to ensure the prosperity of the merchants, fur traders, and planters. With the growing indebtedness of the regime, there seemed little hope for generous subsidies essential to the well-being of the colony. Moreover, if popular demonstrations in New Orleans were needed to pressure the government, the two most likely groups for this purpose, the Germans and the Acadians, would be more disposed to act when their crops had been harvested. Perhaps one cannot dismiss entirely the debilitating effect of the "long, hot summer." At any rate, postponement past October might be fatal to the execution of the scheme. It was known that Spanish troops were being assembled in Havana to permanently occupy Louisiana. If these soldiers were allowed to reach New Orleans, the chances for success would be remote, if not nil. It was necessary, therefore, to act first.

What had held up the organization and dispatch of an impressive Spanish command to Louisiana? Its presence might well have been the key to Spanish control. At the outset Grimaldi had counted on the enlistment of the French troops stationed in the colony under Aubry. When this failed, no other recourse remained but to form a battalion of Spanish soldiers to supplement the meager force in the province. In December, 1766, Ulloa had notified the secretary of state of the size of the force that he believed was requisite for the occupation, some seven hundred men with various pieces of artillery.

The organization and transportation of a contingent of troops from Spain to Louisiana remained unfulfilled by the end of October, 1768. At fault was the characteristic procrastination of the crown, which had failed to react promptly in this emergency, as it had failed similarly in the dispatch of the *situado*. Although Grimaldi should bear some responsibility, the separation of

Louisiana from the administration of the rest of the Indies may have further complicated the channels of bureaucratic communication. Despite repeated requests for troops by Ulloa to Grimaldi and Bucareli, the enlistment for the province proceeded slowly.[10] By the end of the spring of 1768 some soldiers had arrived in Cuba. In June, Grimaldi notified Arriaga that the remainder of the troops were gathered in Cádiz for embarkation, some of them being ironically of French origin, and were scheduled to sail in mail-carrying vessels to the assembly point in Havana. The desperate economic conditions of the summer prompted Ulloa to appeal again to the secretary of state for haste in the dispatch of troops "because each day new reasons for dissatisfaction and unhappiness arise from this mixed government." At the instigation of Bucareli, Ulloa agreed to await the completion of the cadre in Havana before its transportation to Louisiana.[11] In December, 1768, the ranks of the battalion were still unfilled.[12] Without the additional Spanish troops on the scene, the execution of the conspiracy was far easier.

In the early fall the organizers of the plot laid the groundwork for wider support. To win adherents, La Frenière and Pierre Caresse drew up a memorial containing a list of grievances against Ulloa. Once enough signatures had been procured, it would be presented to the Superior Council for discussion and approval.[13] Toward the end of October, many merchants and ship operators had signed the document, which also called for the expulsion of the Spanish governor.

With startling speed, the conspiracy against the Spanish governor, so long in the making, unfolded. On October 21 a colonist, disgruntled over an unfavorable decision of the Superior

10. See correspondence between Arriaga and various officials of the army and navy, July 23, 1767–April 21, 1768, all in Leg. 2542, Audiencia de Sto. Domingo, AGI.

11. Grimaldi to Arriaga, June 8, 1768, and Ulloa to Grimaldi, July 20, 1768, both *ibid.;* Ulloa to Bucareli, July 2, 1768, in Dispatches of the Spanish Governors of Louisiana, I.

12. At the end of the year it consisted of 8 officers, 17 sergeants, 26 corporals, and 363 soldiers. See Rodríguez, *Primeros años,* 270.

13. Proceso incoado contra los sublevados, in Leg. 2543, Audiencia de Sto. Domingo, AGI.

Council in his business affairs, confided to Ulloa rumors of a plot. Unwilling to give credence to a report from this apparently prejudiced source, the governor took no action until the twenty-fifth, when he learned elsewhere of dissension among the Germans. He immediately dispatched Gilbert de St. Maxent, a reliable ally of the Spanish, to La Côte des Allemands, or the German Coast, with enough funds to pay off the debts incurred by the regime. Upon his arrival there he was seized by those involved in the conspiracy and imprisoned until its successful outcome.[14]

There was little doubt now that the situation was serious. Upon learning of the treatment of St. Maxent, Governor Ulloa realized for the first time the strength of the opposition to his government. He sent word at once to Aubry of what was happening, conferred with him at length, but obtained no promise of energetic action to suppress the movement. The French governor was apparently unconvinced that events would go beyond a formal protest against Spanish policies. Moreover, the few French troops, only ninety in the city and these mainly old veterans incapable of real combat, militated against adoption of a strong stand. Nor was Ulloa's miniscule force in a position to curb the insurgents, since practically all the soldiers were at posts in the interior and of the sailors only ten or twelve were aboard the *Volante*. Thus the combined French and Spanish forces in the capital totaling only about one hundred men were too small to deal with a large-scale uprising.[15]

Events had now reached a crucial stage for the conspirators. The concentration of rebels in the city was imperative in order to overturn the regime before troops could be sent from Havana or recalled from the frontier posts to create a counterbalance. A sizable popular demonstration in the capital was essential. According to a prearranged plan, two captains of the militia, Judice

14. Rodríguez, *Primeros años*, 144, 155. Some of the money was paid to the Germans, the rest appropriated by Villeré. After enduring some physical hardships, St. Maxent was released on October 30.
15. "Noticia de los acaecimientos de la Luisiana," fol. 29.

and André Veret, who had been won over by La Frenière, turned to the Acadians for backing. They falsely told the settlers that the Spanish governor had a large amount of money in the treasury, some of which could be used to redeem the paper currency brought by the Acadians from Canada. Although their money had lost all value long before, they were told that it would be honored in Louisiana. Despite the Spanish assistance in their homesteading, they succumbed to the propaganda and believed that their presence in New Orleans would persuade Ulloa to act in their behalf.[16] No doubt some of the recent immigrants still cherished a resentment against their forced settlement near Natchez.

Propaganda was likewise effective among the Germans living on the farms above the city. Rouget de Villeré, commandant of the district, convinced the farmers that the Spanish governor had no intention of paying for the fruits and vegetables purchased during the year. To see that all of their bills were met, they should appear as a group in New Orleans and present their demands. Although the debt amounted to a small sum, the credulous colonists felt impelled to act in what they thought was their best interest. Both groups were simply waiting for a signal from their leaders to march to the city.[17]

To Ulloa, the only possibility of coping with the insurrectionists lay with Aubry.[18] On October 27 the French commander, reassured of the loyalty of his force after a conference with his officers and men, confronted Foucault and La Freniére, recognized openly as the ringleaders. They informed him that they intended to force Ulloa to leave the colony "with the least possi-

16. *Ibid.*, fols. 32, 33.
17. *Ibid.*, fols. 34, 35.
18. Ulloa's letter of October 26 gave Grimaldi alarming news: "There is no doubt that there is a general conspiracy organized against the sovereignty of His Majesty. The aim is to present a manifesto with charges against me to the Superior Council . . . which will order me to leave with all the Spaniards in the colony remaining thus under the domination of France as before." See Ulloa to Grimaldi, October 26, 1768, in Leg. 2542, Audiencia de Sto. Domingo, AGI. It apparently reached Grimaldi at the same time that he received a full report on the rebellion.

ble disturbance, because things had gone so far that it was impossible to draw back."[19] Other Spanish officials might remain, evidently to ensure the continuance of the partial subsidy that was necessary for the existence of the colony. Aubry protested their decision but did nothing to halt the revolt.

In the development of the movement, the confrontation between Aubry and the conspirators was decisive. In a revolution a turning point is generally reached when an illegal force faces duly constituted authority. In defiance of Aubry's protest, Foucault and La Frenière refused to dissolve their following and abandon their plan to expel the Spanish governor. At the moment the French commander made no move to arrest the traitors. His unwillingness to apply force against the rebels was naturally interpreted as a sign of weakness by the insurgents and ultimately meant the success of the uprising. On the other hand, Aubry's inaction in the crisis might be looked upon by the Spanish government as evidence of disloyalty. Such a compromising position would surely require an explanation in the future. To himself, his justification for a disinclination to act boldly was his tiny command and the belief that his status as a French officer, soon to return to France, required no positive move that might incite bloodshed. Humiliated at being forced to back down, Aubry now endeavored to put the best possible light on events. He maintained thereafter that he had won a partial victory by retaining Spanish sovereignty and avoiding a resort to arms. But he had had no success in disbanding the colonial militia, which had been assembled by the insurrectionists. Five companies, two of which consisted of Germans and Acadians, were in the city under the command of Pierre Marquis, who had been promoted by the Superior Council to the rank of colonel at Foucault's and La Frenière's suggestion.[20]

Although still hopeful of successful negotiations by Aubry, Ulloa made his own preparations against assault by the rebels.

19. Quoted in Rodríguez, *Primeros años*, 159.
20. *Ibid.*, 160, 162.

He ordered all military personnel to go aboard the *Volante* and invited those of Spanish birth and sympathizers among the French population to join in the defense. The packet was readied for action, with her decks cleared and her cannon loaded with shot and pointed at the city. Actually, the ship's position was advantageous. Because of the fall of the river at this time of year, the heavy batteries in the city could not be brought to bear on the vessel, yet the *Volante*'s guns controlled the approaches from the levee to the water's edge. For observation, the militia occupied a two-masted brig, anchored off the bow of the *Volante*. To reinforce his small Spanish contingent, Ulloa asked Aubry's permission to release from the guardhouse twenty Spanish soldiers, who had been imprisoned as deserters, but this was refused on the strange grounds that it might be a provocation to the conspirators.[21] Orders were given by Ulloa for the destruction of important papers and records in case of hostilities. Steps were thus taken to counter any foreseeable acts of violence.

Events now took a more critical turn. On the afternoon of the twenty-eighth, some five hundred Acadians and Germans poured into New Orleans. Urged by the leaders of the conspiracy to make a show of force, they aspired to obtain the consent of the governor to pay the bills and to redeem the worthless Acadian currency. They now reinforced the companies of militia commanded by Marquis. Once in the city, all the insurgents congregated at the home of Francois Chauvin de Léry, another member of the cabal, who supplied them with wine and muskets. The "good Bordeaux" removed their apprehensiveness and qualms over the consequences of revolutionary acts and stiffened their resolve to back their leaders. For many, the long, tiring march from the farms and the excitement of the occasion prompted overindulgence and intoxication—the ideal moment to bring down the curtain on the performance if only there had

21. "Noticia de los acaecimientos de la Luisiana," fols. 41, 42; Rodríguez, *Primeros años*, 163.

been enough Spanish troops at hand, as Ulloa subsequently commented. But this was not to be.

The injection of the popular element was essential for the execution of the plot. At this juncture, to assume more control of the capital, Marquis assumed the authority to patrol the streets with the militia. The cannon at the gates of the city, having been spiked the night before by the insurgents, presented no threat. Aubry, angry and alarmed at the possibility of bloodshed in the streets, hastened to the house of the governor to persuade him to take refuge for the time being aboard the *Volante*. With his wife pregnant and a very small child, Ulloa could hardly be accused of cowardice in avoiding an unequal confrontation with the rebels. As additional precautions, Aubry ordered twenty soldiers to join the Spanish force on the packet, thirty others to guard the central square, and the remainder to be ready to face the Superior Council.[22] In the meantime, he made a final appeal to Foucault and La Frenière to desist from their plans. Whether his remonstrances were as vigorous and outspoken as he subsequently asserted is doubtful, owing to his overly cautious and uninspiring leadership.[23]

On this same day, October 28, at Foucault's request, the Superior Council met to consider the petition signed by a large number of merchants and planters, urging the expulsion of the governor and the restoration of all rights and liberties. In the absence of some councilors it was decided to postpone action on the memorial until the next day. Meanwhile, the council turned over the petition to Huchet de Kernion and Piot de Launay to be studied and reported on at the next meeting. To provide more adequate representation, the leaders recommended the election

22. Rodríguez, *Primeros años*, 166.

23. In his written account of the rebellion to O'Reilly, dated August 20, 1769, he claimed that he had done everything possible to thwart their plans: "I summoned Monsieur Foucault [on October 27] when I asked what part he intended to play in the crisis, and as he replied in an ambiguous manner, I told him that he would lose his position irrevocably if he did not join me in opposing such a rebellion. . . . On the next day [October 28] I orderd Monsieur La Frenière to my house and told him that I would hold him to blame for the loss of the region. I stated to him that the lives of conspirators had always come to a tragic end." See Aubry to O'Reilly, August 20, 1769, quoted *ibid.*, 398.

of six supernumerary members. When this had been complied with, the council adjourned.[24]

The following day the die was cast. At nine o'clock on October 29 the eighteen council members, including the six new representatives, assembled again at Foucault's residence, now the accustomed meeting place, to act on the memorial against the Spanish governor. At Ulloa's insistence, Aubry attended the session in a last-minute effort to convince the assembly of its stupidity and folly in proceeding against the sovereignty of Spain.[25] As part of the scheme of the conspirators, groups of militia and citizenry roamed the streets nearby, shouting defiantly their full support of the council's action. There would be no disruption of the conciliar session by Aubry's soldiers.

As the most significant document of the rebellion, the minutes of the October 29 session of the Superior Council deserve special examination.[26] They contain a full indictment of the Spanish regime, as given in the remonstrance of the merchants and planters, the impassioned harangue by La Frenière in support of the accusations, and the final judgment of the council to remove the executive authority. To the conciliar decree were appended Foucault's reservations and Aubry's protests.

Since the petition of the commercial classes deals with the fundamental question at the heart of the uprising, its recommendations are worthy of note. The arguments to abolish restrictions and restore trade with France and the French islands are difficult to refute.[27] However, to apply the concept of free trade to any part of America might be considered singular in an age dominated by mercantilistic thinking. The petition urges the council to take five important steps to improve the well-being of the colony:

24. These were Pierre Hardi de Boisblanc, Antoine Thomassin, Charles Jean Baptiste Fleurian, Bobé Descloseaux, Joseph Ducros, and François Labarre, evidently men who would support the ouster of the Spanish governor. See Gayarré, *History of Louisiana*, II, 192.

25. Rodríguez, *Primeros años*, 166.

26. Gayarré, *History of Louisiana*, 11, 367–83, includes a translation of the proceedings.

27. Clark, *New Orleans, 1718–1812*, 168.

1. That the privileges and exemptions which the colony has enjoyed, since the cession made by the Company [of the Indies] to His Most Christian Majesty, be maintained, without any innovations being suffered to interrupt their course and disturb the security of the citizens.

2. That passports and permissions be granted from the governor and commissioners of His Most Christian Majesty to such captains of vessels as shall set sail from the colony to any portion of France or America whatever.

3. That any ship from any port of France or America whatever, shall have free entrance into the river, whether it sail directly for the colony, or only put in accidentally, according to the custom which has hitherto prevailed.

4. That freedom of trade with all nations under the government of His Most Christian Majesty be granted to all the citizens, in conformity to the King's orders to the late M. D'Abbadie, registered in the archives of the city, and likewise in conformity to the letter of His Grace the Duke of Choiseul, addressed to the same M. D'Abbadie, and dated the 9th of February, 1766.

5. That M. Ulloa be declared to have in many points infringed and usurped the authority hitherto possessed by the government and council of the colony, because all the laws, ordinances, and customs direct, that said authority shall not be exercised by any officer until he shall have complied with all the formalities prescribed, and this condition M. Ulloa has not observed.[28]

In the deliberations and discussion of the council, La Frenière played a major role. With his commanding physical presence, his ringing voice, and his natural eloquence, the attorney general argued convincingly for the expulsion of the Spanish governor. If Foucault was in a roughly general way the Robespierre of the revolution, La Frenière was its Danton. The legal reasoning in his harangue followed two main lines: (1) the competence of the Superior Council as a judicial body, or Parlement, to receive grievances against the governor; and (2) the validity of the complaints of the mercantile elements and other segments of the population. His exposition of these points was comprehensive and emotional. Interspersed with derogatory references to the personality of the governor, it had at times a psychotic quality. His peroration, provided in part below, is to a large extent a reiteration of the demands of the merchants and traders:

28. Gayarré, *History of Louisiana,* II, 374.

Having maturely weighed all this, I require in behalf of the King:

That the sentences pronounced by the councilors nominated for this purpose, and put in execution against Mess. Cadis and Leblanc, subjects of France, be declared encroachments upon the authority of our Sovereign Lord, the King, and destructive of the respect due to his supreme justice, seated in the Superior Council, in as much as they violate the laws, forms, and customs of the colony, confirmed and guaranteed by the solemn act of cession.

That M. Ulloa be declared to have violated our laws, forms and customs, and the orders of His Catholic Majesty, in relation to the act of cession, as it appears by his letter, dated from Havana, on the 10th of July, 1765.

That he be declared usurper of illegal authority, by causing subjects of France to be punished, and oppressed, without having previously complied with the laws, forms, and customs, in having his powers, titles, and provisions registered by the Supreme Council, with the copy of the act of cession.

That M. Ulloa, Commissioner of His Catholic Majesty, be enjoined to leave the colony in the frigate in which he came, without delay, to avoid accidents or new clamors, and to go and give an account of his conduct to His Catholic Majesty; and, with regard to the different posts established by the said M. Ulloa, that he be desired to leave in writing such orders as he shall think necessary; and that he be declared responsible for all the events which he might have foreseen; and that Mess. Aubry and Foucault be requested, and even summoned, in the name of our Sovereign Lord, the King, to continue to govern and administer the colony as heretofore.[29]

The conciliar resolution for the expulsion of the governor is the third and final section of the recorded proceedings. It repeats, in the main, the accusations and charges of the attorney general and the mercantile group and stipulates the interim restoration of French authority, although granting permission to the lesser Spanish officials, Gayarré, Loyola, and Martin Navarro, to remain until orders were received from Madrid. As this is a lengthy document, only salient parts are selected:

---

29. *Ibid.*, 381. Cadis and Leblanc, the two persons singled out in the remonstrance as having been unjustly treated by Ulloa, were French colonists engaged in the slave trade with Martinique. Contrary to decrees of the Superior Council and to orders from Spain, they imported Negroes of such undesirable or vicious character that Ulloa compelled both traders to send back a number of blacks, much to La Frenière's discomfiture, he being an agent for the two. See "Noticia de los acaecimientos de la Luisiana," fol. 70.

The Council . . . has declared and declares that the sentences rendered by the councilors nominated by M. Ulloa and carried into execution against Mess. Cadis and Leblanc, subjects of France, to be encroachments upon the authority of our Sovereign Lord, the King, and destructive of the respect due to his supreme justice vested in the Superior Council; has declared and declares him an usurper of illegal authority in causing subjects of France to be punished and oppressed, without having previously complied with the laws and forms, having neither produced his powers, titles and provisions, nor caused them to be registered, and that, to the prejudice of the privileges insured to them by the said act of cession: and to prevent any violence of the populace, and avoid any dangerous tumult, the Council, with its usual prudence, finds itself obliged to enjoin, as in fact it enjoins, M. Ulloa to quit the colony allowing him only the space of three days, either in the frigate of His Catholic Majesty in which he came, or in whatever vessel he shall think proper, and go and give an account of his conduct to His Catholic Majesty. It has likewise ordained and it ordains that, with regard to the posts established by him in the upper part of the river, he shall leave such orders as he judges expedient, making him at the same time responsible for all the events which he might have foreseen. It has requested and requests Mess. Aubry and Foucault, and even summoned them in the name of our Sovereign Lord, the King, to continue to command and govern the colony as they did heretofore. At the same time, it expressly forbids all those who fit out vessels, and all captains of ships, to despatch any vessel with any other passport than that of M. Foucault, who is to do the office of intendant commissary; it has also ordered and orders, that the taking possession for His Catholic Majesty can neither be proposed nor attempted by any means, without new orders from His Most Christian Majesty; that, in consequence, M. Ulloa shall embark in the space of three days in whatever ship he shall think proper.[30]

Despite La Frenière's efforts, the two most prominent members of the council, the French governor and the commissary, dissented from its judgment. Outvoted, almost ignored, Aubry insisted nevertheless on having his protest registered in the formal account of the proceedings: "I protest against the decree of the Council, which dismisses Don Antonio de Ulloa from this colony; their Most Christian and Catholic Majesties will be offended at the treatment inflicted on a person of his character; and notwithstanding the small force which I have at my disposal,

30. Gayarré, *History of Louisiana*, II, 381–83.

I would, with all my might, oppose his departure, were I not apprehensive of endangering his life, as well as the lives of all the Spaniards in this country."[31] Having voiced his full opposition to the action of the council, Aubry stalked from the chamber. He had given due warning to the representatives of the impending wrath of the two European monarchs.

On the other hand, Foucault's dissent proposed a modification of the action to be taken against the Spanish governor. Although the Superior Council might suspend Ulloa's authority, it was beyond its power and jurisdiction to force his departure from the colony. From a practical standpoint, Ulloa would be exercising wisdom in sailing for Cuba, as the commissary had already suggested. It is clear that Foucault was aware of the possible adverse repercussion in the courts of Madrid and Versailles. Secretly in full sympathy with the aims of the conspirators, he nevertheless posed as a moderate, an official of the old regime who was acting in accord with his orders from France and with the legal prescriptions and formalities surrounding the assumption of authority in the colony. As the treasurer of the French province, he understood the extreme need for Spanish pesos to maintain the government. So that his position might not be construed in the future as having been fully consonant with that of the rebels, he had his vote incorporated in the record:

> The intention of the King, our master, being that the colony should belong, fully and without reserve, to His Catholic Majesty, by virtue of the treaty of cession, my opinion is, that none of the Spanish officers who have come here by order of their government, can be legally sent away; that, considering the causes of discontent enumerated in the petition of the citizens, and Ulloa's omission to take possession of the colony with the usual formalities, he, the said Ulloa, should be prohibited from exercising the powers of Governor, in anything relating to the French subjects now in Louisiana, or who may come thereto, hereafter, either as colonists or not: and that everything appertaining to the commerce carried on by the French and other nations with the colony, be regulated as it was before his arrival; nevertheless, that all the officers of the Spanish administration should continue their respective functions, in order to provide for the supplies

31. *Ibid.,* 383.

necessary to the town and to the posts, for the payment of all salaries, and for the expenses of the French troops which will continue to serve, and of the works which will be deemed proper; this, until the decision of the courts of France and Spain be known, reserving to the delegates of the people the right to address His Catholic Majesty in the most respectful and lawful manner, in order to obtain the privileges they claim.[32]

Of the three sections of the proceedings, La Frenière's oration bears most scrutiny, since his ideas and legal arguments were embodied in the conciliar resolution. His reasoning was intended to provide a legal justification for the removal of the governor. Was the Superior Council competent to judge the constitutionality of the Spanish regime? Although Ulloa had addressed a courteous letter to the council in July, 1765, announcing his proposed arrival in the colony, he never accepted this body as one with important judicial or legislative powers and secretly worked for its abolition. Anyone who has examined the correspondence of the French minister of marine with the colony must conclude that Versailles looked on the governor and the commissary as the real instruments of royal authority. As for the Spanish obligation to preserve the customs, laws, and institutions of the colony, it should be recalled that the cession was unconditional. On the lack of fulfillment of the formalities of possession, a proclamation of authority in the capital and raising the flag of the Spanish Bourbons, La Frenière was right. But in actuality, in the acceptance of Spanish funds and general acknowledgment of orders and decrees, Louisiana was a Spanish dependency. Hence, many of his arguments were without foundation.

One is impressed by the venom and antipathy directed throughout the controversy toward the Spanish governor by his enemies. The terms "tyrant," "oppressor," and "usurper" crop up frequently in the documents and records of the revolt. According to his accusers, he was guilty not only of breaking the laws of the realm and of a pact between two sovereign powers, but also of behaving contrary to the mores and customs of the

32. *Ibid.*, 204.

country. It would be difficult to gather evidence to uphold the condemnation by his critics of his character and behavior. The facts of his pre- and post-Louisiana career repudiate the charges of graft, excessive severity in enforcing decrees, and even moral dereliction implied by his opponents. What idiosyncracy in his conduct or putative expression of superiority was responsible for this unbridled assault on his personal character, one may never know. Popular irrationality of this nature occurs in all times, with variations only in intensity and duration. It was unquestionably an invidious reflection on the political and social conditions in Louisiana in the eighteenth century. Undoubtedly, the successful machinations against Kerlérec constituted a precedent for the removal of the Spanish official. Unchecked in the past, the leaders of the conspiracy turned to force as a solution to their economic and social ills.

Execution of the expulsion decree represented the last and irrevocable step in the unfolding of the revolt. Would the Spanish governor comply with an order from the Superior Council calling for his withdrawal from the colony within three days? In the minds of the plotters a show of military strength, combined with demonstrations by a hostile populace, would suffice to attain this goal. It is not inconceivable that the determined rebels would have resorted to force to remove Spanish authority. At 2:00 P.M. on October 29, the conciliar scribe delivered a copy of the order to Ulloa aboard the *Volante*. To celebrate the issuance of the decree, Foucault invited the council members to a repast in his apartment.[33] Meanwhile, units of the militia paraded in the streets, and groups of Germans and Acadians, either indulging their thirst anew or recovering from the effects of the heady wine of the night before, roamed unsteadily in various sectors of the city. Shouts of "Vive le roi" and "Vive Louis le bien-aimé" were heard, together with cries of "Vive le bon vin de Bordeaux" and "A bas le poison de Catalogne."[34] Faced with what seemed to be strong popular opposition, the Spanish gov-

---

33. *Ibid.*, 205. I have been unable to locate a copy of the order for the expulsion.
34. Villiers, *Les dernières années*, 263.

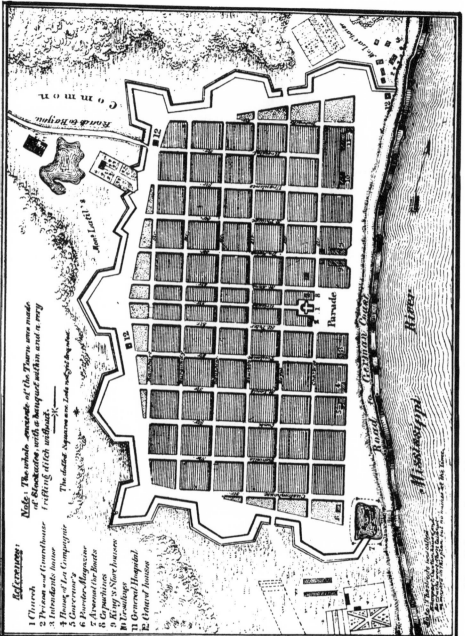

New Orleans about 1770

ernor capitulated. Without sufficient Spanish troops at hand, unable to count on the loyalty of the French regulars, and with his family a distinct liability in the event of hostilities, he had perhaps no alternative.[35] The Spanish commissary Loyola was ordered to end the subsidy to the French officials and soldiers in the city and the outposts and to terminate the delivery of supplies to the Acadians and gifts to the Indians. Only at the solicitation of Aubry was any exception to be made.[36] Ulloa also issued orders for the Spanish troops to evacuate the outposts and return to Havana.

On November 1 Governor Ulloa took his last look at New Orleans. He did not know this, for he must have thought that he would return to the city with the expeditionary force in Havana to reoccupy the province. Accompanied by his family and some close advisers, including the Capuchins, he sailed down the river.[37] But it was on a French frigate, the *César,* which happened to be in New Orleans and was bound for Havana. The *Volante* unfortunately needed repairs and could not have made the trip across the Gulf safely. According to Aubry, the commander of the French militia, Marquis, intended to escort Ulloa's ship to the sea and occupy Balize by ousting the Spanish garrison. Only by a dint of threats did Aubry avert this open insult and possible armed clash. It was the first occasion in which his orders had been obeyed by the militia. At Balize the French vessel halted, apparently to secure additional supplies for the voyage and await more favorable weather. News of the delay reached New Orleans and incited fears that the governor was simply stalling for time, until Havana could be notified and Spanish troops, already assembled in Cuba, could be dispatched in large numbers to

35. Aubry, in his explanation of events to the minister of marine, estimated the number of armed men in the town to be nine hundred. See Aubry to Praslin, November 25, 1768, in C13A48, Colonies, AN. In a later version of the incident to O'Reilly, he increased the number to one thousand. See Aubry to O'Reilly, August 20, 1769, in Rodríguez, *Primeros años,* 399.

36. Ulloa to Loyola, October 30, 1768, in Leg. 3883, Estado, AHN.

37. Creole tradition had it that some bold rebels at daybreak managed to cut the mooring lines and set the vessel adrift. The discovery several years ago of an ancient anchor in the river immediately revived the old legend.

suppress the movement. Before Marquis' militia could approach Balize, Ulloa and his entourage had set sail. On December 3, after a voyage of over three weeks, described by one of the passengers as a "painful navigation," the governor and his party entered the harbor of the Cuban capital.[38]

So far the rebel cause had been victorious. In the expulsion of Governor Ulloa the insurgents had attained their immediate goal. Notwithstanding this success, the future was fraught with uncertainty, with the critical problems of setting up a viable, temporary regime and of reestablishing a permanent relationship with Spain and France.

38. Aubry to Praslin, November 25, 1768, in C13A48, Colonies, AN; Bucareli to Grimaldi, December 4, 1768, in Leg. 2542, Audiencia de Sto. Domingo, AGI.

IX

Isolation and Disillusionment

With the departure of Antonio de Ulloa, the leaders of the rebellion were free to inaugurate a government to their liking. In the October 29 decree of the Superior Council, there was no declaration of independence or separation from Spain. The intent of the conciliar act was ostensibly to restore the authority of the French governor and the commissary. The presence of the lesser Spanish officials would serve as a surety for the good behavior of Spain and for the continuation of some kind of subsidy for the colony. Such action would make it easier to bring about retrocession or to negotiate with the authorities in Cuba for more favorable treatment in the framework of mercantilism. Essential to this plan was the attitude of Aubry. He himself confessed that he had lost prestige and his power was limited, but as commander of the regular troops he was inevitably involved. There was little doubt about the firm, behind-the-scenes support for the insurrection from Foucault, who, with an eye on the revolution's effect in Europe, did not wish to appear an extremist. His conduct permitted La Frenière to accept the plaudits of the public and the Superior Council as the foremost figure in the victory over the Spanish governor.

In this turbulent situation the real government was a mélange of diverse elements. Undeniably, a major component in the administration of affairs was the Superior Council, which arrogated to itself executive and legislative prerogatives in addition to its traditional judicial functions. Its frequent sessions and its issuance of numerous *mémoires, adresses, requêtes,* and *arrêts* testified to its expanding role during the crisis. As long as the colonial militia obeyed its directives, the council could enforce its decrees. Participating in its deliberations as colonial officials were Foucault and La Frenière, both of whom entertained motives of personal gain. It was impossible for the council to ignore the formal status of Aubry, because he commanded troops still under arms and capable of deployment if all authority threatened to break down.

To broaden its support among the citizenry, the Superior Council now resorted to an expedient familiar to revolutionary bodies: it enlarged its membership. Although the legality of the procedure is uncertain, during November eight syndics were selected to take part in the conciliar deliberations. These were men who had participated directly in the uprising or had given ample evidence of their anti-Spanish feelings. Among them were Pierre Marquis, Joseph Villeré, Balthasar Masan, Pierre Caresse, Denis de Laronde, and Pierre Poupet. Following the election of these new members, the council held only closed meetings.[1]

In the second week after Ulloa's departure, between November 8 and 13, the council considered the charges against the Spanish governor. Piot de Launay, one of the councilors, drew up the bill of information registering for this purpose twenty-one depositions from aggrieved persons. Included were the complaints of ship captains and pilots against maritime regulations, of merchants engaged in the slave trade, of Acadians forced to live across the river from the English fort at Natchez, and of sailors forced to serve in Piernas' expedition to the Missouri. Most of the charges were petty, exaggerated, and, according to Aubry, without foundation.[2] On November 12, the council, from the depositions and other documents at hand, prepared

1. Rodríguez, *Primeros años,* 235, 236.

2. Among other things, it was charged that he had acted cruelly by excluding three children from living with their families in the city and forcing them to dwell far from the inhabited area because they were afflicted with leprosy. Another deposition came from Father Dagobert, vicar general and curate, who affirmed that Ulloa's marriage to the Peruvian heiress was illegal. See *ibid.,* 183, and Gayarré, *History of Louisiana,* II, 220.

the *Très humbles représentations qu'adressent au roi notre très honoré et souverain seigneur les gens tenant son conseil superieur à la Nouvelle Orléans.* When Aubry got hold of a copy, he hastened to the printer and angrily demanded that certain phrases offensive to the Spanish crown be deleted or amended. The objectionable passage read as follows: "Charged with our hatred which he [Ulloa] has so justly merited, cannot his nation reproach him for having failed in the implementation of Spanish policy, which, soft and insinuating in principle, becomes tyrannical when the yoke is imposed?" Because of Aubry's threats, the printer toned down the accusations against Spain in later copies: "Charged with our hatred which he has so justly merited, his nation can still reproach him for having failed in the rules of policy in forcing us by his tyranny to fear all Spanish government."[3]

On November 22, the Superior Council dictated a letter to Praslin, urging him to present to the French king the petition from the council and a memorial from the merchants and planters. The *Très humbles représentations* was a defense of conciliar action in expelling the Spanish governor.[4] In the petition the council stated that Louisiana had been prosperous and well off before the Spaniards came. The policies of Governor Ulloa had led to the ruin of commerce and agriculture. Of special significance in causing this condition, the petitioners asserted, was the issuance on September 6, 1766, of an order that was "illegal." Ulloa's attitude became that of a tyrant. Moreover, "he had the greatest contempt for the Superior Council. He sought to deprive it of power and tried, without legal authority and in violation of a letter from Your Majesty, to create and establish a new body of councilors." The council next dealt with the charges of unwarranted control of the slave traffic and of mistreatment of the Acadians, both of which added to the misery of the colony. Finally, when "all hearts were reduced to despair ... the planters, merchants, artisans, and workmen united in drawing up a

3. Villiers, *Les dernières années,* 274; Fortier, *A History of Louisiana,* I, 198.
4. Gayarré, *Histoire de la Louisiane,* I, 211–29, has the full text of the letter and the memorial.

remonstrance to the Superior Council." After a justificatory account of proceedings against the governor, it concluded with an impassioned plea for the retrocession of the colony: "Deign, Sire, to receive in your royal and paternal breast your children who have no other desire than to die your subjects."[5]

Designed to be more effective in its appeal to the crown was the *Mémoire des habitants et négociants de la Louisiane sur l'evénement du 29 octobre, 1768.*[6] Less emotional, it aimed to convince the royal councilors that retrocession was advisable, using arguments based on common sense and economic gain for France and for the colonials. Copies of it were run off by the royal printer, Denis Braud, with the approval of the commissary and were distributed throughout New Orleans. Although repetitious and somewhat overdone in its praise of Louis, "le Bien Aimé," it presented a cogent exposition of the causes of the extreme discontent of the landed and mercantile groups. Despite its general objectivity in the discussion of Spanish commercial policies, there were many defamatory references to the personality and character of Ulloa.

The memorial was primarily a condemnation of Spanish mercantilism. Incorporating Louisiana into the closed economic system would spell the inevitable decline in its prosperity, since Spain and its possessions could never provide a sound, lasting market for colonial products. Interference with the fur trade and the shipment of timber had already affected the income of the colonists. The decree of March, 1768, although a concession to free trade in permitting commodities unabsorbed in the Iberian Peninsula to be sold to foreign countries, in reality hindered commerce by increasing costs due to unloading in a Spanish port and reloading for shipment to other markets, thereby doubling the price of commissions, insurance, storage, and other services. Objection was raised also to limiting navigation at the mouth of the Mississippi to a single pass, delaying the movement of ships

5. *Ibid.,* 218, 224, 225, 227, 228.
6. Fortier, *A History of Louisiana,* I, 177–204, has a complete translation of the document.

and resulting in incidents of stranding on the sandbars and wrecks. As in other representations, the regulation of the slave trade came under fire. The last part of the remonstrance was a concise presentation of the strongest reasons for the retrocession of the province. It disclosed an insight into the Spanish *raison d'état* for accepting the colony in 1762 and into the potential value of Louisiana for the French Empire. Was the possession of Louisiana vital to Spain for the protection of colonial wealth? To counter the argument of imperial security was essential: "Inferior in its products to the rich countries that Spain possesses, our country could only be a rampart of Mexico. Nor would this rampart be impenetrable to the forces of His Britannic Majesty, who, already master of the country to the east of the Mississippi, would share the navigation of the river with Spain and who has establishments to which the access is not alone by the mouth of the river, but also by the immediate proximity of the other countries of the north, where her domination is established."[7]

To the contrary, the return of the province to France would enhance Spanish security: "The retention of this colony by France protects in a better way the possessions of Spain on this side than the cession made to that crown. The disadvantageous impressions of Spain, already received by the savage nations, which have drawn upon M. Rios [Riu], Spanish captain, commandant at the Illinois, not only insults but threats, would range the savages, in case of attack, with the hostile party. On the contrary, those people would always march with the French soldiers, without asking for whom one wishes to fight. That is the true rampart."[8] There were positive benefits and advantages for France in annulling the concession. Napoleon a half century later could hardly have phrased a more succinct statement of the utility of Louisiana to the mother country:

The loss of Canada having closed that outlet to the manufactures with which France abounds, the preservation of Louisiana may repair in a short time a

7. *Ibid.,* 187, 188, 200.
8. *Ibid.,* 200.

loss so hurtful to the national industry. The efforts of the true Frenchmen established here, and those who come every day to establish themselves, may easily increase this trade of the Missouri, opened already with happy results, and to the aggrandizement of which are lacking the encouragement and aid which the French domination alone can procure. Even the savages from Canada come every day to trade at the Illinois for French goods, which they prefer to those that the English carry to their villages. Let one cease to forge shackles for our activity, and soon the English will cease to sell to France the peltries she consumes. Our manufacturers, in exporting them, will find an assured sale, which will bring profit; and in the peltries—to which may be added our indigo, our sugar, our cotton—they will have the raw material that feeds factories and gives work to laborers. If then, the ability for manufactures in the kingdom is so well recognized that it has drawn to them at all times a particular protection from the sovereign, is it not in the political order that this protection be extended to preserve for them resources, for which it would use perhaps the power of the state, if it were a question of acquiring them?[9]

This was not the last of the *mémoires* drawn up by the rebels to vindicate their position vis-à-vis Spanish sovereignty. The Superior Council also composed legal defenses of itself for Duc Louis Philippe d'Orleans, presumably a friend, and for the Parlement de Paris. Although the council's first memorial was almost identical in sentiment and expression to others also promulgated, its second could be interpreted as a challenge to the constitutionality of the act of cession. In denouncing Spanish absolutism, the authors by inference criticized the parallel political theory of the French monarchy that relegated the high court in Paris, or Parlement, to an inferior status in governmental affairs: The citizens of Louisiana "knew that a Spanish governor has no more rights than his own will, and that, haughty and despotic, he looks down on all men who are beneath him as base slaves, who must obey his first precept, however void of reason or absurd." Although ideas of this nature might find sympathy among the judges of the high court, these sentiments would have the opposite effect on the monarch and the royal council.

Although the revolutionists defended the expulsion of Ulloa

9. *Ibid.*, 201, 202.

primarily on the grounds that his government was illegal because he had failed to take formal possession of the colony, they upheld their action by another appeal to political theory. A recently discovered document, "Manifeste des habitants, négociants, et colons de la province de la Louisiane au sujet de la révolution qui est arrivée le 29 octobre, 1768," not only challenges regalian rights in the transfer of the region to Spain, but advocates the right of resistance to tyranny. The Treaty of Fontainebleau is denounced as invalid, being contrary to the laws of nations and the customs of provinces, and as a violation of a fundamental law of the French monarchy, the inalienability of the royal domain. The document justifies revolt against the Spanish regime on the grounds of natural law, which—as expounded by the Spanish Jesuit Francisco Suárez and the Dutch jurist Hugo Grotius—declares men to be born free and equal. Suárez asserted the right of revolution by the people in the event of extreme injustice and despotism. Such an interpretation is strained in the case of Grotius, although he postulated patriotism and liberty as natural rights. In the protest against Ulloa, a theory of popular sovereignty is expressed. But, strangely enough, no clear reference is made to Jean Jacques Rousseau's *Contrat social,* published in 1762, or to *De l'esprit des lois,* published in 1748 and written by Charles Louis de Secondat, the baron de Montesquieu.

The manifesto's authorship and exact date of composition are matters of conjecture. The organization of the material and the familiarity with both French constitutional law and the concepts of political philosophy point to a person of a legal mentality. Such a one might be Julien Doucet, a lawyer and relative newcomer to the colony, who was actually accused by the Spanish prosecutor in the conspirators' trial of having drawn up such a remonstrance. The deposition of the Spanish official Esteban Gayarré contains additional proof of the charge, naming Doucet as one who "had been responsible for the composition of most of the memorials of the rebels." For his part in the rebellion Doucet was sentenced to ten years' imprisonment. Internal evidence, particularly references to the struggle by the Swiss cantons for freedom against the Austrians, suggests the Swiss militia officer Pierre Marquis, who openly advocated a republic as the ideal form of government. Possibly the two men collaborated on the document. How long the manifesto appeared after the uprising is uncertain. Nor do we know how widely it was circulated, since its radical tone detracted from its reception by the mercantile-landed group. Its existence indicates, however, a greater acquaintance with political theory and philosophy among the insurrectionists than has hitherto been supposed.[10]

After preparing the petition to the Parlement, the next step for the revolutionists was to appoint delegates to plead their case at Versailles. Although Ulloa had left New Orleans by November 1, the rebels apparently felt no great sense of urgency to defend their cause before the French court. In retrospect, to delay for any length of time was a mistake. As soon as a vessel could reach Cádiz from Havana, the Spanish court would relay the news of the insurrection across the Pyrenees to Paris. The Spanish version might prove difficult to refute or modify. The colonists seemingly had a momentary grasp of the need for haste when, only a few days after the epochal meeting of the Superior Council, the dissatisfied groups named their respective delegates to the committee bound for France: Julien Lesassier for the Superior Council, Pin St. Lette for the planters, and Jean Milhet, a wealthy merchant, for the traders. To present his dissident views, Aubry selected de Lapeyrière, a knight of Saint Louis and an officer of the garrison.[11]

Before leaving for France, the anti-Spanish members of the

10. Father Charles O'Neill of Loyola University, who came across this document in the Archivo General de Indias, graciously allowed me to examine it before his delivery of a paper, "Louisiana Rebellion of 1768: A Prelude to 1775?" at the Louisiana Historical Association's annual meeting, March 26, 1976, in Lafayette. For more references on this topic, see William A. Dunning, *A History of Political Theory from Luther to Montesquieu* (New York and London, 1910), II, 132–91; William F. Church, "The Decline of the French Jurists as Political Theorists, 1660–1789," *French Historical Studies,* V (Spring, 1967), 1–40; Rodríguez, *Primeros años,* 390.

11. Gayarré, *History of Louisiana,* II, 211.

conciliar delegation sought to agree on the grounds for the defense of the uprising and on the most artful approach to the crown, all of which involved considerable time. Another cause for postponement was the forlorn hope of support from the British in West Florida. In the summer of 1768, Bienville Noyan, a brother of Jean Baptiste Noyan, and Masan had journeyed to Pensacola to determine the attitude of the British officials concerning a successful revolt in the colony. The British position was noncommittal. Despite this uncertainty, a second delegation set out shortly after Governor Ulloa's expulsion to confer with Brigadier Haldimand at Pensacola. The English commander flatly rejected an invitation from the colonists to occupy, even temporarily, the province on the grounds of dangerous repercussions in Europe and on the inadequacy of the force at his command.[12] Notwithstanding, some British officials in West Florida were unduly sanguine over the prospects of annexing the province to the British Empire. One of these was Lieutenant Governor Montfort Browne, who perceived distinct advantages from the removal of Spanish sovereignty from the region.[13] Haldimand's decision was well taken, for it is inconceivable that English occupation would not have provoked a contretemps between Spain and Great Britain. There was actually little chance of any wholesale migration of settlers to English

12. Rodríguez, *Primeros años*, 224. In September the British, in order to concentrate forces on the Atlantic seaboard, had evacuated Natchez and Manchac and had a relatively small number of soldiers at Pensacola and Mobile, too few in fact for any serious undertaking in Louisiana. See Gayarré, *History of Louisiana*, II, 227, 228.

13. Browne was elated at the prospective benefits for British trade and for the general consolidation of England's position on the Gulf. Giving an account of the rebellion to the ministry in February, he declared that he had been told that "the whole Province of Louisiana have Deputed fifty of the Principal Inhabitants to make a Representation to me of their Grievances which is now preparing for the Press demanding to become English subjects and to settle at the Natchez, having heard from the great Distance it is from Pensacola that it is to be made a Separate Government." In a second communication a few days later, he reiterated his conviction that English domination of the region was inevitable: "The Inhabitants of New Orleans are much inclined to Become British subjects . . . and if they are not so Disposed by Choice, it is apprehended they must Shortly be so from Necessity, should the Crown of Spain Resolve to punish their . . . Defiance." See Browne to Hillsborough, February 25, February 28, 1769, both in Correspondence of the British Governors of West Florida, DLXXV, PRO.

territory, even though this fear crops up in the Franco-Spanish diplomatic correspondence. It is extremely unlikely that one important segment of the population, the Acadians, who had exiled themselves from their homeland in the North with much hardship, would voluntarily have accepted English sovereignty.[14]

Disheartened over the opposition of the British authorities to intervention in the uprising, the delegation set sail for France toward the end of November from New Orleans in the brigantine bearing the appropriate name of *Patriote*. Because of frequent stops at landings along the river to indulge in acts of jubilation, the vessel did not anchor at Balize until the middle of December. To the alarm of the crew and passengers, the ship began to leak badly. Repairs took time and, in consequence, the brigantine did not enter the blue waters of the Gulf until mid-January. Rough weather and the unseaworthiness of the vessel caused protracted delays in the voyage to France, so that the delegation did not reach Paris to appeal to the king until April. Meanwhile, the French court had already learned of the insurrection by the end of January from Spanish sources.[15]

It is evident that, between the time the news was received and the delegates arrived, Choiseul had given some thought to the future of Louisiana. One of his advisers, Comte Jean Baptiste d'Estaing, had broached the proposal of a semiindependent republic for liberated Louisiana in a memorial of March 10, 1769. This was the view also of Comte Florent Louis Marie de Châtelet. The new government would be essentially a Franco-

---

14. How they would have fared under Haldimand is debatable. A Swiss Protestant and soldier of fortune who had lived in Canada, he spoke French and knew something of French law and customs. But, when appointed governor of Canada in 1778, he denigrated the French Canadians on one occasion: "No people in the world are more bigoted in their laws and usages. The clergy especially have an attachment for France concealed under their zeal for the preservation of their religion." Quoted in Mason Wade, *The French Canadians, 1760–1767* (Rev. ed., 2 vols.; Toronto, 1968), I, 80. This would not have augured well for the treatment of the French population of Louisiana in 1769.

15. Rodríguez, *Primeros años*, 224–27. There is no suggestion in the official correspondence between the minister of marine and the colonial officers that France favored the retrocession.

Spanish protectorate, with Louisiana governing itself in domestic matters but directed by the Family Compact in foreign relations. The port of New Orleans would be duty free, open to all and hence able to provide through its lucrative trade the funds necessary to maintain an administration. Consequently, both France and Spain would be free of the expenses of government, the bugbear of the past and probably the future. A distinct advantage for the safety of the French and Spanish colonial empires would be the encouragement of revolution in the English colonies, "disclosing to colonials who wish to be free neighbors freer than they." It was assumed that the existence of this semiautonomous regime would not create ambitions for similar status in the Caribbean colonies of France and Spain, which had evinced little disloyalty in the past. The conclusion of the memorial was that "what occurred in Louisiana seems one of the happier circumstances for the conservation of the Spanish and French colonies."[16] Although Choiseul was sympathetic from the first to the cause of the Louisianians and possibly toyed with the idea of a protectorate, he took no risks in preserving the Family Compact. Upon learning of the Spanish determination to reclaim Louisiana, he dropped the project and refused to consider seriously any joint policy for the future.

In the meantime, unaware of the official attitude of the French government toward the insurrection, the delegation from Louisiana arrived in Paris. It proved impossible to obtain a reception with Choiseul. Praslin reluctantly gave a private audience to a member of the group who was an old friend. In official quarters the petitioners met with complete silence. The cold neutrality or indifference that marked the attitude of the crown toward the delegates was not altogether the case with other groups. Upon arrival in the capital, the representatives dispatched letters to various chambers of commerce throughout the country having an interest in colonial trade, particularly to

16. Pierre Boulle, "French Reactions to the Louisiana Revolution of 1768," in John F. McDermott (ed.), *The French in the Mississippi Valley* (Urbana, 1965), 148–53.

Paris, La Rochelle, Nantes, Marseille, and Rouen. These communications besought aid and support in the retrocession of the colony to France. The results were meager. Typical was the attitude of La Rochelle, which felt it necessary to confer with the bureau in Marseille: "We can only consider [the events in New Orleans] through the commercial angle . . . [it was] such a delicate subject . . . that only united action could be risked." The Paris bureau resolved to leave the matter to the government, offering to give its counsel when called upon. The crown made no move to consult these bodies.[17] The lack of a positive response from this significant sector of the public bespoke the long experience of the French mercantile world, which had never succeeded in a long-term exploitation of Louisiana.

The populace of Paris refused also to subscribe completely to the crown's negativism toward the appeals of the colony. Because of the traditional ties with Louisiana, public opinion sided with the colonists. Gazettes and journals in the capital carried accounts of the uprising favorable to the revolutionists and critical of Spanish policy.[18] Despite the popular clamor, the dispirited delegates realized how futile and ineffective were their pleas and, somewhat fearful of the future, none returned to the colony.[19]

If an English protectorate could not be devised, the colonists in Louisiana had perforce for the moment to rely on themselves. The alternatives were now complete independence or renewal of governmental ties with France. To a very small minority the

17. *Ibid.,* 153–55.

18. Grimaldi complained to Choiseul of the lack of censorship exercised by the French crown, which might endanger Franco-Spanish relations: "These writers [the deputies] not only had succeeded in publishing them [the articles] but in inserting into various gazettes an article from Paris, portraying our government and our nation in most horrible colors. The liberty which the deputies of the colony enjoy in Paris may have contributed a great deal to the ease in which their injurious denunciations are spread around. And the absence of any move against them may persuade our emulators that that government does not disapprove of them." It was expected that the Spanish ambassador would bring this to Choiseul's attention. See Grimaldi to Fuentes, June 8, 1769, in Leg. 3883, Estado, AHN.

19. Rodríguez, *Primeros años,* 227.

ideal solution was to found a republic. Logically, the inspiration for this came from a Swiss adventurer, Pierre Marquis, who because of his birth and education was acquainted with this type of government in his homeland and who had no compelling reason to feel a strong attachment to France. Although he disavowed advocating this revolutionary project during the subsequent trial of the conspirators, circumstances of the moment lend credence to the validity of the accusation.[20] Apparently, the scheme did not reach the stage where a detailed plan for such a government was publicly presented. Despite the vagueness of the proposal, both La Frenière and Foucault felt compelled to attack its feasibility through the publication of a memorial. They contended that the colony lacked the financial resources to maintain an independent regime.[21] Owing to the arguments of the leaders of the revolt and to the lack of English aid, support for a republic among the rebels dwindled away and the plan was dropped. Perhaps as a gesture to the populace and to the extremists, the Superior Council agreed at this juncture to select the eight syndics who had the powers and attributes of regular council members.

As time passed, the gravity of the economic situation dawned upon the conspirators. Trade was languishing and, in consequence, prices for staples and manufactured articles mounted. The immediate threat to the permanence of the regime was financial. Without a reliable source of funds, it would be impossible to sustain an administration. The *situado* left by the Spanish governor was small and was, moreover, assigned to maintain the Spanish officials, the crew of the *Volante*, the remnants of the military contingent drawn in from the outposts, and the French soldiers under Aubry. When the next ship with specie from

20. See acusación de promotor fiscal, in Leg. 2543, Audiencia de Sto. Domingo, AGI.
21. Finances constituted the major argument against an autonomous government: "What are the means to realize it [independence]? The colony has no currency, no minerals; some say that a currency can be made from paper but can anyone take seriously such an absurdity! What value can the paper have? If there are no stocks of specie or metal to back up the value of the paper, no one will accept it." Quoted in Villiers, *Les dernières années*, 285.

Havana would put in was uncertain, in view of the hostile acts against representatives of the Spanish crown. To confiscate the wealth of Spaniards and their sympathizers, the usual resort of revolutionary regimes, was unfeasible, since little existed and since, if it were taken over and sold, only a modicum of funds would be raised because of the general shortage of specie. Furthermore, recourse to such stringent measures might have serious repercussions on the development of a favorable attitude in France. Until the French crown resumed sovereignty, the most promising panacea for the financial ills was the founding of a bank.

The concept of a financial institution, called the Banque du Mont de Piété, was bold but impractical. Its chief promoters were Pierre Hardi de Boisblanc and Pierre Poupet, both men of some means and experience in finance. The primary purposes of the scheme were to create a currency and to provide necessary loans and credit to merchants and landowners. Capital for the bank was to come from well-to-do colonists, who for a small interest would deposit one-half the income from their land or business. There was a partial precedent for this in the issuance of notes by the Company of the Indies, which in the end, however, had foundered in a morass of indebtedness. The bank's success depended on capital, a dubious assumption in this economically depressed region.[22]

The future of this financial expedient was not long in doubt. In February, 1769, Aubry, more pessimistic than ever over the prospects of the colony, predicted the bank's demise. The precarious political state of the colony and the fluctuating income from commerce and crops militated against investor confidence. There was also the firm opposition of foreign merchants, who desired a sound currency, to conduct trade with the colony.[23] It was well known, moreover, in New Orleans business circles that some of those most active in the founding of the bank owed large

22. Rodríguez, *Primeros años,* 238–41.
23. See Proceso incoado contra los sublevados, in Leg. 2543, Audiencia de Sto. Domingo, AGI.

sums and would profit by the extension of credit. After the initial failure of the bank to attract any sizable capital, even La Frenière lost heart, and without his support the institution collapsed.[24] Had the bank succeeded it might have afforded temporary financial stability, but it could not per se have forestalled the downfall of the regime.

The last futile gesture of Hispanophobia was the forced exit of the frigate *Volante*. To the hostile colonists it was an ominous symbol of Spanish sovereignty as long as it remained at New Orleans. The move to expel the vessel had a practical purpose as well, for the ship might serve as a rallying point of resistance for Spanish officials, the soldiers from the evacuated posts, and the citizens still loyal to the Spanish crown. With its guns the *Volante* precluded the full resumption of contraband trade, an important source of revenue for the insurgents. Had the ship been seaworthy it would have undoubtedly transported the Spanish governor to Cuba and thus would have been no problem. But the need for repairs was too urgent.

Soon after the flight of Governor Ulloa, the Superior Council attempted to persuade the captain of the frigate to follow suit. On November 4, the council volunteered to assist the crew in installing a mast and planking the bottom. When the ship was still riding at anchor in December, some of the rebels threatened to seize it and set it adrift.[25] There is no tangible proof to support the theory that the Spanish were deliberately stalling the repairs to preserve the reality of their presence in the province. Finally, the disaffected, to speed up the ship's departure, drew up a petition to the council, recommending forcible action. But Aubry's warning of the dire consequences of sanctioning interference with the efforts at ship repair temporarily muted the demands: "I do not wish to think that those who put their signatures to this petition intend to seek to employ violence

24. La Frenière, Foucault, and Marquis were heavily in debt. Hardi de Boisblanc, on the other hand, owned property in the city and in the province. See Rodríguez, *Primeros años*, 243, 242.

25. *Ibid.*, 244, 245.

against a frigate of the king of Spain; I believe them too good citizens to dare commit an act that would draw upon this country the indignation and vengeance of the two greatest monarchs in Europe."[26]

The respite for the *Volante* was not long. La Frenière and Foucault redoubled their efforts to force the last visible sign of Spanish armed power and might to disappear. Agents were dispatched to arouse the Indians and to keep alive the resentment of the Germans and Acadians. According to the Spanish commissary Loyola, the council met secretly on February 25 to reconsider measures to deal with the frigate. Although no decision was announced publicly, the subsequent intensification of public hostility suggests the nature of conciliar deliberation. Again, threats were made to cut the moorings of the ship and set it adrift if it did not sail. Loyola informed Grimaldi of the unfriendly manifestations in the city, which were accompanied by "curses and insults against this country. . . . These are heard every day and are a source of mortification to those who have the honor of being its citizens."[27] In April the campaign of the conspirators bore fruit. But there had been time for the workmen to make the *Volante* ready to ride the swift currents of the river and the waves of the Gulf and to accommodate the officials and soldiers for the trip to Havana. On April 20, 1769, the frigate raised anchor and proceeded downstream to Balize and eventually to the Cuban capital. According to Captain Acosta, the vessel left at 7:00 A.M., an hour earlier than planned, because of numerous threats to sever the mooring cable.[28] At the last

26. Statement of Aubry, December 17, 1768, in Leg. 3883, Estado AHN.
27. Loyola to Grimaldi, March 1, 1769, *ibid.*
28. Rodríguez, *Primeros años,* 259. On behalf of the Spanish officials and crew, Acosta dashed off a note of thanks to Aubry for his measures ensuring their safety: "I wish to express the eternal gratitude of all the Spaniards accompanying me—a gratitude that we will always remember—for what you have done since October 29 in avoiding clashes with the rebels and upholding the dignity and honor of the king, my lord. You have acted with an energy and firmness that I doubt that any other than you could have succeeded." The tiny garrison from the port on the Missouri did not arrive in New Orleans until May 9, so were unable to take passage on the *Volante.* See Acosta to Aubry, May 8, 1769, and Aubry to Praslin, May 23, 1769, both in C13A49, Colonies, AN.

minute, however, the rebels detained Loyola, Gayarré, and Navarro, resolving to hold them as hostages against punitive measures by Spain.

With the retreat of the *Volante* down the winding river, the conspirators breathed more easily. Yet there was reason for perturbation and soul searching. No word had been received from the deputies, who were to present the petitions for retrocession to the crown. Had the ship foundered in a storm en route to France, or was the silence an indication of the negative response of Louis XV? What was the reaction in Spain to a deliberate affront to its representative? These were questions for which the leaders of the rebellion had no answers. The economy was also a continual cause for worry. Unquestionably, conditions had worsened. In spite of removing restrictions imposed by the Spanish, foreign trade had not increased. The lack of specie with which to pay for foreign imports was only too apparent. There were no funds with which to meet the costs of administration. Toward the end of March Foucault pleaded with Praslin to succour the extraordinary needs of the colony: "You will judge, Monseigneur, from all the details that I have the honor to give you and from those furnished by Monsieur Aubry, that our position is indeed a cruel one, in fact, it is beyond the power of description, absolutely without money, provisions, munitions, merchandise, no funds to pay the soldiers and to take care of all those other aims indispensable for the administration of this unfortunate colony." In May, Aubry informed his superiors in Paris that the situation was so desperate financially that he had had to pay his men from his own fortune. The attempt by the council to procure funds through special import duties or levies was an exercise in futility.[29]

Even before the exit of the *Volante* from the scene, there had been misgivings among the conspirators over the outcome of the revolt. Late in March, Foucault, who by now had had second

---

29. Foucault to Praslin, March 24, 1769, and Aubry to Praslin, May 23, 1769, both *ibid.*; Rodríguez, *Primeros años*, 250.

thoughts about his role in the events of October, sought to vindicate himself in the eyes of the French minister of marine:

> I believe that persons poorly informed of the state of affairs might blame me for having summoned the Superior Council in regard to different petitions, but I must expect more justice from those who realize that the effective force of the garrison and the Spanish was only at the most 150 men and the greater part of unfriendly disposition; and there were at the least 1,000 colonists who, moved by a kind of fury against Monsieur de Ulloa and through association against all the other Spaniards, were resolved to obtain their end by force if they were unable to do this by means of the council. I believe that in a situation so harassing and unfortunate I did everything to induce the crowd to be content with the exile of Monsieur de Ulloa and his followers, which I could not prevent.[30]

It was his conviction that the colonists "did not wish to live under the domination of Spain after the enmity that Monsieur de Ulloa has created through his conduct; they seek to escape by going to the French colonies and to the English, our too close neighbors." To change the attitude of the settlers, Foucault recommended that Spain adopt a conciliatory policy. His plan envisaged a preliminary step by France, the dispatch of French troops to the colony, a month or two before the entrance of the Spanish reoccupation command. This would have a soothing effect on the turbulent spirits of the settlers. The French crown, to avoid additional expenses, might detach several battalions destined for St. Domingue to Louisiana. But more important was the absolute concession by Spain of "free trade and other privileges which the colonists have always enjoyed."[31] Undoubtedly, some of the rebels shared his view.

Although the commissary Foucault endeavored to mend his fences, the attorney general La Frenière made no overt move in this direction. On the contrary, he solicited sympathy and support for the movement from officials in St. Domingue. In a communication of May 23, 1769, Aubry reported to Praslin that

---

30. Foucault to Praslin, March 24, 1769, in C13A49, Colonies, AN.
31. The audacious Foucault even suggested the name of the Spanish consul at Bordeaux as the colony's intendant. See *ibid.*

La Frenière had received a letter from the attorney general of the Council of Port-au-Prince in which the latter "highly approves of the conduct of the members of the council and the settlers, which encourages them in their uprising and in their disobedience to the king's order." Loyola notified Bucareli later that the French crown had removed the Dominican officer from his position and had ordered his recall to France as a sign of its displeasure.[32] Despite these gestures, La Frenière must have had forebodings, for it is unthinkable that he was blind to the dangerous isolation of the colony. But, as the public figure who had championed more vigorously than anyone else in the council the expulsion of the Spanish governor, he felt impelled to maintain a resolute posture.

If the leaders of the revolt now had doubts of its ultimate success, the populace soon began to adopt similar views. Among the colonists, elation was succeeded by disillusionment and finally by resignation and despair. Aubry's letter to Praslin, written in the middle of April, analyzes the state of the public mind in this precarious period: "The people are repentant.... The part of the rebels grows smaller every day and the state of matters has changed that ... with three hundred more men and funds to pay for the expenditures and debts, I can promise you that the act of possession would take place peacefully and the inhabitants would remain calm, provided there is an assurance of pardon ... except for the twelve who would flee quickly to avoid the punishment that their criminal conduct exposes them to."[33]

May, June, and half of July passed without direct word from the governments of Spain and France. The longer the silence from the European capitals the greater was the anxiety over the future of the colony. The period of waiting terminated abruptly on July 19 with the startling intelligence that General Alexander O'Reilly, with a force of more than two thousand men, had arrived at the mouth of the Mississippi. Clearly, Spain intended

32. Aubry to Praslin, May 23, 1769, *ibid.;* Loyola to Bucareli, June 30, 1769, in Leg. 3883, Estado, AHN.
33. Aubry to Praslin, April 14, 1769, in C13A49, Colonies, AN.

to reoccupy the province ceded by the Treaty of Fontainebleau.

The experiment in what amounted to virtual self-rule under nominal French sovereignty could not be termed successful. The leaders of the revolt had negotiated for aid ineffectively with the British at Pensacola and had at hand no evidence of a modification of French policy toward retrocession. Economic conditions were, by and large, much worse than they had been in October. The scheme to found a bank had fallen through because of the scarcity of silver coins in the city and the desire of foreign merchants for a currency supported by the French or Spanish treasury. Contraband, a source of income in the past, no longer flourished because of the lack of specie and the extended sojourn of the *Volante* at New Orleans. The prospect of reoccupation aroused fear in the small coterie of rebels for their personal safety, although no blood had been spilled when Ulloa had been expelled. Some colonists, who had gone along with the rebels, albeit unenthusiastically, inwardly rejoiced that the period of uncertainty was at an end. Political stability and security now seemed assured. The nature of the second Spanish regime, whether conciliatory or repressive, depended on the resolves of Grimaldi and the Council of State, backed by Charles III, and on the measures applied by the military commander to implement that policy.

X

Restoration of
Spanish Rule

Napoleon's formula for decisive victory was known in Europe long before his famous campaign across the Alps. The use of speed, surprise, and concentrated force reflected the determination of the Spanish court to reestablish its authority in Louisiana at any cost. Although stern pacification might be difficult, involving possible bloodshed initially and creating enduring latent hostility to authority among the French settlers, it was believed to be well worth the effort.

Manifestly, the development of a policy by Spain toward Louisiana had diplomatic complications from the first. Since the colony had belonged to France originally, it behooved the crown to maintain contact with, but not necessarily to act in concert with, the court at Versailles. The attitude of Spain's rival and neighbor on the Gulf could not be taken for granted, as the French pioneers might appeal for aid from that quarter or might migrate to West Florida should the reimposition of Spanish rule be too onerous. To Grimaldi, an architect of the Treaty of Fontainebleau, was reserved the solution of these diplomatic entanglements and the adoption of a firm policy toward the colony. By the end of January, 1769, he learned of the uprising from a Spanish Capuchin, who had accompanied Governor Ulloa in his flight from New Orleans. The governor himself followed the friar to Europe and by the middle of February was in Cádiz, awaiting orders before setting out for Madrid to give a personal account of the event to the court.[1] By the end of March,

1. The officials in Havana were taken aback by the suddenness of the insurrection against Ulloa. On December 6 a conference, attended by the high-ranking military and

Grimaldi had received Ulloa's detailed story of the plot and his recommendations for a future course of action.[2]

To preclude any friction with his ally, Grimaldi on February 2 notified the French ambassador d'Ossun of the occurrence of the insurrection. Presumably, he tendered also a copy of Ulloa's preliminary version of the event.[3] The report reached Versailles by the sixth of the month, thus anticipating by a number of weeks direct information from the colonists. During the second week of February, the conde de Fuentes, Spanish ambassador to France, received a lengthy dispatch from Grimaldi with an account of the uprising: "We have learned by the latest mail that a revolution has occurred in Louisiana, as a result of which Don Antonio de Ulloa, who had not yet taken formal possession of the colony, was forced to leave and find refuge in Havana. It appears that the French settlers have taken as pretext the decrees that had been promulgated at the king's command to arrange commerce between the colony and Spain, claiming that these destroyed the illicit trade between this same colony and our possessions in America."[4]

---

naval officers, took place at the palace of Captain General Bucareli to plan a course of action. Ulloa, in giving his views of the causes of the revolt, stressed the economic plight of the colonists. See copy of minutes of the conference, enclosed in Bucareli to Arriaga, December 10, 1768, in Leg. 2542, Audiencia de Sto. Domingo, AGI. The viceroy of New Spain, to whom Ulloa had written on December 10, was likewise nonplussed by the events in New Orleans: "Strange indeed is the incident to which you refer in your letter . . . in the knowledge that such affairs require heavy expenditures, I shall do all that I can to provide assistance with funds." See Croix to Ulloa, January 4, 1769, in Leg. 149A, Papeles de Cuba, AGI.

Although it would seem logical, as Bucareli suggested, for Ulloa to remain in Havana to observe happenings in New Orleans and to be ready to lead a force for reoccupation, he was determined to go to Spain as soon as possible to give Grimaldi a true version of the rebellion: "France may be inclined to excuse those vassals so that the crime may seem less atrocious; this excuse must not reflect on the decree of the king who decides upon the way in which trade should be carried on between Spain and the colony through orders dispatched by Your Excellency . . . and [thus] France, situated close at hand, and everyone else will understand, without harboring ill feeling, the lack of any basis for their alleged excuses, and that no sovereign could permit or tolerate the acceptance of law dictated by vassals . . . a people who do not submit to law or kingship." Ulloa to Grimaldi, December 10, 1768, and Bucareli to Arriaga, December 10, 1768, both in Leg. 2542, Audiencia de Sto. Domingo, AGI.

2. Grimaldi to Bucareli, March 25, 1769, in Leg. 1630, Indiferente, AGI.

3. D'Ossun to Choiseul, February 2, 1769, in Correspondance Politique, Espagne, DLVI, Archives de Ministère des Affaires Etrangères, Paris, hereinafter cited as AAE.

4. Grimaldi to Fuentes, February 6, 1769, in Leg. 6972, Estado, AGS.

The French reply to Grimaldi's dispatch was not immediate. In a communication to d'Ossun, dated February 25, Grimaldi's French counterpart Choiseul acknowledged with some astonishment the news of the rebellion. To say the least, the reference to Louisiana is enigmatic: "For eighteen months there have been no signs of life among the French who have remained in the country. . . . You can assure him [Grimaldi] that the king has resolved to support all the measures that the king his cousin judges suitable to force obedience from the inhabitants of Louisiana."[5] It is wholly unreasonable to conclude that Choiseul was blind to conditions in the colony, in view of the frequent and detailed letters addressed by Aubry and Foucault to the minister of marine, the duc de Praslin. By disclaiming any knowledge of discontent in the colony, the astute Choiseul sought to preserve intact the tranquillity of the Franco-Spanish accord. The dispatch from Versailles was virtually a carte blanche promise of support for any means, coercive or conciliatory, to suppress the revolt. The firmness of the French position could, however, be modified by appeals of the colonists or by the nature of the measures utilized for pacification.

In adjusting Spanish diplomacy to the new situation in Louisiana, Grimaldi could not overlook the interests of the English government. On the same day that he had composed the dispatch to the Spanish minister at Versailles, Grimaldi addressed a note to Felipe Victorio Amadeo Ferrero de Fiesco, the príncipe de Masserano and Spain's representative to the Court of St. James's. It was imperative to inform Masserano of the nature of the uprising, for the English ministry would undoubtedly seek to ascertain from every source Spain's attitude toward recovering the colony. In soft-pedaling the gravity of the revolt, the note reasserted the importance of the economic issue as a primary cause for the disaffection:

> You will hear that the inhabitants of Louisiana have thrown off Spanish rule, but this is not so because we had not yet taken possession of that

5. Choiseul to d'Ossun, February 25, 1769, in Correspondance Politique, Espagne, DLVI, AAE.

province and were simply waiting for the arrival of troops from Cádiz to take this step. In bringing about this situation the major factor was a commercial regulation, and, as it was aimed at eliminating the illicit trade, a source of profit in the past, the inhabitants decided not to give up French rule and for that reason to send deputies to His Most Christian Majesty; and Don Antonio de Ulloa, who was to be our governor, found it convenient to go to Havana.[6]

As one might surmise, the English ministry had already learned of the insurrection through their superior system of communication from Lieutenant Governor Browne at Pensacola and from another source, presumably Russian.[7] Browne's reports glowed with optimism over the possibility of French settlers becoming English subjects because of their extreme dissatisfaction with Spanish rule.

Before Masserano had received Grimaldi's dispatch of February 6, Lord Hillsborough had sounded out the Spanish minister on the future of Louisiana. Although engaged in a policy of retrenchment in colonial administration, the English statesman could not forego the glittering prospect of imperial expansion and the discomfiture of a powerful rival. According to Masserano, it was Hillsborough's suggestion in the initial discussion that "we ought to cede Louisiana to them, as a result of which he would receive no more complaints from English subjects and there would be extinguished a motive that might lead to war." The Spaniard's rejoinder was that England should relinquish her desire for aggrandizement and return Florida, which would lessen the friction between the two countries. Hillsborough then commented that "Florida was of little value, that he preferred the city of New Orleans, with the Mississippi to continue to serve as a boundary between his possessions and ours." In a conversation the following day, the English minister alluded to the manifesto of the inhabitants of New Orleans, in which they had

---

6. Grimaldi to the príncipe de Masserano, February 6, 1769, in Leg. 6972, Estado, AGS. Masserano had learned of the uprising from the Russian minister in London, who had gotten the news from his country's representative in Madrid. See Masserano to Grimaldi, February 21, 1769, in Leg. 6972, Estado, AGS.

7. Masserano to Grimaldi, February 24, 1769, in Leg. 3883, Estado, AHN.

declared that "they would submit happily to France or to England but never to Spain." William Henry Nassau de Zuylestein, the earl of Rockford, another member of the ministry who resumed the talks in Hillsborough's place, declared that "such a rebellion was of the greatest importance for all of Europe because of the consequences that it would have." The Spanish ambassador retorted, "I told him that the citizens of New Orleans had anticipated what the English colonies were ready to undertake, from whom they [the French colonists] had pursued a bad example."[8] On this prophetic note the verbal exchange ended. Masserano had had, indeed, the last word! Believing that Grimaldi was determined to retain the province at all cost, Masserano evinced no softness in the Spanish position. Unless hostilities erupted in Louisiana when Spanish troops appeared or the Family Compact was weakened by other causes, Great Britain stood little chance of finding justification for intervention or of pressuring Spain for territorial concessions.

At this critical moment the future of Louisiana was in the hands of Grimaldi. The retrocession of the colony was not impossible despite the terms of the Treaty of Fontainebleau. Simply by default, through failing to take formal possession, the colony might revert to France or, as a remote contingency, become an independent state under French protection or a joint protectorate of the two powers. From the first, Grimaldi had had apparently no reservations about the desirability of recovering the province. Before receiving an answer from Choiseul concerning the attitude of the French crown, he summoned on February 11 a conference of the chief members of the Council of State to discuss the advisability of retaining Louisiana. To strengthen his position with the king, he requested that each councilor put his view in writing on the course to be followed. Because of Castilian deliberateness or procrastination, it was not until the end of March that the last written opinion had been received.[9]

8. *Ibid.*
9. See Ms. 2829, in Miscelánea de Ayala, Manuscritos de América, BP.

As Grimaldi had hoped, the dictamen of the council was virtually unanimous in favor of retaining the colony. An examination of the affirmative votes discloses a similarity of reasons for reoccupation. Because of the confidence that he enjoyed with the king and his grasp of foreign policy, the conde de Aranda's arguments for retention are worthy of note: (1) Louisiana constituted a natural barrier protecting the valuable region of New Spain from the English colonies and impeding the growth of contraband trade; (2) if by accident the colony became independent, it would set a dangerous example for Mexico; and (3) should Louisiana be returned to France, that country would "on the first occasion cede it to England." With his customary arrogance, Aranda rejected the merits of any consideration to the contrary: "In view of the fact of the acquisition of Louisiana by Spain with the reasons that determined this step and since it may therefore be regarded as property of the crown and joined to the dominion of Mexico, I am of the opinion that it was wise to accept it from France and it is indispensable to retain it at all cost."

Only the secretary of the treasury Miguel de Muzquiz opposed the reincorporation of Louisiana into the empire. With considerable prescience, he pointed out the heavy costs of administration and defense: "If we preserve Louisiana, we will take on an annual expenditure of 300,000 pesos, a constant obligation to provide officials, and the ever-present occasion of having disputes with the English, which will be a handicap to the government." Countering the argument that it was necessary to avenge unilaterally the king's honor, he declared, "The offense is joint in my opinion, that is, to both crowns; if France should retain the province, it is her rightful duty to punish those who have been disobedient to the commands of the monarch."[10] Muzquiz's views constituted the single negative vote. Thus assured of the councilors' backing, Grimaldi proceeded forthwith, with the approval of the king, to appoint Alexander O'Reilly, then inspector

---

10. There was some criticism of Ulloa in the council's discussion. See *ibid.*

general of the army, leader of the expedition and to assemble the requisite ships and men.

O'Reilly's designation as head of the expeditionary force was an acknowledgment by Charles III of the need for swift, conclusive, and perhaps ruthless action to restore Louisiana to Spanish authority. Born in county Meath in 1722, Alexander O'Reilly was one of many Irish soldiers of fortune who migrated to the Continent in the eighteenth century. Enlisting in the Spanish army in Italy, he won the attention of his officers by his bravery and execution of commands. It is not unlikely that his career was helped by his acquaintance with General Richard Wall, an Irish compatriot who preceded Grimaldi in the key position of Spanish secretary of state.[11] O'Reilly's conduct in the invasion of Portugal during the Seven Years' War elicited praise from Charles III, and after the war he received the post of inspector general, with orders to restore discipline and efficiency to the demoralized army. Upon completing his tour of duty to inspect the fortifications in Cuba and Puerto Rico, he returned to Spain and at this moment was the most respected figure in the military. His suppression of popular demonstrations against royal decrees in Madrid raised him still more in the king's esteem. To many at the court his choice was logical and imperative.

Because of the criticism of some of his subsequent policies in Louisiana, an insight into O'Reilly's character and personality seems germane. Portraits reveal a man with a commanding presence, physically stout, well formed, and taller than average. Although he walked with a slight limp, the result of a wound suffered in combat, his handicap in no way retarded his military career.[12] He was energetic, firm in his opinions, and at times confident to the point of arrogance. His contacts with the court at Madrid had given him also a certain polish and courtesy.

---

11. *Diccionario de historia de España desde sus orígenes hasta el fin del reinado de Alfonso XIII* (2 vols.; Madrid, 1952), II, 729. See also Bibiano Torres Ramírez, *Alejandro O'Reilly en las Indias* (Seville, 1969), for the fullest and most recent account of O'Reilly's tour of duty in America. Torres gives his year of birth as 1725 instead of 1722.

12. Torres, *Alejandro O'Reilly*, 6.

Alexander O'Reilly. From the Collection of the Louisiana
State Museum, New Orleans

Coupled with these traits were intelligence and lofty ambition. This latter quality led him to indulge in palace intrigues, marked by unscrupulousness and dissimulation.[13] There is some doubt among historians regarding his military ability. Considering the catastrophic defeat of the Spanish army in Algiers in 1776, which not only spelled the end of his career but brought in its wake the fall of his protector Grimaldi, one would not place him in the first rank among the European generals of his day.

It is important to examine the orders that he received from the king. As they were not specific on the treatment of the rebels in Louisiana, it seems clear that much was left to O'Reilly's discretion and common sense:

THE KING

Don Alexander O'Reilly, Knight Commander of the Order of Alcantara, Lieutenant General of My Armies: Having great confidence in your well known zeal and activity in behalf of my Royal Service, I have decided to send you to America with several missions. Since the most important is to take formal possession of the Colony of Louisiana, which my most worthy Christian and beloved Cousin has ceded to me, I have decided that as soon as you reach the island of Cuba you must obtain the proper number of soldiers and ammunition and other supplies which you feel are necessary, and that after having then taken possession of it in my Royal Name, you must make formal charges and punish according to the law the instigators and accomplices of the uprising which occurred in New Orleans. . . . So that you may carry out my instructions fully, I give you today such power and jurisdiction as shall be necessary for handling each matter, case, and incident . . . for this is my desire.

Dictated at Aranjuez on the
16th day of April of 1769[14]

13. This trait of deception saved his life during his early career as a minor officer in the Spanish army. Severely wounded in battle in an Italian campaign and unable to move, he was approached by an Austrian soldier bent on robbing and killing him. To appeal to the soldier's avarice in hopes of warding off an assault, he claimed that he was the son of a distinguished Spanish nobleman, the duke of Arcos. The ruse succeeded, and O'Reilly was captured and held for ransom. See Rodríguez, *Primeros años*. 295. For additional details of his pre-Louisiana career, see Gayarré, *History of Louisiana*, II, 286–87; David K. Bjork, "Alejandro O'Reilly and the Spanish Occupation of Louisiana, 1769–1770," in George Hammond (ed.), *New Spain and the Anglo-American West* (Lancaster, Pa., 1932), 166; and David K. Texada, *Alejandro O'Reilly and the New Orleans Rebels*, University of Southwestern Louisiana History Series, 2 (Lafayette, 1970), 23–26.

14. Quoted from Texada, *Alejandro O'Reilly*, 26. It is possible, of course, that he received oral orders from the king and Grimaldi supplemented these written orders. At

Having received his orders, O'Reilly sailed from the Galician port of La Coruña aboard the frigate *Palas* toward the end of May and after an uneventful trip across the Atlantic entered Havana harbor on June 24. With the full support of Bucareli, he quickly assembled men and supplies for the expedition. In the unbelievably short period of ten days, the convoy was ready to sail for Louisiana, eloquent testimony to his gift for logistics. The fleet, consisting of 21 ships, transported a contingent of 2,056 men, 46 cannon, food, medical supplies, and in addition a sum of 150,000 pesos to sustain the force on its arrival and to meet any debts of the provincial treasury.[15] Fittingly enough, to avenge the insult to the honor of his sovereign, General O'Reilly chose as his flagship the *Volante,* which had conveyed Ulloa to New Orleans in 1766 and had been in Havana since May. On the afternoon of July 6 the last of the vessels glided past the grim fortress of El Morro. Fair weather enabled the fleet to reach the mouth of the Mississippi on July 20, fourteen days later.

Few secrets in the annals of eighteenth-century Spanish diplomacy were better kept than the dispatch of O'Reilly's force to the Indies in 1769.[16] There were no leaks by disgruntled or disloyal bureaucrats to hamper the crown in enforcing its policy. The prying French ambassador in Madrid accused the secretary of state of "not being candid as to Spanish policy toward Louisiana." D'Ossun reported to Choiseul in the middle of April, "He told me only that Spain had suspended the transfer of funds to New Orleans for the troops and other governmental expenses and that he believed that this suspension would cause great hardship to the chiefs of the uprising." D'Ossun went on, "General O'Reilly will go soon to America to make another inspection of fortifications, arsenals, and troops in Mexico and around the

---

any rate, the general believed that he had a free hand in dealing with the plotters, because he did not bother to seek clarification of his original command or additional instructions after the trial.

15. Gayarré, *History of Louisiana,* II, 296, puts the number of men at 2,600, but his figure may include sailors and other ancillary personnel.

16. The orders for the expulsion of the Jesuits from America in 1767 are perhaps the best example of the complete loyalty of the bureaucracy. Although affecting hundreds of persons and enforced over a large area, they remained a secret until put into execution.

Gulf." When the French government did learn the true intention of O'Reilly's mission, the reoccupation force was already assembling in Havana. In a long letter dated June 8, Grimaldi instructed Fuentes to inform Choiseul of the purpose of Spanish policy and the means to realize it. Regarding the extent of authority conceded to the Irish general, "practicality could not permit an unequivocal definition. But as the king, whose character is known to all the world, is always inclined toward piety, he gave orders that it would be his royal pleasure to proceed with great moderation, being satisfied with expelling from the colony even those who deserved greater punishment." From his Bourbon cousin the Spanish monarch requested that a dispatch be sent to the rebels in Louisiana, disapproving their conduct and demanding that "as vassals they should ask for mercy and live subject to the laws he wished to impose."[17] In reply Choiseul expressed doubt that O'Reilly's mode of action was appropriate, since "a majority of the colonists may cross into English territory." Choiseul agreed, however, to comply with the request for a royal letter to the colonists, exhorting them to lay down their arms and obey the orders of the Spanish crown. To reassure Charles III, the French minister a week later repeated his full support of the plan for reoccupation.[18] It is clear from the foregoing that the French government was not fully aware of the methods to be used in subjugating the colonists. One may infer from Choiseul's letters that he regarded moderation and conciliation as the best means of regaining the loyalty and confidence of the colonists. Privately, Grimaldi could congratulate himself on the subtle handling of the diplomacy of the affair.[19] The veil of secrecy thrown around the organization and dispatch of the

17. D'Ossun to Choiseul, April 17, 1769, in Correspondance Politique, Espagne, DLVI, AAE; Grimaldi to Fuentes, June 8, 1769, in Leg. 3883, Estado, AHN.

18. Choiseul to d'Ossun, July 11, 17, 1769, both in Correspondance Politique, Espagne, DLVII, AAE. D'Ossun did not penetrate the curtain of concealment surrounding the expedition until the first week of July and, like Choiseul, was dubious over the employment of force "without first having tried to win back the minds of the inhabitants of the colony by conciliatory offers." See d'Ossun to Choiseul, July 8, 24, 1769, both in Correspondance Politique, Espagne, DLVII, AAE.

19. He was particularly elated by the energetic manner in which O'Reilly had executed his orders in organizing his force and concealing his movements from the colonists.

expedition had not been penetrated. Spain had afforded Great Britain no excuse or pretext for interference. More important, the French crown by virtue of the Family Compact stood firm in its resolve to fulfill the territorial concessions of the Treaty of Fontainebleau.

Grimaldi's reliance on overwhelming force and his complete concealment of the Spanish countermove proved well founded. The colonists were indeed startled and dismayed at the news of the presence of a hostile fleet at Balize. On July 24 General O'Reilly's aide-de-camp, Lieutenant Colonel Francisco Bouligny, reached New Orleans with a letter for Governor Aubry, notifying him of the general's arrival and of his intention to reoccupy Louisiana. Aubry placed his force at the disposal of the Spanish and promised to cooperate in every way in the restoration of their authority. On July 27, Aubry's senior officer and three representatives of the people, La Frenière, Marquis, and Joseph Milhet, journeyed down the river to confer with O'Reilly on the submission of the colony. La Frenière, as the principal spokesman for the settlers, declared that "the colony never had any intention of straying from the profound respect that it professes for the great monarch that Your Excellency represents. The severity of the nature of Don Antonio de Ulloa and the subversion of the privileges assured by the act of cession have been the only cause of the uprisings that occurred in the colony." This volte-face by the erstwhile conspirators was evidently intended to establish a basis for conciliation. Although courteous, O'Reilly was not influenced by this sudden show of respect for Spanish authority. His cautious response, with its promise to consider all aspects of the rebellion, seemed reassuring: "Gentlemen, it is not possible for me to judge things without first finding out about the prior circumstances; and, as soon as I arrive in the city, I shall devote all my attention to becoming

---

As he wrote to Fuentes, "The king is very satisfied with the rapidity that one believes very important for the realization of the objective proposed, for it is likely that the inhabitants of the colony were surprised. It is with this in mind that we kept the plan secret here as long as possible. We flatter ourselves that secrecy will have been extremely useful above all when it has been accompanied by promptness in execution." See Grimaldi to Fuentes, August 28, 1769, *ibid.*

informed about everything thoroughly, and you may be sure that my greatest pleasure will be to do good and that I shall regret very much to see myself compelled to do harm to anyone."[20]

After this outwardly friendly interview on the *Volante*, the colonial representatives returned to New Orleans. What was their reaction to this confrontation with O'Reilly? Their actions disclose that they were convinced of the futility of any resistance to the massive power of the Spanish army. Was Spanish policy to be essentially one of clemency to the participants in the rebellion and of general pardon to the populace? What was passing through the minds of La Frenière, Marquis, and Milhet at this critical moment, one will never know. From their later conduct one may infer that they did not foresee the severity of the sentences to be inflicted. No blood had been shed in the expulsion of Governor Ulloa. They had not been arrested on the *Volante* and thrown into prison without a trial. Surely, for their defiance of Spanish authority they expected some punishment that might take the form of fines, confiscation of property, imprisonment, or even banishment from the colony. But not one of the major conspirators attempted to flee to the sanctuary of West Florida, which would have been an instinctive reaction to a threat to life. Their passivity or inaction raises the question of evasiveness by O'Reilly. If he purposely adopted deception as a means of getting his hands on the chief figures in the plot, he was completely successful.[21]

20. A reliable source for this period is Bouligny's own account to O'Reilly, July 26, 1769, in Emile and Rosamunde E. Kuntz Collection, Howard-Tilton Memorial Library, Tulane University, New Orleans. O'Reilly did not believe that the delegates had come in good faith with the sole intent of asking for clemency. In his mind their real purposes were to gauge the possibility of resistance and to ascertain his attitude toward the leaders of the rebellion. Having seen the size of the Spanish force, they abandoned any idea of open opposition. See O'Reilly to Grimaldi, August 31, 1769, in Leg. 2543, Audiencia de Sto. Domingo, AGI. Before leaving Madrid, O'Reilly must have received Grimaldi's version of the insurrection, which was based largely on Ulloa's written reports and interviews. The Spanish minister's opinion of the uprising is perhaps best expressed in a communication to Fuentes: "The true aim of those colonists, and especially that of the prime movers of the sedition, is to live in absolute liberty, without laws, government, good order." See Grimaldi to Fuentes, June 8, 1769, in Leg. 3883, Estado, AHN.

21. One hesitates to agree with Fortier in emphasizing duplicity, yet these were

After notifying the Acadians and the Germans that they must under no circumstances bring armed forces into the city under pain of attack, O'Reilly played his next and most important card. On the night of August 16 the ships in the Spanish convoy lifted anchor and began to move up the river from Balize to New Orleans. Two days later occurred the traditional ceremony of the legal transfer of sovereignty from France to Spain, one that Ulloa had desperately wanted but had lacked the troops to fulfill. Bouligny has left us a brief description of the fanfare and pagentry involved in the procedure:

> Everything was ready for the 18th when possession was taken of the Plaza with all the form and ceremony appropriate. Our troops in the center of the Plaza occupied three sides of a square and the French soldiers closed the square. The General disembarked at 5:30 P.M. and came to the center of the Plaza, where he presented to M. Aubry that which he was waiting for, namely the order of His Catholic Majesty. Immediately, the latter placed at his feet the keys of the city. At the same time Spanish flags were run up in various parts of the city, and the artillery and the troops on the Plaza fired a general salute. After this, our General, with the French commander and all the officers, whose duties permitted them, entered the church, where a Te Deum was sung as an act of Thanksgiving.[22]

After fulfilling all the requirements and proprieties stipulated by international law and custom to establish territorial sovereignty, O'Reilly turned to the chastisement of the leaders of the insurrection. To him this was of grave concern, for the honor and prestige of the monarch of the leading house in Europe were at stake. From a practical viewpoint, given the tradition of lawlessness and disorder, there was no assurance that in a moment of crisis or weakness in Europe the French colonials might not overturn the regime again or act in a fashion detrimental to its well-being. In the interview with La Frenière and his companions on the frigate, the general had nevertheless promised to deal fairly and justly with the members of the conspiracy. On the day following the formal occupation, O'Reilly ordered the

---

intelligent men who believed that they had committed no crime deserving of the supreme penalty, since no blood had been spilled.

22. Bouligny's account of the formality of occupation, quoted in Texada, *Alejandro O'Reilly*, 33.

French governor to furnish him with a complete account of the uprising. Although Aubry did not provide a full list of the plotters, there was enough evidence for formal accusations to be made against the principal figures.[23] General O'Reilly then invited the accused, with the exception of Foucault, to his residence for a conference. Upon their arrival they were shown the charges leveled against them, arrested, and imprisoned. These persons were La Frenière, Pierre Hardi de Boisblanc, Balthasar Masan, Joseph Villeré,[24] Pierre Marquis, Pierre Poupet, Joseph Petit, Pierre Caresse, Julien Jerome Doucet, Jean Milhet, Joseph Milhet, Jean Baptiste Noyan, and Denis Braud.[25]

It was necessary at the same time for the Spanish authorities to have the goodwill of the New Orleans mercantile and propertied classes and of the citizens of the city and province. Hence the general assembled the merchants of New Orleans and promised no punishment for their part in the rebellion.[26] An amnesty was proclaimed for the residents of the city and region who had been "led astray by the intrigues of ambitious . . . people." To impress upon the people the necessity for unqualified obedience to the Spanish crown, O'Reilly ordered all residents of the capital to take a solemn oath of fealty to Charles III. After the oath was given, each person affixed his signature to a formulary, which was duly sent to Spain.[27]

23. O'Reilly to Aubry, August 19, 1769, in Leg. 2543, Audiencia de Sto. Domingo, AGI. It is to O'Reilly's credit that he was determined to secure the evidence from the testimony of witnesses present in the city at that time. "I did not believe it desirable," he informed Grimaldi, "to undertake any judicial inquiry until the formality of possession had taken place, or to avail myself of an *informe* from Ulloa, who as the injured party would be suspected [of prejudice] by all." See O'Reilly to Grimaldi, August 31, 1769, in Leg. 2543, Audiencia de Sto. Domingo, AGI.

24. Villeré, who was not present at O'Reilly's residence, died shortly after the issuance of orders for his arrest under circumstances that are still unclear. Gayarré, *History of Louisiana*, II, 306, leans to the theory that he was the victim of a stroke. The testimony available during the trial points to the fact that he died of wounds received when resisting arrest. His was the first blood to be shed in the revolution. See Rodríguez, *Primeros años*, 339, 340.

25. O'Reilly ordered Braud's release later when it was obvious that he was simply carrying out the orders of the commissary. See Gayarré, *History of Louisiana*, II, 313.

26. Texada, *Alejandro O'Reilly*, 34, 35.

27. Proclamation of amnesty, August 21, 1769, and proclamation, August 23, 1769, both in Leg. 2543, Audiencia de Sto. Domingo, AGI. The clergy was also required to

Only one last detail, an important one, remained for O'Reilly before beginning the trial of the conspirators. This concerned Nicolas Foucault, who along with La Frenière was a principal in the insurrection. On the basis of the document entitled *Mémoire des habitants et négociants de la Louisiane sur l'evénement du 29 octobre, 1768,* printed by Denis Braud on the commissary's orders, and other evidence, O'Reilly commanded Aubry to arrest Foucault. Aubry immediately had this official confined to his house under guard, suspended from his duties as commissary, and replaced by Bobé Descloseaux.[28] One should note that this act was carried out by a French functionary, since Foucault was a French administrator ordered by his government to remain in the colony until financial arrangements had been satisfactorily made with the Spanish crown. O'Reilly wisely recognized Foucault's special jurisdictional status and refrained from treating him as an ordinary prisoner. Nevertheless, O'Reilly secretly hoped to secure from the commissary through Aubry a confession of wrongdoing or, if not this, at least supporting evidence to convict the other conspirators, before Foucault was sent back to France for trial according to the criminal code of that country.

In the dramatic struggle between Spaniard and Frenchman, the trial of the leaders of the rebellion was the main event of the final act. Although O'Reilly believed that those arrested were guilty in varying degrees, the proceedings were not a farce or a foregone conclusion. That the trial was held in private and did not include a jury was consonant with Spanish custom and practice. The key figure in ascertaining guilt or innocence was the *promotor fiscal,* or prosecuting attorney, Felix Del Rey. He was an experienced lawyer who had served in a similar capacity in the *audiencias* of Santo Domingo and New Spain and had accompanied O'Reilly from Havana. The official secretary of the expedition, Francisco Xavier Rodríguez, was his assistant.[29] It was

---

take this oath. See O'Reilly to Munian, August 31, 1769, in Leg. 2543, Audiencia de Sto. Domingo, AGI.

28. O'Reilly to Aubry, August 23, 1769, and Aubry to O'Reilly, August 24, 1769, both *ibid.*

29. O'Reilly to Bucareli, June 27, 1769, in Dispatches of the Spanish Governors of Louisiana, I.

Del Rey's purpose to show that the accused were guilty of treason and sedition in expelling the lawful governor Antonio de Ulloa from Louisiana. To this end the prosecuting attorney counted on the testimony of the French commander Charles Aubry, who was present from the beginning of the uprising and presumably was aware of the attitudes and acts of the accused. In addition, sworn statements were to be given by the Spanish functionaries Esteban Gayarré, the auditor; Martin Navarro, the royal treasurer; Juan José de Loyola, the commissary; and José Melchor de Acosta, captain of the *Volante*. There would be, of course, confessions from persons hoping that last-minute repentance might soften their sentences.

In listing the causes of the rebellion for the court, Aubry asserted that the Superior Council's ambitions were a major factor.[30] To counter any allegation that he was caught off guard by the sudden eruption of events, the French commander declared that he had learned of the plot four days before the revolt was to occur and so informed the Spanish governor. In contradiction, Ulloa's version implies that it was he who apprised Aubry of the dangerous turn of affairs. Every effort was made, so Aubry said, on his part to stifle the uprising. According to him, Ulloa agreed to meet with representatives of the colonists individually to listen to their grievances. Contrary to their promises, the conspirators presented themselves in the city, armed and accompanied by large numbers of settlers. Having only a hundred men in his force to pit against a thousand colonists, Aubry testified that he could do nothing and so was compelled to stand by as the Spanish governor withdrew from New Orleans. He made charges against most of the accused, singling out Foucault—for whom he had a personal antipathy—as the most culpable, since the commissary had backed La Frenière even though he knew that Louisiana was legally Spain's.[31] One must

30. Aubry to O'Reilly, August 20, 1769, in Leg. 2543, Audiencia de Sto. Domingo, AGI.

31. Aubry's testimony is given in Rodríguez, *Primeros años*, 395–402. This is his letter of August 20, 1769, to O'Reilly, attached to O'Reilly's communication to Grimaldi, October 17, 1769, in Leg. 2543, Audiencia de Sto. Domingo, AGI. See also the preceding chapter herein for Ulloa's account of what happened.

not overlook the likelihood of bias in Aubry's version, since he was bent on proving his loyalty to the Spanish regime by removing any suspicion of complicity in or sympathy with the uprising. Damaging testimony against the accused men was given also by the various Spanish officials. In general, to them the chief culprit and ringleader was La Frenière.

From the written and oral evidence presented by the witnesses, Del Rey prepared his case against the accused. In his brief the prosecutor depicted the background of the revolt, summed up the case against each of the prisoners, whether principal or accomplice, and finally cited the Spanish laws concerning treason and sedition with the sentences for those found guilty. As a basic point in his case, he affirmed that Louisiana was legally a Spanish domain by virtue of Ulloa's raising the red and yellow standard of the Spanish Bourbons at Balize and other outposts in the province, even though the fleur-de-lis of the French branch of the family continued to fly at New Orleans, the capital.[32] The leaders of the rebellion had challenged the king's authority, personified by Governor Antonio de Ulloa, an offense punishable by death and the seizure of property by the crown. To the prosecutor there was ample evidence of treason. "The insurrectionists conspired openly against the Realm, drawing the colony away from the Catholic domination, execrating laws, the government, and the nation, with furious invectives, and this is in hatred of the crown . . . which is also covered by this last law: 'In hatred of Him or of the Realm.' " Sedition, or the incitement of the citizenry to rebel against lawful authority, was also punishable by death and confiscation of property. Del Rey claimed that the leaders were guilty of violating this law as well, inasmuch as Louisiana was rightfully a Spanish possession: "That crime was

32. Grimaldi maintained that Spain had not formally taken possession of the colony owing to a lack of troops. Was it therefore necessary for O'Reilly to go through all the formalities of the act of possession when the Spanish forces landed if this had already occurred? There is no doubt, however, that *de facto* Louisiana was a Spanish province even if some of the legal requirements had not been fulfilled. See acusación de promotor fiscal, attached to O'Reilly to Grimaldi, October 28, 1769, in Leg. 2543, Audiencia de Sto. Domingo, AGI.

perpetrated against His Most Catholic Majesty and his State . . . in this colony, which he had gained possession of through the ministry of Don Antonio de Ulloa, and the right to which he held by virtue of the act of cession from His Most Christian King, which [act] was obeyed by the Council and was made public in the colony by his order."[33]

The next step in the trial was the formal interrogation of the prisoners. Del Rey summoned each one in turn, notified him of the charges made by the crown, and permitted him to acknowledge or deny the validity of the allegations. If the accused affirmed his innocence, he was allowed to challenge point by point the charges in the indictment. The judge's decision in the case was, however, final. This procedure was normal in a system of criminal law inherited largely from precepts of Roman jurisprudence.

The oral examination began naturally with those considered to be the central figures in the rebellion. La Frenière, the attorney general, was accused of organizing the plot in collaboration with Foucault, stirring up the people against the Spanish, and taking the lead in the conciliar deliberations of October 29 which led to the ouster of the Spanish governor. To these charges was added the responsibility for drafting the memorial of October 27. From perusing this portion of the proceedings, one gets the impression that the attorney general lost some of his bravado in his appearance before Del Rey.[34] La Frenière was undoubtedly aware that his status in the colony was unlike that of Foucault, who was a permanent official of the ministry of marine and had orders to return to France as soon as the arrangements affecting the currency had been made. La Frenière's position was purely local, its functions associated with the Superior Council. Hence it was impossible for him to claim the jurisdiction of French law and seek a trial in France. Despite the recital of extensive incriminating evidence, La Frenière rejected the charges, claiming

33. Quoted in Texada, *Alejandro O'Reilly*, 46.
34. *Ibid.*, 48.

that Ulloa had been ejected from the colony as a private citizen, not as a Spanish governor, since there was no *de jure* government. As to the authorship of the memorial, he contended that the blame should be assigned to Pierre Caresse. In view of the lengthy testimony to the contrary presented by other witnesses, Del Rey rejected the defense as untenable.[35]

Jean Baptiste Noyan, although a nephew of Jean Baptiste Le Moyne, the sieur de Bienville, was like La Frenière denounced by the prosecutor as a principal in the conspiracy. It was claimed that he had used his influence and powers of persuasion to secure from the council the vote for the governor's expulsion. Specifically, he was charged with having induced the Acadians to arm themselves and then to enter New Orleans to demonstrate against Spanish authority. Noyan did not deny the charges but maintained that his first loyalty was to Louis XV, so that his actions could not be regarded as seditious. Del Rey considered this defense without foundation, for acts of violence against Charles III constituted proof of disloyalty to the French monarch.[36]

Against the Swiss Pierre Marquis, the charges were grave indeed. As colonel of the militia, he had employed the force under his command to threaten the Spanish regime. Not only had he served as a syndic, or deputy, in the Superior Council after Ulloa's ejection, but in defiance of Spain and France had urged the formation of a republic, a form of government contrary to Spanish tradition and history. It was impossible for him to controvert the abundant testimony to his acts, which were well known throughout the city.[37]

A fourth person whom the crown considered an instigator of the plot was Pierre Caresse. His offenses included placing himself at the head of the band of Acadians entering New Orleans to demonstrate against the Spanish regime, serving as one of the new syndics in the council, and finally of composing parts of the

35. Rodríguez, *Primeros años,* 474–82.
36. Texada, *Alejandro O'Reilly,* 49, 50.
37. *Ibid.,* 50.

Mémoire des habitants et négociants. His defense, which was similarly turned down by the prosecutor, followed the pattern of a majority of the accused, namely a denial of the legality of the government established in the colony.[38]

For his part in arousing the citizenry, particularly in persuading the merchants and other prominent people to support the remonstrances to the French crown, Del Rey regarded Joseph Milhet as guilty of serious crimes. Milhet had also, according to the accusation, told the Acadians that it would be in their interest to force the Spanish to leave. These acts constituted sedition. Milhet sought to defend his action by claiming that, as a leader of the militia, he was simply carrying out the orders of his superior, Marquis. In substantiating Milhet's culpability, the crown asserted that his plea was additional evidence of treason, for, in reality, Aubry as governor commanded all the French military units.[39]

The last of the major instigators in the Spanish indictment was Joseph Villeré. His sudden death at the time of his arrest did not prevent the crown from trying him *in absentia*. Not only had he been an agitator among the Germans against the Spanish, but he had prevented Ulloa's agent St. Maxent from paying off the government's debts to the Acadians and the Germans to satisfy their demands and thus forestall a march on New Orleans. There was no plea offered by relatives or friends in mitigation of a charge of treason.[40]

The remaining prisoners were charged by the prosecutor as accomplices, major or minor. Although they contributed to the temporary success of the rebellion, their sentences were obviously to be milder than those imposed on the instigators, consisting of banishment, imprisonment, confiscation of property, or fines. In this group were six persons. Joseph Petit had denounced publicly the commercial decrees and had helped to force the *Volante* to leave, and Balthasar Masan had served as

38. *Ibid.*, 50–52.
39. *Ibid.*, 52, 53.
40. *Ibid.*, 53, 54.

treasurer for the rebels and refrained from coming to Aubry's assistance in a move against the conspirators. Jerome Doucet, the lawyer, and Jean Milhet were both charged with collaborating with the ringleaders. Del Rey accused the former of having had a part in drafting a memorial that justified the act of revolution on the grounds of the right of all people by natural law to throw off the shackles of oppression. In the crown's estimation Milhet had played a minor role in the revolt, having openly criticized the commercial decrees and having been a member of a militia unit taking orders from Marquis rather than from Aubry. It was asserted that Pierre Poupet had acted as fiscal officer for the post-Ulloa regime, even donating funds of his own to the treasury. Although cleared of any part in forming the plot, he confessed having been an armed demonstrator in New Orleans on October 29. The last of those denounced as accomplices was the banker Pierre Hardi de Boisblanc. There was no direct evidence to show that he had taken part in the development of the plot to destroy the Spanish regime, but he had agreed to provide finances for the new government, organizing for this purpose the Banque de Mont de Piété. His intimate association with La Frenière and Foucault was damaging.[41]

During the course of the trial, the Spanish government made a futile attempt to obtain a confession from the French commissary. Less conspicuous than La Frenière in the public eye, Foucault may well have been the brains of the cabal, but because of his secretiveness there has been a tendency to accord him second place in the ranks of the rebels. It was clear to O'Reilly that Foucault could not be treated as an ordinary criminal owing to his status as an important official of the French government. Since August 24 Foucault had been under arrest at Duplantier's house on the wharf, near the Ursuline convent. Acting on orders from O'Reilly, Aubry, accompanied by an officer of the Lisbon regiment and the chief clerk of the Superior Council, proceeded on October 5 to the residence to conduct an interrogatory of the prisoner. Aubry subsequently described Foucault's posture as

41. *Ibid.*, 54–59.

that of a voluntary mute, refusing to answer any question, even his name, age, and position, or to sign the papers of the inquiry. Throughout the inquest he steadfastly maintained that no Spanish court had jurisdiction over a French official, unless specifically ordered to do so from Versailles.

The items in the interrogatory, formulated from the testimony of witnesses, confessions of the accused, and other evidence, point to the commissary's grave implication in the Spanish governor's expulsion from the colony:

1. Did Monsieur Caresse give him on October 25 or 26 the representation of the residents and merchants demanding the withdrawal of Ulloa and all the Spaniards?

2. Did he call a meeting of the Superior Council to discuss Ulloa's exile, knowing that this was not a prerogative of the council?

3. Had he not authorized the election of six new councilors, he himself proposing two of the names?

4. Had he not given a dinner in his apartment to the members of the council to celebrate the passage of the decree [of expulsion], and had he not visited Aubry to congratulate him on taking over the government and marched through the streets to receive the plaudits of the crowd?

5. Had he not given permission for the printing and sale of the seditious *Mémoire des habitants et négociants de la Louisiane sur l'evénement du 29 octobre?*

6. Why did he not join with Aubry in protesting the passage of the decrees expelling Ulloa and the frigate *Volante?*

7. Had he not been since October 29 closely associated with La Frenière, Marquis, and others involved in the plot?

8. Had he not on October 29 advised the colonists to act concerning matters of navigation, functioning of departments, etc., as if France were still governing the colony?

9. Had he not failed to carry out Ulloa's request that all French ships arriving in New Orleans should have licenses from the Spanish secretary of state?

In conclusion, how could he oppose the occupation of the colony by Ulloa when he was expressly ordered to recognize the Spanish official as the new governor?[42]

Although fully convinced of Foucault's culpability, O'Reilly did not believe that he could be held indefinitely in custody in New

---

42. Interrogatory, enclosed in Aubry to Praslin, October 6, 1769, in C13A49, Colonies, AN.

Orleans. It was proper to accede to his plea for a trial by authorities in France. "I am very happy," the general confided to Grimaldi, "that he be judged by his own court.... He is a narrow-minded, conceited person who has deceived nearly everybody here, as it is easy to judge by the extent of his indebtedness ... I am of the opinion that the fear of being unable to pay this off was the chief cause of his misdoings."[43] Accordingly, arrangements were made for the commissary's departure under guard on the French brigantine *Père de Famille* and for his detention and interrogation on arrival in France. Sailing on October 17, the vessel docked at La Rochelle on December 14. On January 10 Foucault was taken to the Bastille, where a three-day interrogatory began on February 14. A full confession exposed his involvement with the plotters, and he was sentenced to prison for an indefinite term.[44]

With this potential troublemaker on the high seas, O'Reilly undoubtedly felt freer to deal with the remaining conspirators. On October 20, he received Del Rey's recommendations on the guilt of the principals and accomplices. Four days later he handed down the sentences: the death penalty for La Frenière, Noyan, Caresse, Joseph Milhet, Marquis, and Villeré (already deceased); ten years' imprisonment for Masan and Doucet; and six years in prison for Jean Milhet, Poupet, and Boisblanc.

Since New Orleans had no public hangman, the death penalty had to be implemented through other means. The execution of the five men was therefore carried out by a firing squad at 3:00 P.M. on October 25, 1769, in the barracks yard of the Lisbon regiment. The official report of the Spanish authorities provides no significant details of the act, no mention of cries of the condemned or outbursts from the citizenry. There is in the archives of the Ursuline convent adjoining the barracks a notation that the sound of a volley came from the direction of the

43. O'Reilly to Grimaldi, October 17, 1769, *ibid.* Aubry put Foucault's debts at sixty thousand livres, a sum owed to a number of persons. See Aubry to Praslin, October 5, 1769, *ibid.*

44. See Interrogatoire fait de l'ordre du roi à Denis Foucault, in Correspondance Politique, Espagne, DLIX, AAE.

military area in the afternoon of that day. According to the clerk of the expedition, the men were "bound by the arms"; after the sentence had been read, first in Spanish and then in French, they were "placed at the spot where they were to suffer the death penalty." Marc de Villiers du Terrage, citing Champigny, Bossu, and other eighteenth-century authors, asserts that the condemned spoke out courageously at the last moment, but states that the accounts differ as to what was actually uttered. It is not unlikely that, given their past course of action, their protestations contained sentiments of allegiance to Louis, "le Bien Aimé."[45]

Even though they had shed no blood, they were given no opportunity to appeal to Charles III for a stay of execution or a commutation of sentence. As part of the final settlement, the property of the convicted conspirators was seized by the crown and sold at auction to provide funds for payment of debts to creditors, of doweries, and of dues to the state.[46] The five persons condemned to imprisonment were taken to Havana for incarceration in El Morro, the Spanish counterpart of the Bastille in the Caribbean. There were, of course, other influential persons in the colony who had either quietly encouraged the rebels or remained neutral in the uprisings. To the crown they constituted a future source of danger and had to be dealt with.[47]

The fate of Charles Aubry might well have been predicted.

45. Rodríguez, *Primeros años*, 342; Fortier, *A History of Louisiana*, I, 226; Villiers, *Les dernières années*, 311–12.

46. Like Foucault, La Frenière was also heavily in debt. See Estado que manifiesta el producto total y distrivución de los bienes sequestrados a los reos de estado, in Leg. 20,854, Consejo de Indias, AHN.

47. In a report to Luis de Unzaga, his successor in Louisiana, the general listed twenty-one persons who were expelled from the colony for suspected sympathy or complicity in the uprising. Three Jews were banished at the same time because of their religious faith and their supposed reputation for sharp dealing. Because of his failure to aid the Spanish in time of crisis and because of his daughter's marriage to Joseph Villeré, d'Arensburg, the commandant of the German settlement, came under suspicion. His family was required to sell its estate on the river above New Orleans and move to Opelousas. The chevalier, because of his advanced age, was permitted to remain in the capital. O'Reilly refused to permit Julien Lesassier, a deputy of the Superior Council to the French court, to return to Louisiana, since he had spoken out in behalf of the colonists in Paris. See O'Reilly to Unzaga, December 17, 1769, and O'Reilly to Arriaga, December 10, 1769, both in Kinnaird (ed.), *Spain in the Mississippi Valley*, II, 103.

Hated by the colonists for his revelations to the Spanish concerning the conspiracy, he could hardly remain in the colony as a private citizen even if he had so wished. Moreover, he had expressed his desire to retire from the army and return to France. Nor could the Spanish authorities, despite his cooperation with O'Reilly, completely forget that he had refused to enlist in the Spanish army in 1766 and that he had been unable to persuade any of his officers or men to. It was in part his lack of boldness and the weakness of the French regime that had compelled Ulloa to rely entirely on the small contingent, which proved inadequate in dealing with the colonial militia and the demonstrators. Consequently, Aubry was permitted to leave New Orleans for France in January, 1770. Unfortunately, the vessel foundered at the mouth of the Garonne River, and he lost his life. The inferences drawn from his lengthy correspondence with the ministry of marine and from other sources make it doubtful that he accumulated a fortune by dishonest means. A letter of June 20, 1768, from Grimaldi to Ulloa authorized payment of three thousand pesos to the French governor for his services when Spanish troops arrived from Havana to take possession of the colony. This sum was turned over to him by O'Reilly in fulfillment of this promise.[48]

For the suppression of the revolt O'Reilly received the approval of the king. He had restored Spanish authority, in the course of which he had punished the traitors and seditionmongers according to the precepts of Castilian law. In a communication of January 27, 1770, Grimaldi conveyed the monarch's gratitude: "The complete justification of the proceed-

---

48. Davis, *Louisiana,* 104. There were no accusations of graft, peculation, or bribery made by the plotters or other witnesses against Aubry during the trial. Had he been as wealthy as Fortier says or as involved, it stands to reason that references to this would have come out in the judicial proceedings. See Fortier, *A History of Louisiana,* I, 220; Kinnaird (ed.), *Spain in the Mississippi Valley,* II, 50; and O'Reilly to Grimaldi, March 1, 1770, in Leg. 2582, Audiencia de Sto. Domingo, AGI. That he had influential friends in France is evident from a letter received by the ministry of marine objecting to invidious references to his conduct in the *affaire de Louisiane* in the *Gazette de Monaco* and requesting that orders be given forcing a retraction of certain statements. See [?] to Praslin, September 21, 1769, in Correspondance Politique, Espagne, DLVII, AAE.

ings against those condemned to death and prison, the moderation in reducing the punishment to what was absolutely necessary to bring about the tranquillity and the good of the province, and your assurance to the rest that no reminders of their crime will subsist, are very comfortable to the pious soul of the King. Your Excellency was well advised of the royal intentions, put them into full effect, and the assurance which I gave him of this may serve as a source of satisfaction."[49] When O'Reilly arrived in Madrid in June, 1770, he was permitted an audience with Charles III and was awarded a purse of two thousand pesos for the successful fulfillment of his mission to Louisiana. For the time being, his star was in the ascendency at the Spanish court.

What was the reaction of the French court to the trial and execution of five prominent colonists in the former province? Assuming that Choiseul's reliance on the Family Compact was a cornerstone for European policy, one would not look for any censure of Spanish action unless it proceeded to the extreme of wholesale deportation. At Grimaldi's insistence, Praslin had written on August 12, 1769, to Aubry and Foucault, demanding

---

49. Grimaldi to O'Reilly, January 27, 1770, in Kinnaird (ed.), *Spain in the Mississippi Valley*, II, 181, 182.

Despite Grimaldi's approval of O'Reilly's measures for quelling the revolt, common sense and circumstantial evidence support the view that the Spanish minister did not anticipate the execution of five prominent citizens of New Orleans: (1) His assurances to the French government before July, 1769, that no punitive steps would be taken, no bloodshed having occurred; (2) the risk of disturbing or even jeopardizing the good relations with France by such an indiscretion; and (3) his repeated efforts to get French approval for O'Reilly's acts. Had this been an Indian uprising in Peru or Mexico, ruthlessness would have been the keynote of the day. I am inclined to judge the general's action as one of "overzealousness," perfectly consonant with the character of an ambitious, aggressive, military opportunist. See Boulle, "French Reactions to the Louisiana Revolution," 156.

That the crown could settle an uprising without resorting to a rigorous application of the law is revealed in the creole revolt against the Caracas Company of Venezuela in 1749. The rebels under a certain Francisco de Leon, inspired by a fear for their economic interests and by personal ambition, threatened the capital with a force of nine thousand men. By adroit diplomacy, the governor managed to disperse the rebels. Despite overt acts of rebellion, the crown sent the leader in chains to Cádiz, where he died after months of imprisonment. His son, who participated also in the insurrection, was forced to serve for an indefinite period in the royal army at Oran as punishment. See Francisco Morales Padrón, *Rebelión contra la compañía de Caracas* (Seville, 1955), 139–42.

that the colonial officials and the people recognize the cession of the region. To a large degree, he maintained, the blame should rest with the Superior Council:

> His Majesty was indignant at what was done against the Spanish governor and well believes that the excesses to which the movement went are the work of the council.... All the estates of the colony had submitted without reservation. Governor Ulloa had been welcomed with greatest signs of jubilation, and the inhabitants, resolved to remain under Spanish rule, enjoyed the greatest tranquillity until October, 1768, and it is then only that, on the occasion of a decree regulating the commerce of the colony and the equipping of ships to be done in European ports, the colony dared to disregard the authority of a governor recognized by all the estates which had hastened to assure him of their homage. The Superior Council, instead of calming these [agitated] minds by resorting to the legitimate route of representation, engaged itself entirely in stirring up the settlers by secret means; it made haste to receive the audacious memorial by which the settlers requested the expulsion of the governor, and it dared to add six members to its body to confirm the decree, branding Ulloa as usurper, on illegal authority, and enjoining him to withdraw from the colony in three days.... It is they above all who must appease the just anger of His Catholic Majesty by hastening to give prompt proof of submission to the orders that His Majesty sends to Louisiana.[50]

Although the letter from Praslin arrived too late in New Orleans to directly assist O'Reilly, it strengthened the feeling in Madrid that its resolute measures for reoccupation were being fully backed by the French crown. On October 5, 1769, Choiseul relayed to Charles III through d'Ossun his best wishes for the fortuitous outcome of O'Reilly's expedition. "We do not desire less sincerely than Spain that the force assigned to M. O'Reilly succeed perfectly according to His Catholic Majesty's plan." In spite of earlier expressions of support, Grimaldi still felt the need to be assured of French backing for Spanish policy. Writing to Fuentes in Paris after learning of O'Reilly's arrival, he declared that "the king was satisfied with the conduct of the general, who has complied with instructions that were given him to

50. Praslin to Aubry and Foucault, August 12, 1769, in C13A49, Colonies, AN. A copy of this letter was sent to Choiseul for dispatch to Spain.

restore the honor and dignity of his sovereign and that of the nation and to mete out justice, tempering this with as much clemency as possible. His Majesty desires that the conduct of O'Reilly merit the approbation of His Most Christian Majesty as it has merited that of His Majesty." Three weeks later Fuentes, upon receiving a note from the French premier reiterating Louis XV's backing, expressed the thanks of Charles III for this statement of policy: "The king my master will see, monsieur, with true pleasure this approval of the king his cousin and he will be very appreciative of the sincere signs of interest and friendship given him in this situation."[51] Grimaldi, with the assurance of French support, had won a diplomatic victory in Europe, despite the potentiality for discord and misunderstanding that existed as a result of Spanish policy in North America. Spain had thus reclaimed Louisiana. With or without the connivance of Grimaldi, O'Reilly had presented Louis XV and the other European powers with a *fait accompli*. There was no stay of execution until the Spanish and French rulers had specifically approved the implementation of the sentences handed down for treason and sedition.

It has been asserted that the unfortunate events in Louisiana from October, 1768, to October, 1769, formed the opening chapter in the history of the movement for independence in North America in the eighteenth century. In retrospect, was it a precursor of the revolution in the English colonies to the north? Were its leaders "patriot-martyrs" for the cause of liberty and independence? It is impossible to support this thesis in its entirety. There was no formal declaration of independence, with the idea of establishing a separate and distinct government. True, the plan for a republic had been proposed by the Swiss-born Pierre Marquis, who headed a small minority of the discontented, but it was speedily turned down as impractical by La Frenière and Foucault. In rejecting Spanish control, the rebels

51. Choiseul to d'Ossun, October 5, 1769, Grimaldi to Fuentes, December 7, 1769, and Fuentes to Choiseul, December 27, 1769, all in Correspondance Politique, Espagne, DLVII, AAE.

advocated retrocession to France as a means of solving their problems, for under the French crown they had enjoyed a period of relaxed authority because of the distance from Europe and the exigencies of the Seven Years' War.

Yet the revolt of 1768 resembles the American Revolution in two ways. Basically, the cause of the uprisings in both sectors of the continent was economic. In Louisiana the imposition of the commercial decrees of 1766 and 1768 threatened to terminate the freedom of trade that the colonists had enjoyed during the years of neglect by France. If enforced, Spanish mercantilism meant an end to profitable exploitation of familiar markets and trade routes and the forced development of unknown markets. The merchant-planter oligarchy in New Orleans, aware that the colony's prosperity depended on foreign trade, regarded the future economy as dismal and unproductive. Unlike in the English colonies, however, their grievances represented the interests of a small group centered in the capital, which limited their revolutionary action to a smaller base of operation. It is dubious also that the leaders in New Orleans were patriot-martyrs, in view of the fact that their personal fortunes hinged on retaining French control. Ulloa and Aubry both contended that La Frenière and Foucault were heavily in debt, the relief of which depended on maintenance of the French ties. Moreover, with its relatively large appointee membership, the Superior Council, which figured prominently in the rebellion, was hardly the counterpart of the more representative English colonial assembly. Notwithstanding these reservations, there was expressed in the resentment toward Spanish authority an inherent localism or regionalism that had developed over a long time. Undoubtedly, the colonists were apprehensive over the adoption of a new official language, code of law, court, and administrative system, even though sharing the same religious faith. It was generally understood that the Superior Council would be abolished and replaced by a Spanish judicial and administrative body. Like the English settlers, the Louisianians cherished the customs, privileges, and rights gained from France during the period of neglect. Perhaps the antagonism to the new system was deeper and more widespread than has hitherto been surmised. The document "Manifeste des habitants, négociants, et colons de la province de la Louisiane au sujet de la révolution qui est arrivée le 29 octobre, 1768," denies the monarch's authority to dispose of Louisiana without the consent of its people and establishes the doctrine of popular sovereignty derived from the possession of natural rights. In harboring feelings of opposition and resentment toward the imposition of European sovereignty, the French and English rebels stood on common ground.[52]

Like the thirteen colonies in 1783, Louisiana in 1769, after the revolt had been quelled, aspired to recovery and rehabilitation. Through the enactment of beneficial decrees, the Spanish crown might seek to make the colony a functioning cog in the imperial machinery and to replace the distrust engendered in the creole mind by the rigorous restoration of authority with loyalty and fidelity to a Spanish Bourbon. As it developed, the foundation of Spanish domination in Louisiana for the next thirty-odd years was the handiwork of Alexander O'Reilly.

52. For an elaboration of this interpretation, see Jo Ann Carrigan's excellent commentary to Alcée Fortier, *A History of Louisiana* (2nd ed., 2 vols.; Baton Rouge, 1966), I, 344–46.

Epilogue

After the purge of the rebels, O'Reilly directed his tremendous energies to achieve stability and prosperity for Louisiana. Time was of the essence, since the cost of the expeditionary force, billeted in the capital, was a drain on the treasury. Ulloa, during his two-and-one-half-year stay in the colony, had recognized its serious political and economic problems and had haltingly sought to alleviate them with the limited means at his command. Having substantial military and financial resources, O'Reilly could restructure the government, modify the commercial system to the colonists' advantage, and improve the defenses along the land and water perimeter.

From the moment that he set foot in the colony, the Spanish general realized the need to modify the provincial government to conform with that of the imperial system. Ulloa had already recommended the elimination of the Superior Council because of its incompetence as a judicial body and because of its reluctance to accept his orders. In a letter of October 17, 1769, O'Reilly notified Arriaga that by virtue of the royal cedula of April 16, 1769, he would abolish the French conciliar institution and replace it with a cabildo, or *ayuntamiento,* comprising two alcaldes to be elected annually, six proprietary *regidores,* or aldermen, and other officials, such as an attorney general and a town clerk.[1] This was the typical local institution, or council, of the Spanish American municipality.

1. O'Reilly to Arriaga, October 17, 1769, in Leg. 2543, Audiencia de Sto. Domingo, AGI.

To assimilate the colony into the empire it would be necessary to fit Louisiana into one of the major governmental units. Accordingly, the captain general of Havana would exercise jurisdiction as he did in Cuba and Florida. Appeals from the various courts would go to a special tribunal in Havana, which included the captain general as president, the auditors of the military and navy departments of the island, the fiscal of the exchequer, and the government secretary. All legal proceedings had to be in Castilian, which, it was believed, would become the language of the population. As an additional step toward assimilation, O'Reilly, in November, 1769, declared null and void the French laws. In their place he issued a code, known as the Code O'Reilly, drawn chiefly from the Laws of the Indies, Alfonso X's *Siete Partidas*, and the French Black Code of 1724. With his characteristic sense of urgency, the general summoned the newly appointed cabildo to its first session on December 1. To house the town council, he ordered the construction of a *casa de cabildo*, or town hall, which was not ready for occupancy until August 17, 1770. It was arranged also that the cabildo should be given land and shops in the city to supplement its income.[2] For the administration of the parishes, forming eleven districts, O'Reilly designated commandants. These officers, with the rank of captain or below, had civil and military powers. Although their primary function was to preserve law and order, they had jurisdiction in some civil cases and served as notary publics, with a right to record inventories and sales of properties of deceased persons. This represented an adaptation of the French local regime.[3] The final step in the transformation of the provincial government was the transfer of supervisory authority from the secretary of state to the minister of the Indies. This did not materialize until the fall of 1770. In a letter of November 24, Grimaldi notified the governor of Louisiana of Charles III's decision to integrate the colony fully into the empire because of its "greater reciprocal

2. Davis, *Louisiana*, 105; Gayarré, *History of Louisiana*, III, 1–26.
3. See James Miller, "Commandant System in Louisiana Under Spain" (M.A. thesis, Louisiana State University, 1965).

commerce [with Cuba] and because of the court of appeals, which is to be established in Havana."[4]

To alleviate the economic distress of the colonists appeared almost as significant to General O'Reilly as the restructuring of the political regime. Had not the commercial decree of March, 1768, been the added weight that had tipped the scales toward revolution? Although the decree was not enforced on his arrival in July, 1769, the general saw the pressing need to establish as soon as possible a viable commercial system to support the colony's economy. Markets must be found for the native products—timber, indigo, cotton, and furs—in order to supply the wherewithal to purchase flour, wine, ironware, arms, and clothing. Logic dictated Havana as the emporium for timber, whence colonial ships might transport Cuban sugar to Spain with a return cargo of wine and other necessities. Export and import duties would be abolished. After O'Reilly's departure, the crown liberalized the rules of commerce, denying to the Louisianians, however, the right to trade directly with the colonial possessions of other powers and with Mexico. In light of the dire needs of the colony, O'Reilly permitted limited trade with French St. Domingue, lowered duties on certain goods and articles, and instituted other measures for the stimulation of foreign commerce, the lifeblood of the economy.[5]

Domestic commerce was less subject to direction from Madrid. Hitherto, smuggling by English and French merchants made up the most lucrative segment of the internal trade. To end this unlawful business, the general expelled from Natchitoches and Opelousas the agents of these houses, who had introduced a quantity of goods into Mexico. The activities of English merchants, in particular, were ended or severely curbed elsewhere in

4. Grimaldi was probably not overcome with grief at relinquishing the direction of the province, although he wrote Governor Unzaga: "I shall not forget the affection with which I have looked after the interests of the province and its inhabitants, and I shall always try to cooperate and with my influence to promote whatever may be conducive to its development, prosperity, and best interests." Grimaldi to Unzaga, November 24, 1770, in Leg. 174, Papeles de Cuba, AGI.

5. Torres, *Alejandro O'Reilly*, 153–55.

the colony. With licenses from the governor, colonial merchants might visit the Indian villages to exchange goods for skins and *aceite*, or oil, provided that they had a reputation for good character and that upon returning to the posts they informed the commandants of the places visited and the nature of the business transacted.[6]

To ensure stability of landholding, General O'Reilly recognized land grants authorized by the French regime. To have done otherwise would have created the groundwork for future rebellions and acts of discontent and disobedience. Regulations for later concessions were stipulated, with reversion to the crown if conditions for use were unfulfilled.[7]

Despite the various remedies adopted by O'Reilly and his successors to assure economic well-being, the colony represented a financial loss to the Spanish exchequer. At the outset it was necessary to settle the debts to the French government, according to the terms of the Treaty of Fontainebleau. Lacking funds from the Spanish treasury, Ulloa had authorized payments for many expenses of the French authorities. To Ulloa's credit, O'Reilly ascribed the excessive charges not to the former's "lack of zeal but to his wish to be always on good terms with the French." A reduction or deletion of many of these items occurred. Similarly, the general lowered the valuation of the tangible property turned over to Spain by France. An inspection of buildings, furnishings, and armaments disclosed much disrepair and uselessness.[8] Consequently, the total amount of the debt to France was far less than anticipated. Obviously, the *situado* from the Spanish treasury, initiated by Ulloa, could not be dropped, only the amount changed. During the three decades of Spanish rule, Louisiana received a greater annual subsidy than any of the other overseas possessions.[9]

6. *Ibid.*, 156, 157.
7. For details of these regulations see *ibid.*, 151–53.
8. *Ibid.*, 163, 165. For example, of the artillery only 30 cannon and 5,121 balls were accepted.
9. For a summary of the expenditures and contractual obligations of the Spanish government in Louisiana from 1766 to 1771, see *ibid.*, 162–71.

Whether larger annual appropriations would have materially improved the defenses of Louisiana in view of the extended wilderness frontier, the Indian question, and the hostility of the English is debatable. Shoring up the barrier proved as perplexing to O'Reilly as to Ulloa. As a veteran military rather than naval officer, O'Reilly perceived more clearly the weaknesses in the colony's strategic situation. The immediate issue was, however, the attitude of the Indians, perturbed over the temporary withdrawal of Spanish sovereignty and discontented over the consequent smaller quantity of gifts and presents for the chiefs.[10] To improve relations with the natives, O'Reilly invited the chieftains of the nations residing within sixty leagues of the capital to meet in New Orleans on October 29, 1769. It was his intention to make them more friendly by presenting gifts and simultaneously to impress them with a show of military might. The solemn pow-wow, presided over by the general, seated in front of his dwelling and surrounded by members of his staff, began at 11:30 A.M. Each chief, accompanied by his braves, approached O'Reilly, dancing, singing, and brandishing his tomahawk and spear menacingly. The remainder of the ritual of friendship and allegiance is aptly depicted by the general's secretary:

> When he [the chief] had deposited at His Excellency's feet all his weapons, he saluted the general with a flag, which is a small painted stick with some feathers spread out like a fan, and waving it over his head in a circular fashion and touching him with it four times on the chest, he handed over the symbol to His Excellency; afterwards he presented His Excellency with a lighted pipe, which the chief held while His Excellency smoked it in order not to look down on their customs; finally each chieftain shook hands with His Excellency, which is the best sign of friendship.

Harangues and speeches on a peaceful note by Indians and Spaniards followed. O'Reilly assured the chiefs of their future gifts and authorized to each a medal with the royal image superimposed. A military parade to dazzle the natives concluded the ceremony.[11] Subsequent decrees to discourage itinerant trad-

10. *Ibid.*, 146–48.
11. *Ibid.*, 148.

ers from wanton acts in the villages and to protect the hunting grounds from land claims bound the Indians to the Spanish as dependable allies.

Long-range strategy was determined more by the threat of English encroachment than by the contingency of Indian uprisings. O'Reilly reversed Ulloa's policy by concentrating Spanish forces in a few places and, in consequence, abandoning many of the forts constructed earlier. This had the double advantage of making the capital more impregnable and of reducing the heavy outlay to maintain the remote outposts. One of the lesser forts abolished was that of Natchez, and another was at Manchac, both considered useless in the event of an English assault and costly to keep up. The nerve center of the defense system was New Orleans, garrisoned by the Batallón Fijo de Luisiana, the recruiting for which was begun during Ulloa's regime and concluded by December, 1769, and by various companies of militia. The French soldiers, a poorly trained and physically unfit lot, on whom Ulloa had mistakenly relied, returned to France.[12] In the protection of the city, heavy artillery, consisting of twelve Spanish cannons plus twenty-five French pieces, was to play a minor role.

Of the outlying forts, three were regarded as worthy of retention after some alterations. Solely from a strategic standpoint, Balize, located at the mouth of the Mississippi, held great possibilities. After reconnoitering the terrain in 1766, Ulloa had concluded that the original site chosen by the French was unsuitable and had established on a small island in the river a new base, known as Isla Real Católica de San Carlos. Knowing of Ulloa's strenuous efforts to secure the base in the mud and sand against the strong currents, O'Reilly ordered a committee of engineers to inspect the post and report on its utility. It was their consensus that the fort be abandoned because the nature of the soil rendered construction of permanent fortifications impossible and because enemy warships could enter the river beyond the reach of the island's cannon. O'Reilly concurred in their recommenda-

12. *Ibid.*, 130–33.

tion to select a site on higher ground very close to the old French fort. By March, 1770, the new post was ready for occupancy.[13] The remaining posts were those in the Illinois country and along the Arkansas River. Owing to the long stretches of territory to be guarded in the North, the Illinois post had three subdivisions, St. Louis, Ste. Genevieve, and the old fort on the Missouri, all under a military commander responsible to the governor, with small garrisons of Spanish regulars supplemented in time of crisis by two companies of militia at St. Louis and Ste. Genevieve. The most precarious of all was the fort on the Arkansas, having few soldiers and dependent on the Illinois post for supplies.[14]

In thus reorganizing the defenses of Louisiana, O'Reilly modified fundamental principles that he had used in Cuba and Puerto Rico. The geography, proximity of the English, and the limited population of Louisiana dictated a new approach. Primarily, he depended on local militia to support the regular troops. A new procedure for the Spanish Empire in the eighteenth century, it was less expensive than maintaining regular military establishments but dangerous if revolutionary sentiment existed. Contrary to the practice in the West Indies, no strong fortification in any way comparable to El Morro in Havana was erected in the colony. In the main, a stockade and a ditch sufficed to shelter the riflemen and the cannoneers. "The defense of the province should consist uniquely of its defenders."[15]

Minor matters that necessitated O'Reilly's intervention were the status of the church and the improvement of public health. Ulloa, although recognizing the indifference and laxness of the French Capuchins, lacked the funds to build chapels and to bring in more missionaries. To care for the religious needs of the

13. See Reconocimiento del actual puesto de la Balissa, situado en la embocadura del rio de San luis de Misisipy, in Leg. 1223, Audiencia de Sto. Domingo, AGI. For a thorough treatment of the difficulties encountered by pilots and engineers in utilizing the entrance to the river, see Walter M. Lowrey, "Navigational Problems at the Mouth of the Mississippi River, 1698–1880" (Ph.D. dissertation, Vanderbilt University, 1956).

14. Torres, *Alejandro O'Reilly*, 136–38.

15. *Ibid.*, 140, 141.

population, O'Reilly created new parishes and requested additional priests from France. None of these arrived during his residence in Louisiana. In 1772 the province became part of the bishopric of Cuba. Primary schools were to be established in New Orleans, and higher standards were imposed for practitioners of medicine.[16]

To terminate his Louisiana assignment as expeditiously as possible had always been O'Reilly's objective. As was customary with Spanish officials, he had followed Ulloa's example and made an inspection of the colony. Unable to go in person to the distant settlements because of the time involved, he had dispatched small commissions to look into affairs, take an oath of allegiance from the inhabitants, and report to the capital. He himself had gone in January to Pointe Coupée, along the way visiting the German Coast and the Acadian region. His own observations and the reports from agents convinced O'Reilly of the wisdom of withdrawing troops from the province as soon as feasible. As early as October, 1769, contingents of soldiers were permitted to return to Havana, and in a few months the great majority had left Louisiana. In November, 1769, at royal command, he designated Luis de Unzaga, colonel of the Regimiento Fijo de la Habana, governor of Louisiana. During the first week of March, O'Reilly, with units of his expeditionary force, sailed from New Orleans, arriving in Havana on the twenty-third, and by June he was once again in Cádiz.[17]

General O'Reilly's subsequent career in Spain belied the promise of his earlier achievements. With his reputation as pacificator and proconsul established, he returned to Madrid as the man of the hour. In high favor with Charles III and Grimaldi, he could not, however, resist the temptation to participate in the dangerous game of court intrigue, and, had war broken out

16. *Ibid.,* 173–79.
17. *Ibid.,* 114, 115, 181, 182, 183. One may speculate on the failure of O'Reilly to receive appointment as viceroy of New Spain, his name having been mentioned for this lucrative post. Perhaps his egocentric personality impelled him to undertake a role in a larger political theater where the stakes were higher. But his decision may have been guided by other reasons, the king's desire to have him at the court and the birth of his son.

between Spain and England over the Falkland Islands, he probably would have become the supreme commander of the Spanish army. In 1774 the occasion for military glory presented itself in a war with Algeria. Through influential friends at court he was appointed general of the invading force, but inadequate planning, poor tactics in landing operations, and lack of discipline among the troops resulted in a fiasco for Spain. O'Reilly was removed from command, and his protector Grimaldi resigned in disgrace. Until his death in 1794 the general occupied only minor posts in the government.[18]

Meanwhile, the severe policy followed toward those implicated in the conspiracy in Louisiana eased somewhat. Relatives and friends of the convicted appealed to have the sentences of the prisoners in El Morro reduced. In June, 1770, the French ambassador in Madrid learned from O'Reilly himself that the general favored a more lenient attitude. D'Ossun then besought Choiseul to indicate the policy of the French crown toward clemency: "I am overwhelmed with petitions by friends and relatives of some of the prisoners. Be so good, monsieur, as to let me know if you approve my taking steps in their behalf and in particular for Monsieur Hardi de Boisblanc and a Monsieur Masan, whose crimes do not appear very serious." Choiseul's prompt response may well have intimated his genuine feeling regarding the prisoners: "They have doubtless merited the punishment meted out to them, but if this generous prince will bear in mind that they manifested a patriotic zeal and preference for their former lord and hence are less guilty, he will believe without hesitation that his duty is to show clemency and give them their liberty, with permission to retire to France."[19] Sharing these views, d'Ossun promised to exert his influence at the court in their behalf at once: "I see from your dispatch, monsieur, the compassion that the French from Louisiana, perhaps more unfortunate than guilty, who are prisoners in

18. Rodríguez, *Primeros años,* 301–18.
19. D'Ossun to Choiseul, June 11, 1770, and Choiseul to d'Ossun, June 26, 1770, both in Correspondance Politique, Espagne, DLIX, AAE.

Havana, arouses in you; it is certainly enough to authorize and increase the wish that I had to work to obtain greater clemency from His Catholic Majesty." Toward the end of July, Choiseul forwarded a copy of Foucault's interrogatory at the Bastille to Madrid, appealing for clemency for the prisoner in view of the "exemplary punishment handed the majority of the guilty ones."[20] Grimaldi's reply was to leave the commissary's sentence to the judgment of the French crown: "However criminal was M. Foucault's behavior in the revolution in Louisiana, since he was a subject of the French government and employed by its ministry, it is His Catholic Majesty's intention not to intervene in the decision as to his fate . . . with the sole condition that he not return to Louisiana at any future time or for any reason." Near the end of August the secretary of state agreed to release the prisoners in Havana.[21] It was not until December 12 that Captain General Bucareli notified Arriaga that those incarcerated in El Morro had been freed and put aboard a vessel for Puerto Rico with St. Domingue or France as the ultimate destination. Under no condition were they to return to Louisiana, nor was there to be any restitution of property.[22] The archplotter Foucault, after remaining in prison in Paris for a year and a half, also secured his freedom and was permitted to perform duties in the ministry of marine.[23] From its overtures for clemency and its action toward Foucault, one may infer that the French crown did not look on the revolt through Spanish eyes. It could not, of course, condone an uprising against a lawful sovereign. But did the punishment fit the crime?

Whether Ulloa approved of the severity of O'Reilly's policy in quelling the insurrection we may never know. There is appar-

20. D'Ossun to Choiseul, July 7, 1770, and Choiseul to d'Ossun, July 25, 1770, both *ibid.,* DLX.
21. Grimaldi to Fuentes, August 19, 20, 1770, both enclosed in Fuentes to Choiseul, August 31, 1770, *ibid.*
22. Bucareli to Arriaga, December 12, 1770, in Kinnaird (ed.), *Spain in the Mississippi Valley,* II, 189.
23. Villiers, *Les dernières années,* 315. Since he served as intendant of the Ile de France et Bourbon in 1776, his restitution must have been complete. See Lemieux, "The Office of Commissaire Ordonnateur," 68.

ently no letter extant in his voluminous correspondence to suggest vindication or disapproval. After O'Reilly's departure for America in 1769, Ulloa had no connection with Louisiana and, so far as is known, proffered no advice on its administration. The crown did not blame him for the disastrous outcome of its first effort to occupy the province. At Grimaldi's suggestion, Charles III exonerated Ulloa from any charge of maladministration. Hence the *residencia,* the usual legal examination of a Spanish official held at the expiration of his duties, did not take place.[24] It is obvious that the French government, basing its opinion on Aubry's and Foucault's detailed reports, would not hold him in high esteem as an administrator.[25]

Although he had "ploughed the sea"—to use Simon Bolivar's famous phrase—in his efforts to govern Louisiana, Antonio de Ulloa continued to enjoy the favor and goodwill of the monarchy. The crown perceived the advantage of utilizing his diverse talents as a naval officer, scientific observer, and author. In 1769 he was promoted to the rank of rear admiral and eventually to that of admiral of the fleet. Some eight years later, in 1777, the ministry entrusted him with the command of the last important flota to Vera Cruz, which he fulfilled to its satisfac-

24. In Additional Manuscripts 20,986, No. 16, British Museum, London. See Appendix herein for a translation of this important document. Although without salutation or signature, it is evident from internal references and content that this is an exoneration by Grimaldi of all charges.

25. A resumé, dated September 5, 1769, and drawn up for Louis XV, portrays Ulloa "as a man of merit, knowledge, and talent, but contrary to the custom of his nation, he is extremely quick-tempered [*vif*] and does not listen to remonstrances that are made to him, which displeases those who have business with him." See Feuille au roi sur la conduite de Ulloa et la rébellion survenue à la Louisiane, in C13A49, Colonies, AN. A memorial, prepared for the ministry in April, 1769, apropos of the request from the Spanish ambassador at Versailles that the French government send a note of disapproval to the Superior Council, suggests that the Spanish government follow customary procedure in dispatching a new appointee, who must work with Aubry and, above all, who must "register with the Superior Council the documentary evidence of his commission to avoid the reproach that was made to Ulloa of not having clarified his status by an act spoken and legal." See Mémoire au sujet de la conduite a tenir vis-à-vis de l'Espagne par rapport aux troubles survenus à la Louisiane, in C13A49, Colonies B, AN. Another resumé of September 5, 1769, roundly criticizes all those holding office in the colonial administration, except Aubry, for their roles in the uprising. See Feuille au Roi sur la rébellion survenue à la Louisiane, in C13A49, Colonies, AN.

tion, returning safely to Seville the following year with one of the richest cargoes of silver of the eighteenth century. The outbreak of war between Spain and England in 1779, which was long overdue, saw him at the head of a squadron operating against English raiders in the Azores. His failure to pursue retreating English vessels brought on a court-martial, in which his name was finally cleared of any implication of cowardice or timidity.[26]

His scientific and literary contributions, extending over a quarter of a century, overshadowed those as a naval officer. Although much of this was published, some reposes in manuscript in the Spanish archives. Utilizing data compiled from his meticulous observations in Peru, Ecuador, Panama, and Louisiana, he published in 1772 the *Noticias Americanas*.[27] This is a primary source of information for geographers, ethnologists, anthropologists, and sociologists interested in the American scene during the eighteenth century. One of his most ambitious projects was to prepare a survey of the navies of Europe, with a description of ships, bases, and armaments and with a preface containing a plea for disarmament. The Spanish ministry, to whom it was submitted, vetoed publication on the grounds that national security might be affected by disclosing the state of the armada and the various naval bases.[28] Because of his wide knowledge of New Spain, he was given the responsibility of formulating queries in an exhaustive interrogatory for the provincial authorities, designed to ascertain facts relating to the geography and natural history of the regions. Other important writings still in manuscript are treatises on Indian labor in the mines of Peru and the nature and properties of the metal platinum. His last work to be published was *Conversaciones de Ulloa con sus tres hijos en servicio de la marina*, a storehouse of information on ships, tides, weather, and indispensable advice

26. Guillén, *Los tenientes de navío*, 239, 240.
27. The full title is *Noticias Americanas: Entretenimientos phísicos-históricos sobre la América meridional y la septentrional oriental* (Madrid, 1772). This is not to be confused with the *Noticias secretas de América*, the joint work of Ulloa and Jorge Juan.
28. In Leg. 375, Marina, AGS.

for young naval officers. A founder of the museum of natural history in Madrid, he was responsible for much of the royal collection and for conducting significant experiments in electricity and magnetism. His reputation as a scientist led to his election either as member or as corresponding member of all the important academies of science in Europe.[29] On his death in 1795 he was buried, fittingly enough, in Cádiz, the traditional center of Spanish naval might. Subsequently, his name was enshrined where it should be in the pantheon of Spain's naval heroes at the naval academy in the same city. In many ways Ulloa exemplified the highest type of bureaucratic official of the Spanish Empire in the eighteenth century. Having a military background like many of Charles III's appointees, he cherished above all the ideals of obedience, probity, and honor. His unswerving devotion to his sovereign compensated for a lack of tact and diplomacy in dealing with his subordinates.

To Antonio de Ulloa and, to a far greater extent, Alexander O'Reilly, the key to the security of New Orleans and the whole of Louisiana was "the defenders," or the people of the province. More than upon concrete bastions or heavy armaments, the safety of this sector of the perimeter of the empire depended on the fidelity of the population, which was primarily French. Ulloa's compromising policy, dictated from military weakness and influenced by unfortunate traits of his personality, led to his expulsion. The club-and-carrot posture of O'Reilly could begrudgingly force submission. But wise government in the long run had to create goodwill and good relations throughout the region. "It will require time as well as trouble and Expense before they [the Spanish] will reconcile the Indians to their Interests, or conciliate the Affection of the French, who are certainly at present very adverse to their Government," General Gage commented to Lord Hillsborough in the autumn of 1769.[30]

29. Guillén, *Los tenientes de navío*, 239–42.
30. Gage to Hillsborough, October 7, 1769, in Carter (ed.), *The Correspondence of General Thomas Gage*, I, 239.

Sound policies and strong administrators could mean the difference between a potentially hostile or rebellious population and a loyal one. Greater efficiency in the government, an aftermath of most revolutionary movements and best exemplified in the French Revolution two decades later, holds true in Louisiana. Contrary to the old saying, the Spanish did learn from experience in Louisiana. Despite its inclusion in the exclusive imperial trade system, the crown permitted the province to enjoy unusual commercial privileges from time to time, mainly to foster the exchange of products with France and French possessions in the Caribbean. Agriculture was encouraged by expanding the cultivation of indigo and sugar. Although these measures were helpful to the economy, they did not prevent the colony from having a consistently unfavorable balance of trade, which necessitated a large annual *situado* of from 200,000 to 400,000 pesos. It was clearly recognized that the sparseness of the population was a distinct drawback to the development of the region. To fill this need, the crown authorized land grants to American settlers if they accepted Spanish sovereignty. Had the original plan of inducing emigrants from the Iberian Peninsula to colonize the region been successful, the history of Louisiana might well have been different. Proof that a lesson in administration was drawn from the events of October, 1768, is the high quality of appointments to office made by José Gálvez, the sagacious minister of the Indies, and his successors. Exceptionally able persons, including Luis de Unzaga, Bernardo de Gálvez, Esteban Miró, Francisco de Carondelet, and Manuel Gayoso de Lemos followed in the footsteps of O'Reilly. Vigorous, suave, cultured, diplomatic, well-trained either as soldiers or bureaucrats, they understood the art of governing. They curried the favor of the influential creole families, even to the point of intermarriage, contrary to the regular practice of the crown forbidding the marriage of a high official to someone from the district to which he had been appointed. Yet, despite these beneficent measures and overtures of *rapprochement,* the Spanish crown never completely trusted the creoles after the rebellion of

1768. Nor could the French in New Orleans easily forget the treatment of its leading citizens in 1769.

Paradoxically, the laurels of victory in this contest between Spaniard and Frenchman went to the conquered rather than to the conquerors. Gallic traditions, language, and way of life triumphed, notwithstanding the contributions made by Spain to economic development, architecture, and concepts of jurisprudence. The traumatic experience of the transfer of sovereignty had, additionally, a unique compensation by making the culture and outlook of contemporary Louisiana more cosmopolitan.

Appendix

Exoneration of Antonio de Ulloa

June 19, 1770

[Grimaldi to Ulloa:]

In your letter of the fourth of this month you state that you have learned that Lieutenant General Alexander O'Reilly had recovered Louisiana, executing the commission that the king had assigned to him, and that you have news of what was done by him in the colony and of the measures taken in matters of justice and war and in the handling of our interests. I cannot do less than tell you that it has been in conformity in total or in part with the ideas and policies that you had when you were governor as may be deduced from the letters you wrote. It is now your request that if any charge is being drawn up against your conduct, it should be sent you for a rejoinder.

I have at hand all that you indicate, because they are the major points that had not been erased from my thoughts and memory and because the letters from you and the answers that I gave you by order of the king are still at hand. Also, I have present everything that the lieutenant general wrote from Louisiana and proposed, and the *informes* that he has made in person since his return, and comparing one with the other, I can tell you that you may rest assured as to your conduct in that assignment, and that neither the said lieutenant general makes any charges nor does any complaint arise from the papers which came earlier and which prove that you gave much thought to the orders that have now been given or ones like those, and that the disturbances that have occurred have been the result of the linking of that colony with other dominions of His Majesty in America and of the subjection to its laws and different type of administration which after the uprising and your departure it was found convenient to impose. For these reasons you may be satisfied that the king has neither changed his opinion of you nor wishes to refrain from availing himself of your talents and acuteness of observation.

Note: Translated by author from Additional Manuscripts 20,968, No. 16, British Museum, London.

Bibliography

DICTIONARIES, ENCYCLOPEDIAS, AND SPECIAL GUIDES

Alvord, Clarence. "Eighteenth-Century French Records in the Archives of Illinois." *American Historical Association Annual Report,* I (1905), 353–66.

Beers, Henry P. *The French in North America: A Bibliographical Guide to French Archives, Reproductions, and Research Missions.* Baton Rouge, 1957.

Chéruel, A. *Dictionnaire historique des institutions, moeurs, et coutumes de la France.* 2 vols. Paris, 1855.

Diccionario de historia de España desde sus orígenes hasta el fin del reinado de Alfonso XIII. 2 vols. Madrid, 1952.

Domínguez Bordona, Jesús. *Catálago de la Biblioteca de Palacio: Manuscritos de América.* Vol. IX. Madrid, 1935.

Gayangos y Arce, Pascual de. *Catalogue of the Manuscripts in the Spanish Language in the British Museum.* 4 vols. London, 1875–93.

Handbook of Latin American Studies. 32 vols. Vols. I–XIII, Cambridge, Mass., 1936–51; vols. XIV–XXXII, Gainesville, Fla., 1951–70.

Harisse, Henry. *Notes pour servir à l'histoire et à la bibliographie et à la cartographie de la Nouvelle France et des pays adjacents.* Paris, 1872.

Lanctot, Gustave. *L'oeuvre de la France en Amérique du Nord.* Montreal, 1951.

Leland, Waldo S. *Guide to Materials for American History in the Libraries and Archives of Paris.* 2 vols. Washington, D.C., 1932, 1943.

Marion, Marcel. *Dictionnaire des institutions de la France au XVIIe et XVIIIe siècles.* Paris, 1923.

O'Neill, Charles E., *et al. Catálago de documentos del Archivo General de Indias, sección V, Gobierno, Audiencia de Santo Domingo sobre la época española de Luisiana.* New Orleans, 1969.

Ouvrage élaboré par l'association des archivistes français: Manuel d'archivistique: Théorie et practique des archives publiques en France. Paris, 1970.

Surrey, N. M. Miller. *Calendar of Manuscripts in Paris Archives and Libraries Relating to the History of the Mississippi Valley.* 2 vols. Washington, D.C., 1926, 1928.

PRIMARY SOURCES

ARCHIVES

Archives de Ministère des Affaires Etrangères, Paris
　Correspondance Politique, Espagne. Vols. DLVI, DLVII, DLIX, DLX.
Archives Nationales, Paris
　Colonies. C13A45, C13A46, C13A48, C13A49 (transcripts in Library of Congress).
　Lettres Envoyées.
Archivo General de Indias, Seville
　Audiencia de Lima. Legajos 590, 775.
　Audiencia de Quito. Legajo 133.
　Audiencia de Sto. Domingo. Legajos 1194, 1221, 1223, 2078, 2088, 2542, 2543, 2357, 2557, 2585, 2594, 2666.
　Indiferente. Legajos 1630, 1631.
　Papeles de Cuba. Legajos 109, 124A, 149A, 174, 174A, 187, 187A, 1055.
Archivo General de la Nación, Mexico City
　Correspondencia de los Virreyes. Ser. 1, Vol. XIII.
Archivo General de Simancas, Simancas
　Marina. Legajos 26, 377, 712.
　Estado. Legajo 6972.
Archivo Histórico Nacional, Madrid
　Consejo de Indias. Legajo 20,854.
　Estado. Legajos 3883, 3889.
Biblioteca de Palacio, Madrid
　Manuscritos de América. Miscelánea de Ayala. Manuscritos 2827, 2829.
　América del Sur. Manuscrito 1468.
Biblioteca Nacional, Madrid
　Manuscritos 17,606, 18,182, 19,246, 19,247, 19,248.
British Museum, London
　Additional Manuscripts 20,986, No. 16.
Howard-Tilton Memorial Library, Tulane University, New Orleans
　French Judicial Records (microfilm).
　Kuntz, Emile and Rosamunde E., Collection.
Louisiana State Museum of History, New Orleans
　Spanish Manuscripts. Mississippi Valley, 1765–1803.
　Spanish Judicial Records. August 18, 1769–December 31, 1803.
Louisiana State University Library, Baton Rouge
　Dispatches of the Spanish Governors of Louisiana. 11 vols. W.P.A. Survey of Federal Archives in Louisiana.
Loyola University Library, New Orleans
　Documents from Archivo General de Indias, Audiencia de Sto. Domingo, pertaining to Louisiana (microfilm).

New Orleans Public Library, New Orleans
Records and Deliberations of the Cabildo, 1769–1803.
New York Public Library, New York City
"Journal des dépenses de la colonie de la Nouvelle Orléans, année, 1766."
Manuscript.
Public Record Office, London
Correspondence of the British Governors of West Florida. Vols. DLXXV,
DLXXVII, DXCV.

PRINTED DOCUMENTS AND CONTEMPORARY WORKS

Alvord, Clarence W., and Clarence E. Carter, eds. *The Critical Period, 1763–
1765.* Collections of the Illinois State Historical Library, X. Springfield, Ill.,
1915.
————. *The New Regime, 1765–1767.* Collections of the Illinois State Historical
Library, XI. Springfield, Ill., 1916.
————. *Trade and Politics, 1767–1769.* Collections of the Illinois State Historical
Library, XVI. Springfield, Ill., 1921.
Baillardel, A., and A. Prioult. *Le chevalier de Pradel: Vie d'un colon français en
Louisiane au XVIIIe siècle d'après sa correspondance et celle de sa famille.* Paris,
1928.
Carter, Clarence, ed. *The Correspondence of General Thomas Gage with the Sec-
retaries of State, and with the War Office and the Treasury, 1763–1775.* 2 vols. New
Haven, 1931–33.
Champigny, Jean Bochart. "Memoir of the Present State of Louisiana." In B. F.
French, ed. *Historical Collections of Louisiana Embracing Transactions of Many
Rare and Valuable Documents Relating to the Natural, Civil, and Political History of
That State, Compiled with Historical and Biographical Notes.* 5 vols. New York,
1846–53.
Kinnaird, Lawrence, ed. *Spain in the Mississippi Valley, 1765–1794.* American
Historical Association Report for 1945, II–IV. Washington, D.C., 1946–49.
La Condamine, Charles de. *Histoire des pyramides de Quito.* Paris, 1751.
"Records of the Superior Council." *Louisiana Historical Quarterly,* II–XXII.
Ulloa, Antonio de. *Conversaciones de Ulloa con sus tres hijos en sevicio de la marina.*
Madrid, 1795.
————. *Noticias Américanas: Entretenimientos phísicos-históricos sobre la América
meridional y la septentrional oriental.* Madrid, 1772.
Ulloa, Antonio de, and Jorge Juan. *Noticias secretas de América.* Buenos Aires,
1953.
————. *Relación histórica del viaje a la América meridional, hecho de orden de S. M.
para medir algunos grados de meridiano terrestre, y venir por ellos en conocimiento de
la verdadera figura de la tierra, con otras varias observaciones astronómicas y físicas.*
4 vols. Madrid, 1748.

Ulloa, Bernardo de. *Restablecimiento de las fábricas, y comercio español: Errores que se padecen en las causales de su cadencia.* Madrid, 1740.

SECONDARY SOURCES

BOOKS

Alcázar Molina, Cayetano. *Los virreinatos en el siglo XVIII.* ed. Antonio Ballesteros. Barcelona, 1945.

Alden, John R. *General Gage in America: Being Principally a History of His Role in the American Revolution.* Baton Rouge, 1948.

———. *John Stuart and the Southern Colonial Frontier: A Study of Indian Relations, War, Trade, and Land Problems in the Southern Wilderness, 1754–1775.* Ann Arbor, 1944.

Ballesteros y Beretta, Antonio. *Historia de España y su influencia en la historia universal.* 2nd ed., 11 vols. Barcelona and Buenos Aires, 1929–50.

Bobb, Bernard E. *The Viceregency of Antonio María Bucareli in New Spain, 1771–1779.* Austin, 1962.

Caughey, John W. *Bernardo de Gálvez in Louisiana, 1776–1783.* Berkeley, 1934.

Chambers, H. E. *A History of Louisiana.* 3 vols. Chicago and New York, 1925.

Bolton, Herbert E., ed. *Athanese de Mézières and the Louisiana-Texas Frontier, 1768–1780.* 2 vols. Cleveland, 1913–14.

Clark, John G. *New Orleans, 1718–1812: An Economic History.* Baton Rouge, 1970.

Coxe, William. *Memoirs of the Kings of Spain of the House of Bourbon from the Accession of Philip V to the Death of Charles III, 1700 to 1788.* 5 vols. London, 1815.

Davis, Edwin A. *Louisiana: A Narrative History.* 3rd ed. Baton Rouge, 1971.

De Ville, Winston. *Louisiana Troops, 1720–1770.* Ft. Worth, 1965.

Fortier, Alcée. *A History of Louisiana.* 4 vols. New York, 1904.

———. *A History of Louisiana.* Introd. Jo Ann Carrigan. 2 vols. Baton Rouge, 1966.

———. *Louisiana, Comprising Sketches of Parishes, Towns, Events, Institutions, and Persons, Arranged in Cyclopedic Form.* 2 vols. Atlanta, 1909.

———. *Louisiana, Comprising Sketches of Parishes, Towns, Events, Institutions, and Persons, Arranged in Cyclopedic Form.* With supplementary biographical information. 3 vols. N.p., 1914.

Gayarré, Charles. *Histoire de la Louisiane.* 2 vols. New Orleans, 1846–47.

———. *History of Louisiana.* 5th ed., 4 vols. New Orleans, 1965.

Giraud, Marcel. *Histoire de la Louisiane française, 1698–1721.* 3 vols. Paris, 1953–66.

Guillén, Julio F. *Los tenientes de navío Jorge Juan y Santacilia y Antonio de Ulloa y de la Torre-Guiral y la medición del meridiano.* Madrid, 1936.

Holmes, Jack D. L. *Gayoso: The Life of a Spanish Governor in the Mississippi Valley, 1789–1799.* Baton Rouge, 1965.

Houck, Louis. *A History of Missouri.* 2 vols. Chicago, 1908.

Howard, Clinton N. *The British Development of West Florida, 1763–1769.* Berkeley, 1917.

Hussey, Roland D. *The Caracas Company, 1728–1784: A Study in the History of Monopolistic Trade.* Cambridge, Mass., 1934.

Johnson, Cecil. *British West Florida, 1763–1783.* New Haven, 1943.

King, Grace. *Creole Families of New Orleans.* New York, 1921.

Lauvrière, Emile. *Histoire de la Louisiane française, 1673–1939.* Baton Rouge, 1940.

Lyon, E. Wilson. *Louisiana in French History, 1759–1804.* Norman, Okla., 1934.

Martin, François-Xavier. *The History of Louisiana from the Earliest Period.* New Orleans, 1963.

Moore, J. Preston. *The Cabildo in Peru Under the Bourbons: A Study in the Decline and Resurgence of Local Government in the Audiencia of Lima, 1700–1824,* Durham, N.C., 1966.

————. *The Cabildo in Peru Under the Hapsburgs: A Study in the Origins and Powers of the Town Council in the Viceroyalty of Peru, 1530–1700.* Durham, N.C., 1954.

Morales Padrón, Francisco. *Rebelión contra la compañía de Caracas.* Seville, 1955.

O'Neill, Charles E. *Church and State in French Colonial Louisiana: Policy and Politics to 1732.* New Haven, 1966.

Phares, Ross. *Cavalier in the Wilderness: The Story of the Explorer and Trader Louis Juchereau de St. Denis.* Gloucester, Mass., 1970.

Ramsey, John F. *Anglo-French Relations, 1763–1770: A Study in Choiseul's Foreign Policy.* University of California Publications in History. Berkeley, 1939.

Rodríguez Casado, Vicente. *Primeros años de dominación española en la Luisiana.* Madrid, 1942.

Rubio, Jerónimo. *Un amigo español de La Condamine: Armona.* Madrid, 1952.

Sosin, Jack. *Whitehall and the Wilderness: The Middle West in British Colonial Policy, 1760–1775.* Lincoln, 1961.

Surrey, N. M. Miller. *The Commerce of Louisiana During the French Regime, 1699–1763.* Columbia University Studies in History, Economics, and Public Law, LXXI, 1. New York, 1916.

TePaske, John. *The Governorship of Spanish Florida, 1700–1763.* Durham, N.C., 1964.

Texada, David K. *Alejandro O'Reilly and the New Orleans Rebels.* University of Southwestern Louisiana History Series, 2. Lafayette, 1970.

Tocqueville, Alexis de. *Democracy in America.* Abr., ed., and introd. Andrew Hacker. New York, 1964.

Torres Ramírez, Bibiano. *Alejandro O'Reilly en las Indias.* Seville, 1969.

Villiers du Terrage, Marc de. *Les dernières années de la Louisiane française.* Paris, 1903.

Wade, Mason. *The French Canadians, 1760–1767.* Rev. ed., 2 vols. Toronto, 1968.

Whitaker, Arthur P. *The Huancavelica Mercury Mine: A Contribution to the History of the Bourbon Renaissance in the Spanish Empire.* Cambridge, Mass., 1941.

ARTICLES

Aiton, Arthur S. "The Diplomacy of the Louisiana Cession." *American Historical Review,* XXXVI (July, 1931), 701–20.

———. "Spanish Colonial Reorganization Under the Family Compact." *Hispanic American Historical Review,* XII (August, 1932), 269–80.

Bjork, David K. "Alejandro O'Reilly and the Spanish Occupation of Louisiana, 1769–1770." In George Hammond, ed. *New Spain and the Anglo-American West.* Lancaster, Pa., 1932.

Boulle, Pierre. "French Reactions to the Louisiana Revolution of 1768." In John F. McDermott, ed. *The French in the Mississippi Valley.* Urbana, 1965. Pp. 143–57.

———. "Some Eighteenth-Century French Views of Louisiana." In John F. McDermott, ed. *Frenchmen and French Ways in the Mississippi Valley.* Urbana, 1969. Pp. 15–27.

Brown, Douglas S. "The Iberville Canal Project: Its Relation to the Anglo-French Commercial Rivalry in the Mississippi Valley, 1763–1775." *Mississippi Valley Historical Review,* XXXII (March, 1946), 491–516.

Chandler, R. E. "End of an Odyssey: Acadians Arrive in St. Gabriel, La." *Louisiana History,* XIV (Winter, 1973), 69–87.

Giraud, Marcel. "France and Louisiana in the Eighteenth Century." *Mississippi Valley Historical Review,* XXXVI (March, 1950), 657–74.

Hardy, James D., Jr. "The Superior Council in Colonial Louisiana." In John F. McDermott, ed. *Frenchmen and French Ways in the Mississippi Valley.* Urbana, 1969. Pp. 87–101.

Holmes, Jack D. L. "Some Economic Problems of the Spanish Governors of Louisiana." *Hispanic American Historical Review,* XLII (November, 1962), 521–43.

Le Conte, René. "The Germans in Louisiana in the Eighteenth Century." Trans. and ed. Glenn Conrad. *Louisiana History,* VIII (Winter, 1967), 67–84.

Lowrey, Walter M. "The Engineers and the Mississippi." *Louisiana History,* V (Summer, 1964), 233–55.

Micelle, Jerry A. "From Law Court to Local Government: Metamorphosis of the Superior Council of French Louisiana." *Louisiana History,* IX (Spring, 1968), 85–108.

Moore, J. Preston. "Anglo-Spanish Rivalry on the Louisiana Frontier, 1763–1768." In John F. McDermott, ed. *The Spanish in the Mississippi Valley, 1762–1804.* Urbana, 1974. Pp. 72–86.

———. "Antonio de Ulloa: Profile of the First Spanish Governor of Louisiana." *Louisiana History,* VIII (Summer, 1967), 189–218.

Nasatir, Abraham. "Government Employees and Salaries in Spanish Louisiana." *Louisiana Historical Quarterly,* XXIX (October, 1946), 885–1040.

Rea, Robert. "Military Deserters from British West Florida." *Louisiana History,* IX (Spring, 1968), 123–37.

Rodríguez Casado, Vicente. "Costumbres de los habitantes de Nueva Orleans en el comienzo de la dominación española." *Miscelánea, Revisita de Indias,* II (October–December, 1941), 170–79.

Shepherd, William R. "The Cession of Louisiana to Spain." *Political Science Quarterly,* XIX (September, 1904), 439–58.

Whitaker, Arthur P. "Antonio de Ulloa." *Hispanic American Historical Review,* XV (May, 1935), 155–94.

———. "Antonio de Ulloa, the *Deliverance,* and the Royal Society." *Hispanic American Historical Review,* XLVI (November, 1966), 357–70.

Wilson, Samuel. "Almonester: Philanthropist and Builder in New Orleans." In John F. McDermott, ed. *The Spanish in the Mississippi Valley, 1762–1804.* Urbana, 1974. Pp. 183–271.

Winston, James. "The Causes and Results of the Revolution of 1768 in Louisiana." *Louisiana Historical Quarterly,* XV (April, 1932), 181–213.

UNPUBLISHED THESES AND DISSERTATIONS

Bjork, David K. "The Establishment of Spanish Rule in Louisiana." Ph.D. dissertation, University of California, Berkeley, 1923.

Lemieux, Donald. "The Office of Commissaire Ordonnateur in French Louisiana, 1731–1763: A Study in French Colonial Administration." Ph.D. dissertation, Louisiana State University, 1972.

Lowrey, Walter M. "Navigational Problems at the Mouth of the Mississippi River, 1698–1880." Ph.D. dissertation, Vanderbilt University, 1956.

Miller, James. "Commandant System in Louisiana Under Spain." M.A. thesis, Louisiana State University, 1965.

Smith, Ronald D. "French Interest in Louisiana from Choiseul to Napoleon." Ph.D. dissertation, University of Michigan, 1964.

Index